W9-BNE-298

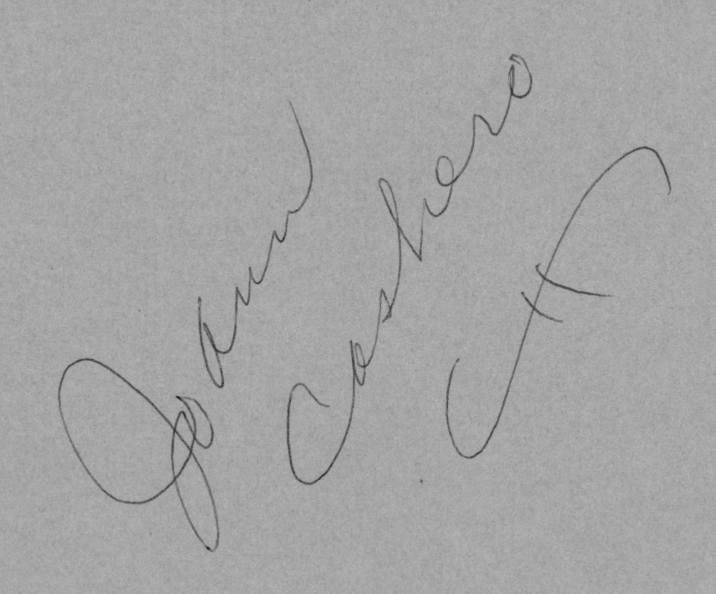

101
Easy SCRAP CROCHET Projects™
HOUSE of WHITE BIRCHES
PUBLISHERS SINCE 1947

101 Easy Scrap Crochet Projects

Editor: Laura Scott
Pattern Editor: Maggie Petsch Chasalow
Editorial Assistant: June Sprunger
Copy Editor: Cathy Reef
Editorial Coordinators: Myra Moore, Tanya Turner

Photography: Tammy Christian, Jennifer Fourman, Jeff Chilcote
Photography Stylist: Arlou Wittwer
Photography Assistant: Linda Quinlan

Production Coordinator: Brenda Gallmeyer
Book Design: Shaun Venish
Production Artist: Pam Gregory
Production Assistants: Shirley Blalock, Dana Brotherton, Carol Dailey
Traffic Coordinator: Sandra Beres

Publishers: Carl H. Muselman, Arthur K. Muselman
Chief Executive Officer: John Robinson
Marketing Director: Scott Moss
Editorial Director: Vivian Rothe
Production Director: George Hague

Printed in the United States of America
First Printing: 1999
Library of Congress Number: 99-94091
ISBN: 1-882138-42-2

Just a Note

Does your mind ever wander to that stash of scrap yarn you have tucked away in a spare closet or in a box under the bed? Do you think, "Someday I'm going to do something with all that yarn ..." and then put it out of your mind until a family member asks you about it again?

*I can never bring myself to throw away perfectly good yarn or thread, even if I only have a few yards of it left, so my collection grows year after year. If you're like me in this regard, then good news is here for us both—*101 Easy Scrap Crochet Projects.

This book was specially planned and the patterns carefully selected to give you more than 100 great crochet project ideas for using up all that leftover yarn and thread. Not only will you delight your family when you finally use all that scrap yarn, you will also delight them when you share the wonderful items you have crocheted.

Take, for example, that typical teenage daughter or granddaughter of yours. Won't she be surprised when she opens her birthday gift of a retro-style vest, just like the ones at her favorite store, made from your stash of scrap yarn? This collection of projects includes everything from in-style vests to cozy afghans to pretty doilies to kitchen table sets to cuddly dolls and so much more.

Warm regards,

Laura Scott

Editor,
101 Easy Scrap Crochet Projects

I hope you have as much fun picking and choosing the projects you'll make and which colors to use as my staff and I had in putting this collection together!

Contents

Scrap Afghans

Mended Hearts....7
Dreamy Stripes....10
Autumn Glory....13
Scrap Happy Pinwheels....14
Happy Times....17
Random Acts of Kindness....18
Pastel Stripes....20
Parfait Baby Afghan....22
Granny's Scrap Basket....24

All Through the House

Painted Daisies Runner....28
Windowsill Tissue Box Cover....30
Diagonal Stripes Rug....32
Floral Window Shade Trim....34
Pastel Garden Centerpiece....36
Loves Me, Loves Me Not....38
Dainty Peach Doily....40
Angelfish Pillow....42
Reversible Rag Rug....44

Scrap Fashions

Zesty Zigzag Cardigan....46
String of Clusters Pullover....49
Flower Garden Bolero....52
Windowpane Tunic....55
Mini-Entrelacs for Kids....58
Country Warmth Set....60
Strawberry Motifs....63
Fluffy Slippers....64
Fluttering Butterflies Motifs....66
Accents in Blue Blouse Edging....68
Rosebuds 'n' Beads T-Shirt....70
Dressed-Up Doggies....73

Little Darlings

Flower Friends....76
Snipper Keeper....78
Miniature Coverlet....79
Cutie Pie Clothespin Dolls....80
Bunny Delight....82
Fashion Doll Fun....85
Itzy-Bitzy Bear....86
Key Chain Combo....88
Booties for Baby....90
Happy Hair Doll....92
Yo-yo Bunny....93

Kitchen Accents

Butterfly's Fancy Table Set....99
Butterfly Magnets....103
Best-Dressed Bottle....104
Waffle Pot Holder....106
Citrus Pot Holder....107
Hot Pepper Hot Pad....108
Starburst Hot Pad....109
Dainty Dishcloths....111
Bag Lady....115
Farm Animal Magnets....117
Jute Jar Lid Covers....122
Piggyback....124
Granny's Scrap Bag Apron....126
Confetti Place Mat....128
Sitting Pretty Table Set....130

Tiny Treasures

Cornflower & Cream Doily....136
Daisy in the Sun Doily....138
Needle Me On Pincushion....139
Rosebud Hair Accent....142
Forget-Me-Not Trinket Box....143
Brimming With Roses Hat....144
Tresses Trio....146
Wild Rose Sachet....149
Pansy Garden Doily....151
Pineapple Rose Doily....152
Chain of Daisies Chest....155
Circles Chatelaine....157
Double-Tiered Star Scrunchies....159
Miniature Rose Crib Set....160
Rose Garden Accessories....164

Christmas Wish List

Gingerbread Swag....168
Gold Glitter Stockings....172
Country Christmas Booties....174
Potpourri Pillows....176
Tiny Tannenbaum....179
Petite Christmas Coasters....180
Decorative Candy Dish....181
Christmas Cuties....182
Ho-Ho-Ho Wall Hanging....185
Jolly Holiday Cushion....186
Christmas Treasures....187

General Instructions....190
Buyer's Guide....190
Stitch Guide....191
Special Thanks....192

Scrap Afghans

Nothing cleans out a basket of odd balls of yarn as quickly or as wonderfully as a gorgeous scrap afghan. Crochet any of the following nine beauties and enjoy the colorful results for years to come!

Mended Hearts

Design by Darla Fanton

Projects stitched by hand have a way of conveying a special message that only comes with the time and effort put into them. This lovely comforter can be so much more than a beautiful decoration for your room—it can truly help mend a heart.

See photo on next page.

Let's Begin!

Experience Level: Intermediate

Finished Measurements: Approximately 51" x 71"

Materials

- Spinrite Bernat Berella "4" worsted weight yarn: 17 oz winter white #8941 (MC), 14½ oz dark denim #8793 (A), 3½ oz midnight blue #8805 (B) and approximately 7–11 yds each of assorted CCs for each section of each heart
- Size K/10½ crochet hook or size needed to obtain gauge
- Tapestry needle

Gauge: 15 sts and 14 rows = 5" in hdc

To save time, take time to check gauge.

Pattern Notes

Join rnds with a sl st unless otherwise stated.

To change color in hdc, work last hdc before color change until last 3 lps before final yo rem on hook, drop working color to WS, yo with next color, complete hdc.

Use a separate ball of color for each section. Do not carry color not in use across back of work. Fasten off each color when it is no longer needed.

When working from charts, read all odd-numbered (RS) rows from right to left, all even-numbered (WS) rows from left to right.

Panel A (make 3)

Row 1 (RS): With MC, ch 26, hdc in 3rd ch from hook and in each rem ch across, turn. (25 hdc, counting last 2 chs of foundation ch as first hdc)

Row 2: Ch 2 (counts as first hdc throughout), hdc in each rem st across, turn. (25 hdc)

Rows 3–23: Work from Chart A, (page 9) changing colors as indicated; at end of Row 23, change to A, fasten off MC, turn.

Rows 24–27: Rep Row 2; at end of Row 27, change to MC, fasten off A, turn.

Rows 28–50: Continue to work from Chart A, changing colors as indicated; at end of Row 50, change to A, fasten off MC.

Rows 51–54: Rep Rows 24–27.

Rows 55 & 56: Rep Row 2.

Rows 57–185: Rep Rows 3–56 alternately, ending with a Row 23; do not change to A at end of Row 185; fasten off.

Panel B (make 2)

Rows 1–185: Rep Rows 1–185 for panel A, working from Chart B instead of Chart A.

Panel C (make 4)

Row 1 (RS): With A, ch 6, hdc in 3rd ch from hook and in each rem ch across, turn. (5 hdc, counting last 2 chs of foundation ch as first hdc)

Rows 2–23: Rep Row 2 of panel A, changing to B in last st of Row 23, turn. (5 hdc)

Rows 24–27: Rep Row 2 of panel A, changing to A in last st of Row 27, turn. (5 hdc)

Row 28: Rep Row 2 of panel A.

Rows 29–185: Rep Rows 2–28 alternately, ending with a Row 23; do not change to B in last st of Row 185; fasten off.

With tapestry needle and B, work blanket stitch around outside of each heart and featherstitch along patch lines.

Assembly

With tapestry needle and A, beg at right side, sew panels tog in following order: panel A, panel C, panel B, panel C, panel A, panel C, panel B, panel C, panel A.

Border

Rnd 1: With RS facing, attach A with a sl st in any corner, ch 3 (counts as first hdc, ch-1), hdc in same st, hdc evenly sp around, working [hdc, ch 1, hdc] in each corner, join in 2nd ch of beg ch-3.

Rnds 2–4: Ch 2, hdc in each st around, working [hdc, ch 1, hdc] in each corner ch-1 sp, join in 2nd ch of beg ch-2; at end of Rnd 4, change to B in last st.

Rnd 5: Rep Rnd 2; fasten off. ❤

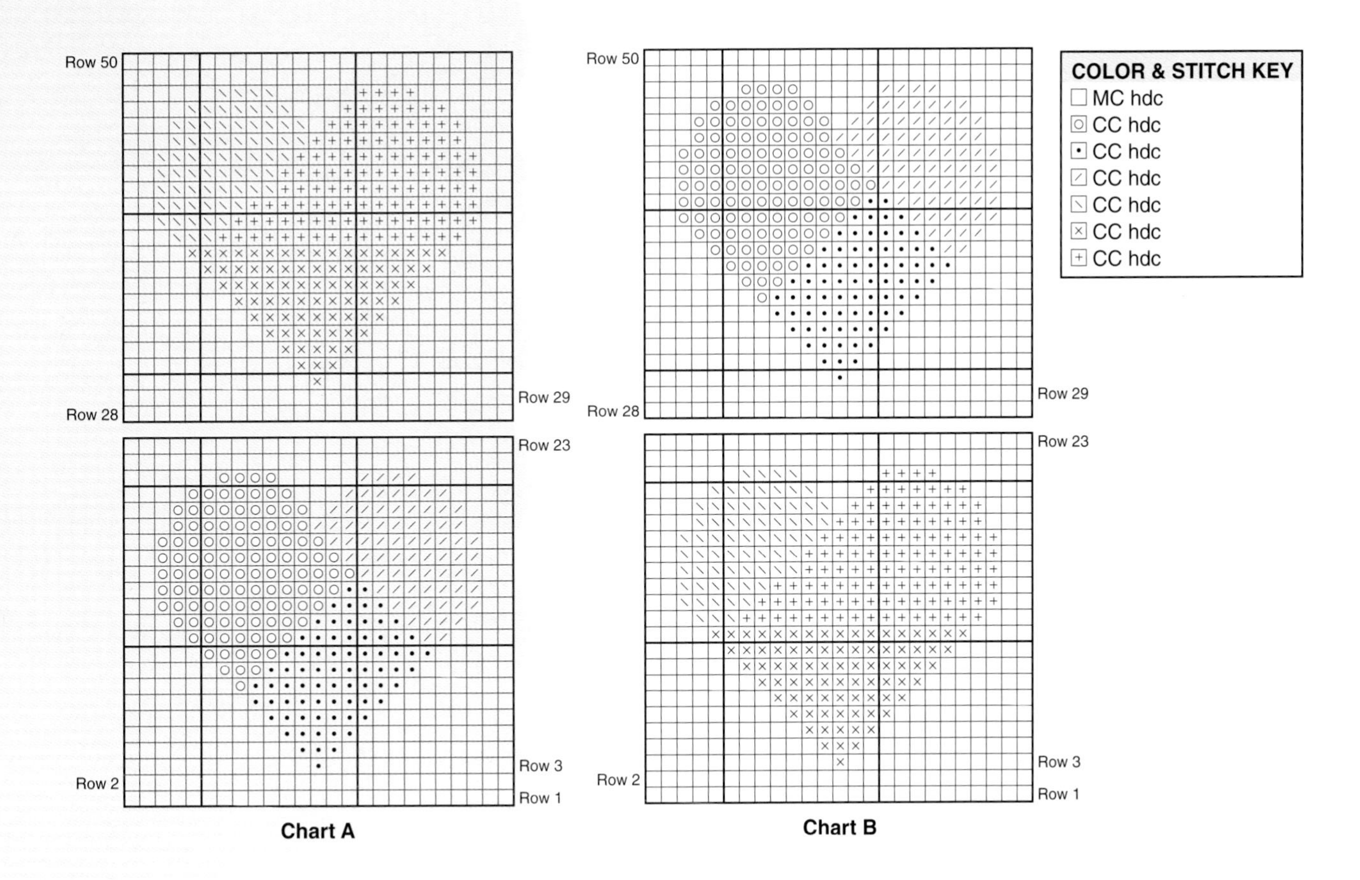

Finishing Techniques

By Jocelyn Sass

There are probably many ways in which all of us could improve our crochet skills, and one of those ways is in the techniques we use to finish our items after they have been so lovingly crocheted. Taking enough time to finish our crochet project neatly and carefully may be the most important part of our finished design. Here are some hints that can help to achieve a smooth, finished look.

When making borders, either for an afghan or another item, make sure there are enough stitches in the ends of rows so the work will lie perfectly flat.

Sew items together neatly and carefully, making sure stitches are neither too loose nor too tight. I prefer using a blunt-end metal needle called a #16 tapestry needle.

When crocheting limbs, other body parts or extra pieces for stuffed dolls and toys, leave about a 10" length of yarn when fastening off. Use this length to sew pieces on securely, and take extra stitches when needed to shape arms, etc., in the proper direction. Leave longer lengths of yarn on afghan squares and strips for sewing together later.

One of the most important finishing techniques is weaving in loose yarn ends so they won't come out. Over the years, I have tried many different techniques and have found that the best way to make them neat, and yet stay put, is to use a combination of weaving and sewing.

Thread a tapestry needle with the yarn end and, working on the back, weave in and out of the same color stitches for about 2", then take a small stitch to secure. Now turn needle and, working in the opposite direction, weave back to just before the starting point. Cut yarn at that point.

Yarn ends for stuffed items may be hidden more easily. The knots and ends are buried into the piece, a technique borrowed from quilting. Thread the needle, poke into the piece close to the knot, push needle into and through the item (stuffing and all), and come up and out several inches away. Pull knot end into piece until buried and clip excess yarn.

Dreamy Stripes

Design by Aline Suplinskas

Soothing country colors against a creamy white background are sure to make this an afghan that will bring you pleasant dreams. Whether daydreaming while curled up in a favorite chair or dozing in the recliner, you'll enjoy the warmth and the feel of this afghan.

Let's Begin!

Experience Level: Beginner

Finished Measurements: Approximately 48½" x 51"

Materials

- Worsted weight yarn: approximately 24½ oz of white (MC) and 3 oz each of 3 shades of rose, 3 shades of blue, 2 shades of green and 2 shades of berry (CCs)
- Size I/9 crochet hook or size needed to obtain gauge

Gauge 7 dc cls = 4"

To save time, take time to check gauge.

Pattern Notes

Each 2-row stripe requires approximately 37 yds.

To change color in sc, insert hook in indicated st, yo with working color, draw up a lp, drop working color to WS, yo with next color, complete sc.

Join rnds with a sl st unless otherwise indicated.

Pattern Stitch

Dc cl: Holding back on hook last lp of each st, 3 dc in indicated st or sp, yo, draw through all 4 lps on hook.

Afghan

Row 1 (RS): With any CC, ch 170, dc cl in 6th ch from hook, [ch 1, sk next ch, dc cl in next ch] rep across to last 2 chs, ch 1, sk next ch, dc in last ch, ch 1, turn. (82 dc cls)

Row 2: Sc in first st, [ch 1, sc in next dc cl] rep across to last dc cl, ch 1, sk last ch of foundation ch, sc in next ch, changing to MC in last sc, fasten off CC, turn.

Row 3: Ch 4 (counts as first dc, ch-1 throughout), sk first ch-1 sp, dc cl in next sc, [ch 1, sk next ch-1 sp, dc cl in next sc] rep across to last 2 sts, ch 1, sk last ch-1 sp, dc in last st, ch 1, turn. (82 dc cls)

Row 4: Sc in first st, [ch 1, sc in next dc cl] rep across to last dc cl, ch 1, sk next ch of turning ch-4, sc in 3rd ch of turning ch-4, changing to next CC in last sc, fasten off MC, turn.

Rows 5 & 6: Rep Rows 3 and 4, changing to MC in last sc of Row 6, fasten off CC, turn.

Rows 7–110: Rep Rows 3–6 alternately; at end of Row 110, change to MC, fasten off CC, ch 1, turn.

Border

Rnd 1: [Sc, ch 1, sc] in first st, *ch 1, [sc in next ch-1 sp, ch 1] rep across to next corner, [sc, ch 1, sc] in last sc, ch 1; working over ends of rows, [sc over end st of next row, ch 1] rep across to next corner *, [sc, ch 1, sc] in first rem lp of foundation ch, rep from * to *, join in beg sc, fasten off.

Rnd 2: With RS facing, attach any CC with a sl st in first corner ch-1 sp of Rnd 1, ch 1, beg in same sp, *4 sc in corner sp, [2 sc in next sp] rep across to next corner, 4 sc in corner sp, [2 sc in next sp, sc in next sp] rep across to next corner, rep from * around, join in beg sc, fasten off. ❤

Autumn Glory

Design by Melody MacDuffee

Bring to life the colors of fall in this multihued afghan. Richly colored yarns are combined to create this warm cover for crisp autumn days.

Let's Begin!

Experience Level: Intermediate

Finished Measurements: Approximately 51" x 66" including border

Materials

- Worsted weight yarn: 20 oz black (MC) and small amounts each of assorted CCs
- Size K/10½ crochet hook or size needed to obtain gauge

Gauge: 17 dc = 5"

To save time, take time to check gauge.

Pattern Notes

Join rnds with a sl st unless otherwise stated.

To change color in sc, insert hook in indicated st, yo with working color, draw up a lp, drop working color to WS, yo with next color, complete sc.

To change color in dc, work dc until last 2 lps before final yo rem on hook, drop working color to WS, yo with next color, complete dc.

Afghan

Row 1 (RS): With MC, ch 163, sc in 2nd ch from hook and in each rem ch across, changing to first CC in last sc, turn. (162 sc)

Row 2: Ch 3 (does not count as st throughout), sk first 3 sts, dc in back lps only of each of next 3 sts, [ch 3, sk next 3 sts, dc in back lp only of each of next 3 sts] rep across, changing to next CC in last dc, turn.

Row 3: Ch 3, sk first 3 dc, dc over ch-3 into back lp only of each of next 3 sts on row before last, [ch 3, sk next 3 dc, dc over ch-3 into back lp only of each of next 3 sts on row before last] rep across, changing to MC in last dc, turn.

Rows 4–150: Rep Row 3 in the following color sequence: 1 row MC, 1 row next CC, 1 row next CC; do not fasten off at end of Row 150; ch 1, turn.

Row 151: Sc in each of first 3 sts, hdc over ch-3 into back lp only of each of next 3 sts of row before last, [sc in each of next 3 sts, hdc over ch-3 into back lp only of each of next 3 sts of row before last] rep across, do not fasten off.

Edging

First side

Working over ends of rows, work 3 sc over end st of each block of MC and CC to next corner, fasten off.

Second side

With RS facing, working over row ends across opposite long edge, attach MC with a sl st over end st of first block of color, ch 1, beg in same block, work 3 sc over end st of each block of MC and CC to next corner, do not fasten off; ch 1, do not turn.

Border

Working across top of afghan, sc in first st, *[sk 4 sts, 11 dtr in next st, sk 4 sts, sc in next st] rep across to corner, adjusting number of sts sk before corner, if necessary, ending with sc in corner st, rep from * around, join in beg sc, fasten off.

Scrap Happy Pinwheels

Design by Frances Hughes

Go 'round and 'round with color and texture while crocheting this striking afghan. Popcorn stitches around the motifs and in the spokes of the wheels add a wonderful tactile dimension to this afghan.

Let's Begin!

Experience Level: Intermediate

Finished Measurements: Approximately 49" x 58"

Materials

- Worsted weight yarn: 7 (100-gram) skeins black (MC) and small amounts each assorted CCs
- Size G/6 crochet hook or size needed to obtain gauge
- Tapestry needle

Gauge: Motif = 7¾" across widest point

To save time, take time to check gauge.

Pattern Note

Join rnds with a sl st unless otherwise stated.

Pattern Stitch

Popcorn (pc): Work 4 dc in indicated st, remove hook from lp, insert hook from RS to WS in top of first of 4 dc, pick up dropped lp, draw through st on hook.

Motif (make 59)

Rnd 1 (RS): With first CC, ch 4, join to form a ring, ch 3 (counts as first dc throughout), work 11 more dc in ring, join in 3rd ch of beg ch-3, fasten off. (12 dc)

Rnd 2: With RS facing, attach next CC with a sl st in any dc, ch 3, dc in same st, 2 dc in each rem st around, join in 3rd ch of beg ch-3, fasten off. (24 dc)

Rnd 3: With RS facing, attach next CC with a sl st in any dc, ch 2 (counts as first bpdc), fpdc in next dc, [bpdc in next dc, fpdc in next dc] rep around, join in top of beg ch-2, fasten off. (24 sts)

Rnd 4: With RS facing, attach next CC with a sl st in any bpdc, ch 3, 2 dc in same st, fpdc in next fpdc, [3 dc in next bpdc, fpdc in next fpdc] rep around, join in 3rd ch of beg ch-3, fasten off. (48 sts)

Rnd 5: With RS facing, attach next CC with a sl st in center dc of any 3-dc group, ch 3, 3 fpdc over next fpdc, [dc in center dc of next 3-dc group, 3 fpdc over next fpdc] rep around, join in 3rd ch of beg ch-3, fasten off. (48 sts)

Rnd 6: With RS facing, attach next CC with a sl st in 3rd fpdc of any 3-fpdc group, ch 3, dc in each of next 6 sts, 3 fpdc over next fpdc, [dc in each of next 7 sts, 3 fpdc over next fpdc] rep around, join in 3rd ch of beg ch-3, fasten off. (60 sts)

Rnd 7: With RS facing, attach MC with a sl st in center fpdc of any 3-fpdc group, ch 3, 2 dc in same st, *dc in next st, [pc in next st, dc in next st] 4 times **, 3 dc in next st, rep from * around, ending last rep at **, join in 3rd ch of beg ch-3. (72 sts)

Rnd 8: Ch 1, sc in same st as joining and in each rem sc around, working 3 sc in center dc of each 3-dc group, join in beg sc, fasten off. (84 sc)

Half-Motif (make 8)

Row 1 (RS): With first CC, ch 4, 5 dc in 4th ch from hook, fasten off. (6 dc, counting last 3 chs of beg ch-4 as first dc)

Row 2: With RS facing, attach next CC with a sl st in 4th ch of first ch-4, ch 3 (counts as first dc throughout), dc in same st, 2 dc in each rem st across to last st, 3 dc in last st, fasten off. (13 dc)

Row 3: With RS facing, attach next CC with a sl st in 3rd ch of first ch-3, ch 3, dc in same st, bpdc in next st, [fpdc in next st, bpdc in next st] 5 times, 2 dc in last st, fasten off. (15 sts)

Row 4: With RS facing, attach next CC with a sl st in 3rd ch of first ch-3, ch 3, dc in next st, 3 dc in next st, [fpdc in next st, 3 dc in next st] 5 times, dc in each of last 2 dc, fasten off. (27 sts)

Row 5: With RS facing, attach next CC with a sl st in 3rd ch of first ch-3, ch 3, dc in next st, dc in center dc of next 3-dc group, [3 fpdc over next fpdc, dc in center dc of next 3-dc group] 5 times, sk next dc, dc in each of last 2 dc, fasten off. (25 sts)

Row 6: With RS facing, attach next CC with a sl st in 3rd ch of first ch-3, ch 3, dc in each of next 7 sts, [3 fpdc in center fpdc of next 3-fpdc group, dc in each of next 7 sts] twice, dc in last dc, fasten off. (29 sts)

Rnd 7: With RS facing, attach MC with a sl st in 3rd ch of first ch-3, ch 3, 2 dc in same st, *[pc in next st, dc in next st] 4 times, 3 dc in next st *, dc in next st, rep from * to * once, [dc in next st, pc in next st] 4 times, 3 dc in last st; working over row ends, [dc, pc] over end st of same row, [dc, pc] over end st of next row, dc over end st of next row, pc over end st of next row, dc over end st of next row, [pc, dc] over end st of Row 1, dc in first ch of beg ch-4 of Row 1, [dc, pc] over opposite end st of Row 1, [dc over end st of next row, pc over end st of next row] twice, join in 3rd ch of beg ch-3.

Rnd 8: Ch 1, beg in same st as joining, sc in each st around, working 3 sc in center dc of each 3-dc group, join in beg sc, fasten off.

Assembly

With tapestry needle and MC, using joining diagram (page 26) as a guide, whipstitch motifs and half-motifs tog on WS.

Border

Rnd 1: With RS facing, attach MC with a sl st in corner st at right-hand corner of either long edge, ch 1, 2 sc in same st, *sc in each st and hdc in each seam across long edge to next corner, 3 sc in corner st, sc in each st across short edge to next corner, work-

Continued on page 26

Happy Times

Design by Dot Drake

Coordinate your cheery colors and stitch a popcorn stripe in a stripe. You'll be delighted with the new afghan you create and enjoy remembering other projects you made with the same skeins of yarn.

Let's Begin!

Experience Level: Beginner

Finished Measurements: Approximately 40" x 70"

Materials

- Worsted weight yarn: approximately 3 oz white (MC) and 1–2 oz for each CC used
- Size H/8 crochet hook or size needed to obtain gauge

Gauge: 13 sts and 8 rows = 4" in hdc

To save time, take time to check gauge.

Pattern Stitch

P: Ch 5, sl st in 4th ch from hook.

Afghan

Row 1: With MC, work p 114 times, turn.

Row 2: Ch 2 (counts as first hdc throughout), [hdc in next ch st between picots, hdc in rem lp of ch at base of next p] rep across, ending with hdc in last ch st after last p, fasten off MC, turn. (228 hdc)

Row 3: Attach first CC with a sl st in first st of last row, ch 2, hdc in each rem st across, turn. (228 hdc)

Row 4: Ch 2, hdc in each rem st across, fasten off, turn. (228 hdc)

Row 5: Attach next CC with a sl st in first st of last row, ch 1, sc in first st, [tr in next st, sc in next st] rep across to last st, sc in last st, fasten off, turn. (228 sts)

Rows 6 & 7: Rep Rows 3 and 4.

Rows 8–12: Rep Rows 3–7 with next 2 desired CCs.

Rep Rows 8–12 until afghan measures approximately 40".

Next Row: Attach MC with a sl st in first st, rep Row 3, ch 1, turn.

Last Row: Sl st in first hdc, [ch 3, sl st in 3rd ch from hook, sl st in each of next 2 hdc] rep across to last st, sl st in last st, fasten off.

Thrifty Baby Blankets

With your leftover balls of baby yarn, crochet 4" squares in single crochet. Use white baby yarn to single-crochet around each square. When you have enough squares, make a carriage blanket or baby shawl.

Baby Gifts

Wrap baby gifts in receiving blankets instead of wrapping paper.

Personalized Afghans

In the lower right-hand corner of a baby afghan, embroider the baby's name and date of birth.

Sweet-Smelling Afghans

When packing away crocheted baby afghans for later use as gifts, place a sheet of dryer fabric softener in with the afghan. It will smell fresh when opened weeks or months later.

Separate Yarns

When working on afghans with more than one string of yarn, put the balls or skeins into separate plastic bags with a twist tie around the top. This will keep the yarn neat, clean and untangled. You can adjust the twist tie so that your yarn flows smoothly.

Odds & Ends

When starting a new project, keep a basket handy and, as soon as you end up with an odd piece of yarn or leftover skein, crochet a motif—granny square, single-crochet square, striped square, etc. As you continue with your main projects, your motifs will add up. After two afghans, you'll usually have enough motifs to make a third. Name this your "profit" afghan, since the cost of the materials is in the first two afghans!

Random Acts of Kindness

Design by Michele Maks Thompson

This afghan was first crocheted in response to a crisis in upstate New York. Scraps of yarn were randomly selected, and the hand-stitched acts of kindness brought wonderful relief to people in need. Check with a charitable organization in your community to find out who could benefit from your acts of kindness.

Let's Begin!

Experience Level: Beginner

Finished Measurements: Approximately 57" x 59"

Materials

- Worsted weight yarn: 68 oz assorted colors
- Size N/15 crochet hook or size needed to obtain gauge
- Tapestry needle

Gauge: 8 dc = 4" with 2 strands held tog

To save time, take time to check gauge.

Pattern Notes

Afghan is worked from side to side.

Use 2 strands held tog throughout.

When attaching next color and when fastening off previous color at begs and ends of rows, leave 3" lengths for fringe. When changing colors in mid-row, weave ends in on WS with tapestry needle.

To change color in dc, work dc with working color until last 2 lps before final yo rem on hook, drop working color to WS, yo with next color, complete dc.

Afghan

Row 1 (RS): With 1 strand each of any 2 colors held tog, ch 122, dc in 4th ch from hook and in each rem ch across, changing to next 2 colors in last st, fasten off first 2 colors, turn. (120 dc, counting last 3 chs of foundation ch as first dc)

Row 2: Ch 3 (counts as first dc throughout), dc in next st and in each rem st across, changing to next 2 colors in last st, fasten off previous 2 colors, turn. (120 dc)

Rep Row 2 until afghan measures 57" or desired width, fasten off.

Fringe

Tie 3" lengths on top and bottom of afghan with square knots for fringe. Cut 2 (3") lengths of yarn; tie with square knot between first 2 units of fringe at top. Rep for each sp between 2 units of fringe across rem of top and across bottom. Cut 2 (3") lengths of yarn and tie with square knot in first st across either long edge. Rep for each rem st across same long edge and across next long edge. ♥

Pastel Stripes

Design by Rose Pirrone

This dainty thread coverlet is just heavy enough to keep your little one warm on mild days. The solid pastel colors are perfect for displaying the pretty shell stitches.

Let's Begin!

Experience Level: Intermediate

Finished Measurements: Approximately 25" x 33½" including border

Materials

- DMC Baroque crochet cotton size 10 (400 yds per skein): 2 skeins each baby blue #0800, baby yellow #0745 and baby pink #0818, and 1 skein white #0001
- Size 3 steel crochet hook or size needed to obtain gauge

Gauge: 8 dc =1"

To save time, take time to check gauge.

Pattern Notes

Join rnds with a sl st unless otherwise stated.

To change color in dc, work dc until last 2 lps before final yo rem on hook, drop working color to WS, yo with next color, complete dc.

Pattern Stitches

Shell: [2 dc, ch 2, 2 dc] in indicated st or sp.

Beg shell: [Ch 3, dc, ch 2, 2 dc] in indicated st or sp.

Afghan

Row 1 (RS): With baby blue, ch 186, dc in 4th ch from hook and in each rem ch across, turn. (184 dc, counting last 3 chs of foundation ch as first dc)

Rows 2 & 3: Ch 3 (counts as first dc throughout), dc in each rem st across, turn; at end of Row 3, change to baby yellow in last st, fasten off baby blue, turn. (184 dc)

Row 4: Ch 3, dc in each of next 7 sts, *[sk 2 sts, shell in next st] twice, sk 2 sts, dc in each of next 8 sts, rep from * across, turn.

Row 5: Ch 3, dc in each of next 7 sts, *[shell in next shell sp] twice **, dc in each of first 3 dc of next 8-dc group, [fpdc over next st] twice, dc in each of next 3 sts, rep from * across to last 8 sts, ending last rep at **, dc in each of last 8 sts, turn.

Row 6: Ch 3, dc in each of next 7 sts, *[shell in next shell sp] twice **, dc in each of first 3 dc of next 8-dc group, [bpdc over next st] twice, dc in each of next 3 sts, rep from * across to last 8 sts, ending last rep at **, dc in each of last 8 sts, turn.

Rows 7–10: Rep Rows 5 and 6 alternately, changing to baby pink in last st of Row 10, fasten off baby yellow, turn.

Rows 11–17: Rep Rows 5 and 6 alternately, ending with Row 5; change to baby blue in last st of Row 17, fasten off baby pink, turn.

Rows 18–122: Beg with Row 6, rep Rows 5 and 6 alternately in the following color sequence: 7 rows baby blue, 7 rows baby yellow, 7 rows baby pink; change to baby blue in last st of Row 122, turn.

Row 123: Ch 3, dc in each rem dc and post st across, skipping ch-2 sps of shells, turn. (184 dc)

Rows 124 & 125: Ch 3, dc in each rem st across, turn; fasten off at end of Row 125.

Border

Rnd 1: With RS facing, attach white with a sl st in st at upper right corner, beg shell in same st, *[sk 3 sts, shell in next st] rep across to next corner, adjusting number of sts sk before corner st, if necessary; shell in corner st; working over ends of rows, work shells evenly sp across to next corner *, shell in corner st; rep from * to *, join in 3rd ch of beg ch-3.

Rnd 2: Sl st in next dc and in shell sp, beg shell in same sp, [shell in next shell sp] rep around, join in 3rd ch of beg ch-3.

Rnd 3: Sl st in next dc and in shell sp, [ch 3, 4 dc] in same sp, *sc between same shell and next shell **, 5 dc in next shell sp, rep from * around, ending last rep at **, join in 3rd ch of beg ch-3, fasten off white.

Rnd 4: Attach baby blue, baby pink or baby yellow with a sl st in first dc of any 5-dc group, ch 1, beg in same st, *sc in each of first 2 dc of 5-dc group, [sc, ch 3, sc] in center dc, sc in each of next 2 dc, sc over next sc into sp between shells on Rnd 2, rep from * around, join in beg sc, fasten off.

Finishing

Place blanket RS down on thick, padded surface. Steam-press border lightly. ♥

Parfait Baby Afghan

Design by Roberta Maier

Imagine the cool, light flavor of your favorite parfait. Using pastel shades of lightweight baby yarn, stitch this afghan for that same cool, light sensation. The extra-long fringe will help to make this an extra-special cover for a baby in your life.

Let's Begin!

Experience Level: Beginner

Finished Measurements: 36" square not including fringe

Materials

- Baby sport weight yarn: 12 oz white (MC), 4 oz each light blue (A), light green (B) and light yellow (C), and 2 oz each light pink (D) and variegated pastels (E)
- Size F/5 crochet hook or size needed to obtain gauge

Gauge: 4 dc = 1"

To save time, take time to check gauge.

Pattern Notes

Join rnds with a sl st unless otherwise stated.

To change color in sc, insert hook in indicated st, yo with working color, draw up a lp, drop working color to WS, yo with next color, complete dc.

To change color in dc, work dc until last 2 lps before final yo rem on hook, drop working color to WS, yo with next color, complete sc.

Afghan

Row 1 (RS): With MC, ch 138, sc in 2nd ch from hook and in each rem ch across, changing to A in last sc, turn. (137 sc)

Row 2: Ch 3 (counts as first dc throughout), dc in next st, [ch 1, sk 1 sc, dc in each of next 11 sc] 11 times, ch 1, sk next sc, dc in each of last 2 sc, turn.

Row 3: Ch 3, dc in next dc, dc in next ch-1 sp, [ch 1, sk next dc, dc in each of next 9 dc, ch 1, sk next dc, dc in next ch-1 sp] 11 times, dc in each of last 2 sts, turn.

Row 4: Ch 3, dc in each of next 2 dc, dc in next ch-1 sp, *ch 1, sk next dc, dc in each of next 7 dc, ch 1, sk next dc, dc in next ch-1 sp, dc in next dc **, dc in next ch-1 sp, rep from * across to last 2 sts, ending last rep at **, dc in each of last 2 sts, turn.

Row 5: Ch 3, dc in each of next 3 dc, dc in next ch-1 sp, *ch 1, sk next dc, dc in each of next 5 dc, ch 1, sk next dc, dc in next ch-1 sp, dc in each of next 3 dc **, dc in next ch-1 sp, rep from * across to last st, ending last rep at **, dc in last st, turn.

Row 6: Ch 3, dc in each of next 4 dc, dc in next ch-1 sp, *ch 1, sk next dc, dc in each of next 3 dc, ch 1, sk next dc, dc in next ch-1 sp, dc in each of next 5 dc **, dc in next ch-1 sp, rep from * across, ending last rep at **, turn.

Row 7: Ch 3, dc in each of next 5 dc, *dc in next ch-1 sp, ch 1, sk next dc, dc in next dc, ch 1, sk next dc, dc in next ch-1 sp **, dc in each of next 7 dc, rep from * across to last 6 sts, ending last rep at **, dc in each of last 6 sts, turn.

Row 8: Ch 3, dc in each of next 6 dc, *dc in next ch-1 sp, ch 1, sk next dc, dc in next ch-1 sp **, dc in each of next 9 dc, rep from * across to last 7 sts, ending last rep at **, dc in each of last 7 sts, changing to MC in last dc, fasten off A, ch 1, turn.

Row 9: Sc in each dc and each ch-1 sp across, ch 1, turn. (137 sc)

Row 10: Sc in each sc across, ch 1, turn.

Row 11: Rep Row 10, changing to E in last sc, fasten off MC, ch 1, turn.

Row 12: Sc in each sc across, changing to MC in last st, fasten off E, ch 1, turn.

Rows 13–15: Rep Row 10, changing to B in last sc of Row 15, do not ch 1 at end of Row 15; fasten off MC, turn.

Rows 16–29: Rep Rows 2–15, changing to C in last sc of Row 29.

Rows 30–43: Rep Rows 2–15, changing to D in last sc of Row 43.

Rows 44–57: Rep Rows 2–15, changing to C in last sc of Row 57.

Rows 58–71: Rep Rows 2–15, changing to B in last sc of Row 71.

Rows 72–85: Rep Rows 2–15, changing to A in last sc of Row 85.

Rows 86–93: Rep Rows 2–9; fasten off at end of Row 93.

Border

Rnd 1: With RS facing, attach MC with a sl st in first rem lp of foundation ch at bottom right-hand corner, ch 1, 2 sc in same st; *working over row ends, work 2 sc over end st of each dc row and 1 sc over end st of each sc row to next corner *, 3 sc in first st of last row, sc in each st across last row to next corner, 3 sc in last st of last row, rep from * to *, 3 sc in first rem lp of foundation ch, sc in each rem st across bottom, sc in same st as beg sc, join in beg sc, ch 1, turn.

Rnd 2: Ch 1, 2 sc in same st as joining, sc in each rem sc around, working 3 sc in each corner sc, sc in same st as beg sc, join in beg sc, ch 1, turn.

Rnd 3: Rep Rnd 2, changing to E in last sc of rnd, join in beg sc, do not fasten off MC, ch 1, turn.

Rnd 4: Rep Rnd 2, changing to MC in last sc of rnd, join in beg sc, fasten off E, ch 1, turn.

Rnds 5–7: Rep Rnd 2; at end of Rnd 7, fasten off.

Finishing

Fringe

Cut 2 (10") strands of MC. Holding both strands tog, fold in half, insert hook from WS to RS in any sc on last rnd of border, draw folded end of strands through st to form lp, pull free ends through lp, pull to tighten. Rep for each sc around last rnd of border. Trim ends evenly. ❤

Granny's Scrap Basket

Design by Katherine Eng

Stitch this pleasant pattern using eight colors against a stunning black background. The pastel stripes in the border with the small scalloped edge set this afghan apart as a comfortable, yet unique, project.

Let's Begin!

Experience Level: Intermediate

Finished Measurements: Approximately 45" x 63"

Materials

- Worsted weight yarn: 26 oz black (MC) and small amounts (less than 3 oz each) burgundy (A), bright pink (B), medium lavender (C), light lavender (D), medium green (E), light green (F), medium blue (G) and light blue (H)
- Size G/6 crochet hook or size needed to obtain gauge
- Tapestry needle

Gauge: Motif = 5½" square

To save time, take time to check gauge.

Pattern Note

Join rnds with a sl st unless otherwise stated.

Pattern Stitches

Small shell (sm sh): [2 dc, ch 2, 2 dc] in indicated sp or st.

Large shell (lg sh): [3 dc, ch 2, 3 dc] in indicated sp or st.

Motif A (make 20)

Rnd 1 (RS): With A, ch 4, join to form a ring, ch 1, sc in ring, ch 2, [2 sc in ring, ch 2] 3 times, sc in ring, join in beg sc. (8 sc; 4 ch-2 sps)

Rnd 2: Ch 1, sc in same st as joining, *sm sh in next ch-2 sp, sc in next sc, ch 4 **, sc in next sc, rep from * around, ending last rep at **, join in beg sc, fasten off.

Rnd 3: With RS facing, attach MC with a sl st in any sm sh sp, ch 1, sc in same sp, *ch 1, lg sh in next ch-4 sp, ch 1 **, sc in next sm sh sp, rep from * around, ending last rep at **, join in beg sc.

Rnd 4: Ch 1, sc in same st as joining and in each rem dc and ch-1 sp around, working [sc, ch 2, sc] in each lg sh sp, join in beg sc, fasten off. (44 sc)

Rnd 5: With RS facing, attach E with a sl st in 2nd sc to the left of any corner ch-2 sp, ch 1, sc in same st, *ch 1, sk next sc, sc in next sc, ch 1, sk next sc, fpdc over next sc in row before last, ch 1, [sk next sc, sc in next sc, ch 1] twice, [sc, ch 2, sc] in corner ch-2 sp, ch 1, sk next sc **, sc in next sc, rep from * around, ending last rep at **, join in beg sc, ch 1, turn.

Rnd 6: Sl st in next ch-1 sp, ch 1, sc in same sp, ch 1, *[sc, ch 2, sc] in corner ch-2 sp, ch 1, [sc in next ch-1 sp, ch 1] rep across to next corner ch-2 sp, rep from * around, ending with [sc in next ch-1 sp, ch 1] rep across last side, join in beg sc, fasten off.

Rnd 7: With RS facing, attach MC with a sl st in any corner ch-2 sp, ch 1, *[sc, ch 3, sc] in corner ch-2 sp, sc in next sc, [sc in next ch-1 sp, sc in next sc] 3 times, fpdc over next fpdc in row before last, sc in next sc, [sc in next ch-1 sp, sc in next sc] 3 times, rep from * around, join in beg sc, fasten off.

Motif B (make 20)

Rnds 1–8: Rep Rnds 1–8 of motif A, working Rnds 1 and 2 with B, Rnds 3, 4 and 7 with MC and Rnds 5 and 6 with F.

Motif C (make 20)

Rnds 1–8: Rep Rnds 1–8 of motif A, working Rnds 1 and 2 with C, Rnds 3, 4 and 7 with MC and Rnds 5 and 6 with G.

Motif D (make 10)

Rnds 1–8: Rep Rnds 1–8 of motif A, working Rnds 1 and 2 with D, Rnds 3, 4 and 7 with MC and Rnds 5 and 6 with H.

Assembly

With tapestry needle and MC, whipstitch 10 motifs D tog through back lps for center strip. Make 2 strips of 10 motifs each with motif B and whipstitch 1 on each side of center strip. Make 2 strips of 10 motifs each with motif C and whipstitch 1 on each side of last 2 strips. Make 2 strips of 10 motifs each with motif A and whipstitch 1 on each side of last 2 strips.

Border

Rnd 1: With RS facing, attach MC with a sl st near center st of any motif on any edge, ch 3 (counts as first dc throughout), *dc in each sc, each fpdc and each ch-3 sp, and tr in each seam across edge to corner, sm sh in corner ch-3 sp, rep from * around, ending with dc in each sc, fpdc and ch-3 sp, and tr in each seam across to beg ch-3, join in 3rd ch of beg ch-3, fasten off.

Rnd 2: With RS facing, attach D with a sl st in any sm sh sp, ch 1, beg in same sp, *[sc, ch 3, sc] in sm sh sp, ch 1, [sk next st, sc in next st, ch 1] rep across to next sm sh sp, rep from * around, join in beg sc, fasten off.

Rnd 3: With WS facing, attach MC with a sl st in any ch-1 sp near center of any edge, ch 1, sc in same sp, *ch 1, [sc in next ch-1 sp, ch 1] rep across to corner, [sc, ch 3, sc] in corner sp, rep from * around, ending with ch 1, [sc in next ch-1 sp, ch 1] rep across last side to beg sc, join in beg sc, turn.

Rnd 4: Ch 3, dc in each rem sc and ch-1 sp around, working sm sh in each corner ch-3 sp, join in 3rd ch of beg ch-3, fasten off.

Rnd 5: With RS facing, attach H with a sl st in 3rd dc to the left of any sm sh sp, ch 1, sc in same st, *ch 2, [sk 2 sts, sc in next st, ch 2] rep across to next corner, [sc, ch 3, sc] in sm sh sp **, rep from * around, ending last rep at **, ch 2, join in beg sc, fasten off.

Rnd 6: With WS facing, attach MC with a sl st in any ch-2 sp near center of any edge, ch 1, sc in same sp, *ch 2, [sc in next ch-2 sp, ch 2] rep across to corner, [sc, ch 3, sc] in corner sp, rep from * around, ending with ch 2, [sc in next ch-2 sp, ch 2] rep across last side to beg sc, join in beg sc, ch 1, turn.

Rnd 7: *[{Sc, ch 3, sc} in next ch-2 sp, ch 1] rep across to corner, [sc, ch 2, sc, ch 3, sc, ch 2, sc] in corner sp, ch 1, rep from * around, ending with ch 1, [{sc, ch 3, sc} in next ch-2 sp, ch 1] rep across last side to beg sc, join in beg sc, fasten off.

Scrap Happy Pinwheels

Continued from page 15

ing 3 sc at outer point of each motif and skipping 1 sc at each side of each seam between motifs **, 3 sc in corner st, rep from * around, ending last rep at **, sc in same st as beg sc, join in beg sc.

Rnd 2: Ch 1, 2 sc in same st as joining, sc in each st around, working 3 sc in center sc of each 3-sc group and skipping 2 sc at base of each "V" across each short edge, sc in same st as beg sc, join in beg sc.

Rnd 3: Ch 1, beg in same st as joining, reverse sc in each st around, join in beg reverse sc, fasten off.

JOINING KEY
- Motif
- Half-motif

Joining Diagram

All Through the House

Turn your crochet hook into a magic wand as you turn those leftover thread and yarn odds and ends into enchanting home decor pieces from delicate doilies and elegant table runners to throw pillows and accent rugs!

Painted Daisies Runner

Design by Lucille LaFlamme

Assorted pastels surround brighter colors to complete this palette of painted daisies. The unique shape and size of this table runner make it one to distinguish a special table or dresser.

Let's Begin!

Experience Level: Intermediate

Finished Measurements
Approximately 12" x 44"

Materials

- DMC Cebelia crochet cotton size 10 (50 grams per ball):1 ball light yellow #745 (MC), 88 yds each light pink #747 (A) and light blue #818 (B), and 22 yds each dark blue #799 (C), dark pink #3326 (D) and gold #743 (E)
- Size 7 steel crochet hook or size needed to obtain gauge

Gauge: Motif = 3¼" in diameter

To save time, take time to check gauge.

Pattern Note

Join rnds with a sl st unless otherwise stated.

Pattern Stitches

Tr5tog: Holding back on hook last lp of each st, tr in each of next 5 sts, yo, draw through all 6 lps on hook.

Tr6tog: Holding back on hook last lp of each st, tr in each of next 6 sts, yo, draw through all 7 lps on hook.

P: Ch 4, sl st in top of last dc or last sc made.

First Motif

Rnd 1: With MC, ch 9, join to form a ring, ch 1, 16 sc in ring, join in beg sc. (16 sc)

Rnd 2: Ch 7 (counts as first dc, ch-4), [sk next sc, dc in next sc, ch 4] rep around, ending with sk last sc, join in 3rd ch of beg ch-7. (8 ch-4 sps)

Rnd 3: Sl st in first sp, ch 4 (counts as first tr), 5 tr in same sp, ch 3, [6

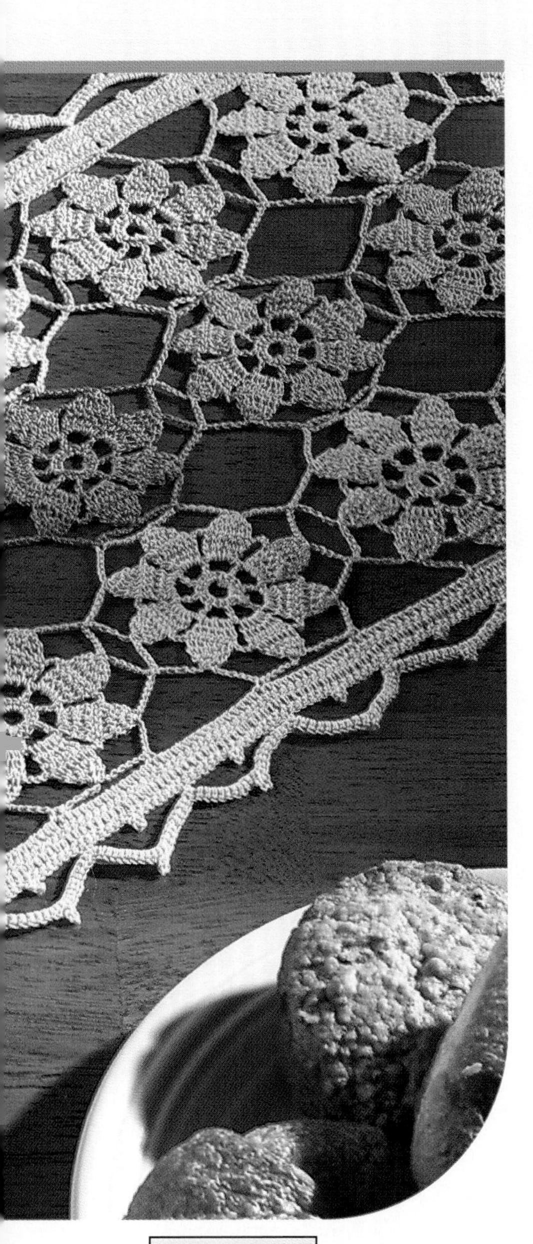

tr in next sp, ch 3] rep around, join in 4th ch of beg ch-4.

Rnd 4: Ch 3, tr5tog, ch 13, [sk ch-3 sp, tr6tog, ch 13] rep around, join in top of tr5tog, fasten off.

Second Motif

Rnds 1–3: With A, rep Rnds 1–3 of first motif.

Rnd 4: Ch 3, tr5tog, ch 6, sl st in 7th ch of corresponding ch-13 on previous motif, ch 6, sk next ch-3 sp on working motif, tr6tog (1 side joined), continue around as for Rnd 4 of first motif.

Rem Motifs

Rnds 1–4: Following joining diagram in numerical order for color, rep Rnds 1–4 of 2nd motif, joining as established on Rnd 4 of 2nd motif on as many sides as are indicated on joining diagram.

Border

Rnd 1: With RS facing, attach MC with a sl st in 7th ch of last free ch-13 lp at top of 30th motif on right-hand end of runner (see joining diagram), ch 1, sc in same ch, *[ch 15, sc in 7th ch of next free ch-13 lp on next motif, {ch 13, sc in 7th ch of next free ch-13 lp on same motif twice}] twice **, [ch 15, sc in 7th ch of next free ch-13 lp on next motif, ch 13, sc in 7th ch of next free ch-13 lp on same motif] 6 times, rep from * to **, ch 15, sc in 7th ch of next free ch-13 lp on next motif ***, [ch 13, sc in 7th ch of next free ch-13 lp on same motif] 5 times, rep from * around to last motif, ending last rep at ***, [ch 13, sc in 7th ch of next free ch-13 lp on same motif] 4 times, ch 15, join in beg sc.

Rnd 2: Ch 3 (counts as first dc throughout), dc in each rem ch and each sc around, join in 3rd ch of beg ch-3.

Rnd 3: Ch 3, dc in each of next 8 dc, p, dc in each of next 15 dc, p, continue around, working dc in each dc and p over center dc of each 13-dc and 15-dc group, join in 3rd ch of beg ch-3. (60 picots)

Rnd 4: Ch 1, sc in same st as joining, *[ch 17, sc in center dc between next 2 picots] 25 times *, [ch 19, sc in center dc between next 2 picots] 5 times, rep from * to *, [ch 19, sc in center dc between next 2 picots] 4 times, ch 19, join in beg sc.

Rnd 5: Ch 1, *[{10 sc, p, 10 sc} over next sp] 25 times, [{11 sc, p, 11 sc} over next st] 5 times, rep from * around, join in beg sc, fasten off. ❤

COLOR KEY
MC Light yellow
A Light pink
B Light blue
C Dark blue
D Dark pink
E Gold
∩ Ch-13 lp

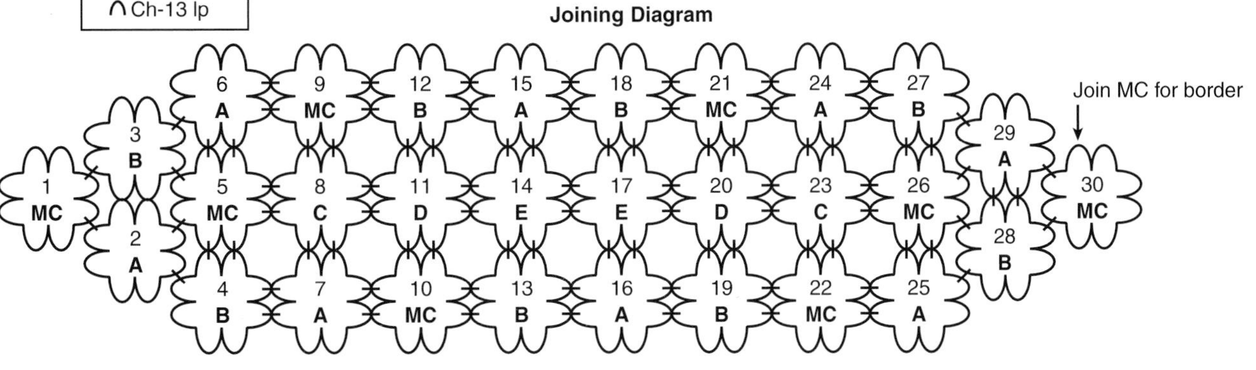

Joining Diagram

Windowsill Tissue Box Cover

Design by Daria McGuire for Women of Design

Open wide the shutters to let the sunshine in! Crochet this lovely window box scene to use as a bright accent in your home.

Let's Begin!

Experience Level: Intermediate

Finished Measurements: Fits boutique-style tissue box

Materials

- Spinrite Bernat Berella "4" worsted weight yarn: 2 oz oak #8796, 1½ oz white #8942, 1 oz black #8994, ½ oz each medium ocean #8762, rose #8922 and light damson #8854, and small amount light tapestry gold #8886
- Size G/6 crochet hook
- Size H/8 crochet hook or size needed to obtain gauge
- Yarn needle

Gauge: 9 sts and 9 rows = 2" in sc with larger hook

To save time, take time to check gauge.

Side (make 3)

Row 1 (WS): With larger hook and oak, ch 22, dc in 4th ch from hook, dc in each rem ch across, turn. (20 dc, counting last 3 chs of foundation ch as first dc)

Row 2: Ch 2 (counts as first hdc throughout), hdc in each of next 3 sts, fpdc over each of next 4 sts, hdc in each of next 4 sts] twice, turn. (20 sts)

Row 3: Ch 3 (counts as first dc throughout), dc in each rem st across, turn. (20 dc)

Row 4: Ch 2, fpdc over each of next 3 dc, hdc in each of next 4 dc, fpdc over each of next 4 dc, hdc in each of next 4 dc, fpdc over each of next 3 dc, hdc in last st, turn.

Row 5: Rep Row 3.

Rows 6–9: Rep Rows 2–5.

Rows 10–12: Rep Rows 2–4, do not fasten off at end of Row 12, do not turn.

Edging

With smaller hook ch 1, sc evenly around outer edge, working 3 sc in each corner, join with sl st in beg sc, fasten off.

Front

Row 1: With larger hook and white, ch 21, sc in 2nd ch from hook and in each rem ch across, ch 1, turn. (20 sc)

Rows 2–21: Sc in each sc across, ch 1, turn, fasten off at end of Row 21.

Edging

With smaller hook, attach black in any st on outer edge of front, ch 1, sc evenly sp around outer edge, working 3 sc in each corner, join with sl st in beg sc, fasten off.

Crossbars

Attach black at side edge of window between Rows 5 and 6, with smaller hook, sl st evenly across to opposite side edge of window, fasten off.

Rep for 2nd crossbar between Rows 13 and 14.

Attach black between 10th and 11th sts on top row of window, sl st evenly from top edge to bottom crossbar, fasten off.

With oak and yarn needle, embroider a double ch-st circle for wreath, following Fig. 1. Using light damson and yarn needle, make 6 triple French knots evenly sp around wreath. Using light tapestry gold, make 6 single French knots evenly sp between light damson French knots, as shown in photo.

Top

Rows 1–5: Rep Rows 1–5 of side.

Row 6: Ch 2, hdc in each of next 4 sts, ch 10, sk 10 sts, hdc in each of last 5 sts, turn.

Row 7: Ch 3, dc in each of next 4 sts, dc in each of next 10 chs, dc in each of last 5 sts, turn. (20 dc)

Row 8: Rep Row 4.

Row 9: Rep Row 3.

Row 10: Rep Row 2.

Row 11: Rep Row 3, do not fasten off, ch 1, turn.

Edgings

With smaller hook, sc evenly sp around outer edge, working 3 sc in each corner, join with sl st in beg sc, fasten off.

Attach oak in any st of ch-10 sp on Row 6, ch 1, sc evenly sp around tissue opening, join with sl st in beg sc, fasten off.

Flower Box

Row 1: With larger hook and black, ch 21, sc in 2nd ch from hook and in each rem ch across, ch 1, turn. (20 sc)

Row 2: Sc in each sc across, ch 1, turn.

Row 3: 2 sc in first st, sc in each of next 18 sts, 2 sc in last st, ch 1, turn. (22 sc)

Rows 4–6: Rep Row 2, do not fasten off at end of last row, do not turn.

With smaller hook, ch 1, sc evenly sp across ends of last 6 rows to bottom, fasten off.

Attach black over end st of row on opposite edge, ch 1, sc evenly sp across, fasten off.

Right Shutter

Row 1: With RS facing, working in front lps only this row, with smaller hook, attach medium ocean in sc at right end of Row 5 of window, ch 1, beg in same st, sc in each of next 17 sc, turn. (17 sc)

Row 2: Ch 5 (counts as first tr, ch-1), sk next sc, tr in next sc, [ch 1, sk next sc, tr in next sc] 7 times, ch 1, turn.

Row 3: Sc in first st, [sc in next ch-1 sp, sc in next st] rep across, ending with sc in each of last 2 chs of beg ch-5, fasten off. (17 sc)

Edging

With smaller hook, RS facing, attach medium ocean at inner edge of shorter side at bottom of shutter, ch 1, sc evenly sp across 3 sides of shutter, fasten off.

Left Shutter

Row 1: With RS facing, working in front lps only this row, with smaller hook, attach medium ocean in sc at top edge of left side of window, beg in same st, sc in each of next 17 sc, ending at Row 5, turn. (17 sc)

Rows 2 & 3: Rep Rows 2 and 3 of right shutter.

Edging

Beg at inner edge of shorter side at top of shutter, work as for edging for right shutter.

Curtain (make 2)

Row 1: With smaller hook and white, ch 8, sc in 2nd ch from hook, [ch 3, sk 2 chs, sc in next ch] twice, turn.

Row 2: Ch 3 (counts as first hdc, ch-1), sc in next ch-3 sp, ch 3, sc in next ch-3 sp, ch 1, hdc in last sc, ch 1, turn.

Row 3: Sc in first hdc, ch 3, sc in next ch-3 sp, ch 3, sc in 2nd ch of beg ch-3, turn.

Rows 4–13: Rep Rows 2 and 3, do not fasten off at end of Row 13, ch 1, turn.

Edging

Sc in first st, ch 1, *[sk next st, sc in next st, ch 1] * rep across last row to corner, 2 sc in corner st, [ch 1, sk next row, sc over end of next row] rep across long edge,

Continued on page 33

Fig. 1

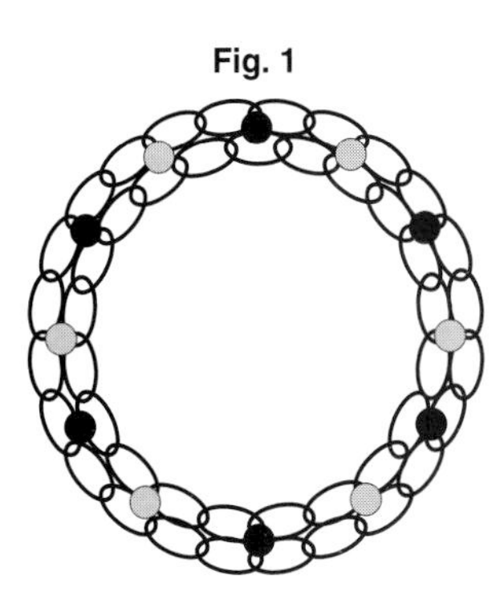

Floral Window Shade Trim

Design by Hélène Rush

Beautify your windows by selecting a fabric to coordinate with the colors of your room. Then add this beautiful crocheted floral trim to create your own individualized window shade.

Let's Begin!

Experience Level: Intermediate

Finished Measurement: 4" wide

Materials

- Sport weight cotton: 2 oz each green (A), yellow (B) and pink (C)
- Size G/6 crochet hook or size needed to obtain gauge
- Window shade roller and hardware
- Cotton fabric in width to fit window shade roller
- Dritz Shademaker heavyweight fusible interfacing
- Dritz HeatnBond ⅝"-wide double-sided fusible tape
- Sewing needle and sewing thread in matching color
- 1¼"-wide masking tape

Gauge: Rnds 1–4 of first motif = 2½" in diameter

To save time, take time to check gauge.

Pattern Note

Join rnds with a sl st unless otherwise stated.

Pattern Stitches

Beg 3-dc cl: Ch 3, holding back on hook last lp of each st, 2 dc in same st or sp, yo, draw through all 3 lps on hook.

3-dc cl: Holding back on hook last lp of each st, 3 dc in indicated st or sp, yo, draw through all 4 lps on hook.

First Motif

Rnd 1 (RS): With B, ch 4, join to form a ring, ch 1, 8 sc in ring, join in back lp only of beg sc. (8 sc)

Rnd 2: Working in back lps only this rnd, ch 1, sc in same st as joining, ch 4, [sc in next sc, ch 4] rep around, join in beg sc. (8 ch-4 sps)

Rnd 3: Sl st in first ch-4 sp, ch 2 (counts as first hdc), [dc, tr, dc, hdc] in same sp, [hdc, dc, tr, dc, hdc] in each rem sp around, join in 2nd ch of beg ch-2, fasten off. (8 petals)

Rnd 4: With RS facing, attach A with a sl st between last hdc made and beg ch-2, beg 3-dc cl in same sp, *ch 2, sc in next tr of next petal, ch 2 **, 3-dc cl between same petal and next petal, rep from * around, ending last rep at **, join in 3rd ch of beg ch-3, fasten off.

Rnd 5: With RS facing, attach C with a sl st in rem lp of any sc on Rnd 1, ch 1, beg in same st, [sc, hdc, dc, hdc, sc] in each rem lp around, join in beg sc, fasten off. (8 petals)

Rem Motifs

Rnds 1–3: Rep Rnds 1–3 of first motif.

Rnd 4: With RS facing, attach A with a sl st between last hdc made and beg ch-2, beg 3-dc cl in same sp, sl st in corresponding 3-dc cl on previous motif, ch 2, sc in next tr of next petal on working motif, sl st in corresponding sc on previous motif, ch 2, 3-dc cl between same petal and next petal on working motif, sl st in corresponding 3-dc cl on previous motif, ch 2, continue around on working motif as for first motif, fasten off.

Rnd 5: Rep Rnd 5 of first motif.

Make and join as many motifs as are necessary for desired length of window shade.

Heading

Row 1: With RS facing, attach A with a sl st in upper 3-dc cl of 2 (3-dc cls) on right-hand side of first motif at right edge, ch 4 (counts as first tr), tr in next sc, *ch 5, sc in next 3-dc cl, 2 sc in next sp, sc in next sc, 2 sc in next sp, sc in next 3-dc cl, ch 5 **; holding back last lp of each st on hook, tr in next sc on same motif, tr in corresponding sc on next motif, yo, draw through all 3 lps on hook, rep from * across, ending last rep at **; holding back on hook last lp of each st, tr in next sc, tr in next 3-dc cl, yo, draw through all 3 lps on hook, ch 1, turn.

Row 2: Sc in first st, *5 sc in next ch-5 sp, sc in each of next 7 sc, 5

sc in next ch-5 sp **, sk next st, rep from * across, ending last rep at **, sc in 4th ch of ch-4, ch 1, turn.

Row 3: Sc in each of first 2 sc, [ch 4, sk next 3 sc, sc in next sc] rep across, ending with ch 4, sc in each of last 2 sc, adjusting number of sts skipped, if necessary, ch 1, turn.

Row 4: Sc in first sc, ch 2, sc in next ch-4 sp, [ch 4, sc in next ch-4 sp] rep across, ending with ch 2, sc in last sc, turn.

Row 5: Ch 3 (counts as first dc), dc in ch-2 sp, 3 dc in each ch-4 sp across, dc in last ch-2 sp, dc in next sc, fasten off.

Finishing

Cut shade interfacing the width of roller plus ⅝" allowance on each side, and cut length to fit window plus 15".

With iron on wool setting, leaving ⅝"-wide allowance free on each side, fuse to WS of fabric using an up-and-down motion, not sliding iron back and forth. Using fusible tape, apply to each side of shade, remove fabric backing, fold allowance toward shade on WS and fuse in place again. Apply fusible tape to lower edge of shade; fold to WS by 1½" to create stick casing. Remove fabric backing and fuse in place.

With sewing needle and thread, sl st edging evenly ¼" from lower edge. Insert stick through casing. Position upper edge of shade straight across shade roller and tape securely in place. ❤

Pastel Garden Centerpiece

Design by Laura Gebhardt

Decorate your home all spring and summer with freshly cut flowers from your garden. A beautiful bouquet set on this delicate centerpiece will be enhanced by the variety of subtle pastel shades crocheted in this lovely design and shape.

Let's Begin!

Experience Level: Intermediate

Finished Measurement: 20" across widest point

Materials

- Crochet cotton size 10: 1 (350-yd) ball white (MC) and 12 yds each lilac (A), pink (B), yellow (C), light blue (D), peach (E) and mint green (F)
- Size 7 steel crochet hook or size needed to obtain gauge

Gauge: Center motif = 2½" in diameter

To save time, take time to check gauge.

Pattern Note

Join rnds with a sl st unless otherwise stated.

Pattern Stitches

Cl: Holding back on hook last lp of each st, 3 dc in indicated sp or st, yo, draw through all 4 lps on hook.

Beg cl: Ch 2, holding back on hook last lp of each st, 2 dc in same sp, yo, draw through all 3 lps on hook.

P: Ch 3, sl st in 3rd ch from hook.

Center Motif

Rnd 1 (RS): With MC, ch 6, join to form a ring, ch 1, 12 sc in ring, join in beg sc. (12 sc)

Rnd 2: Ch 3 (counts as first dc throughout), dc in next sc, [ch 3, dc in each of next 2 sc] rep around, ending with ch 3, join in 3rd ch of beg ch-3. (6 ch-3 sps)

Rnd 3: Sl st in next dc and in ch-3 sp, [beg cl, ch 3, cl] in same sp, *ch 7, [cl, ch 3, cl] in next ch-3 sp, rep from * around, ending with ch 7, join in top of beg cl.

COLOR KEY
MC MC Motif
A Lilac pastel motif
B Pink pastel motif
C Yellow pastel motif
D Light blue pastel motif
E Peach pastel motif
F Mint green pastel motif

Rnd 4: Sl st in ch-3 sp, ch 1, sc in same sp, *[6 dc, ch 3, 6 dc] in next ch-7 sp **, sc in next ch-3 sp, rep from * around, ending last rep at **, join in beg sc, fasten off. (6 petals)

First Pastel Motif

Rnds 1–3: With B, rep Rnds 1–3 of center motif; at end of Rnd 3, fasten off.

Rnd 4: With RS facing, attach MC with a sl st in any ch-3 sp, ch 1, sc in same sp, [6 dc, ch 1] in next ch-7 sp, sl st in corresponding ch-3 sp on previous motif, ch 1, 6 dc in same ch-7 sp on working motif as last 6 dc (1 petal joined), continue around as for Rnd 4 of center motif.

Rem Pastel Motifs

Rnds 1–3: Following joining diagram in numerical order for color, rep Rnds 1–3 of first pastel motif.

Rnd 4: Rep Rnd 4 of first pastel motif, joining as many petals as are indicated on joining diagram.

Rem MC Motifs

Rnds 1–3: Rep Rnds 1–3 of center MC motif.

Rnd 4: With MC, rep Rnd 4 of first pastel motif, joining as many petals as are indicated on joining diagram.

Follow joining diagram in numerical order until all motifs have been completed.

Continued on page 41

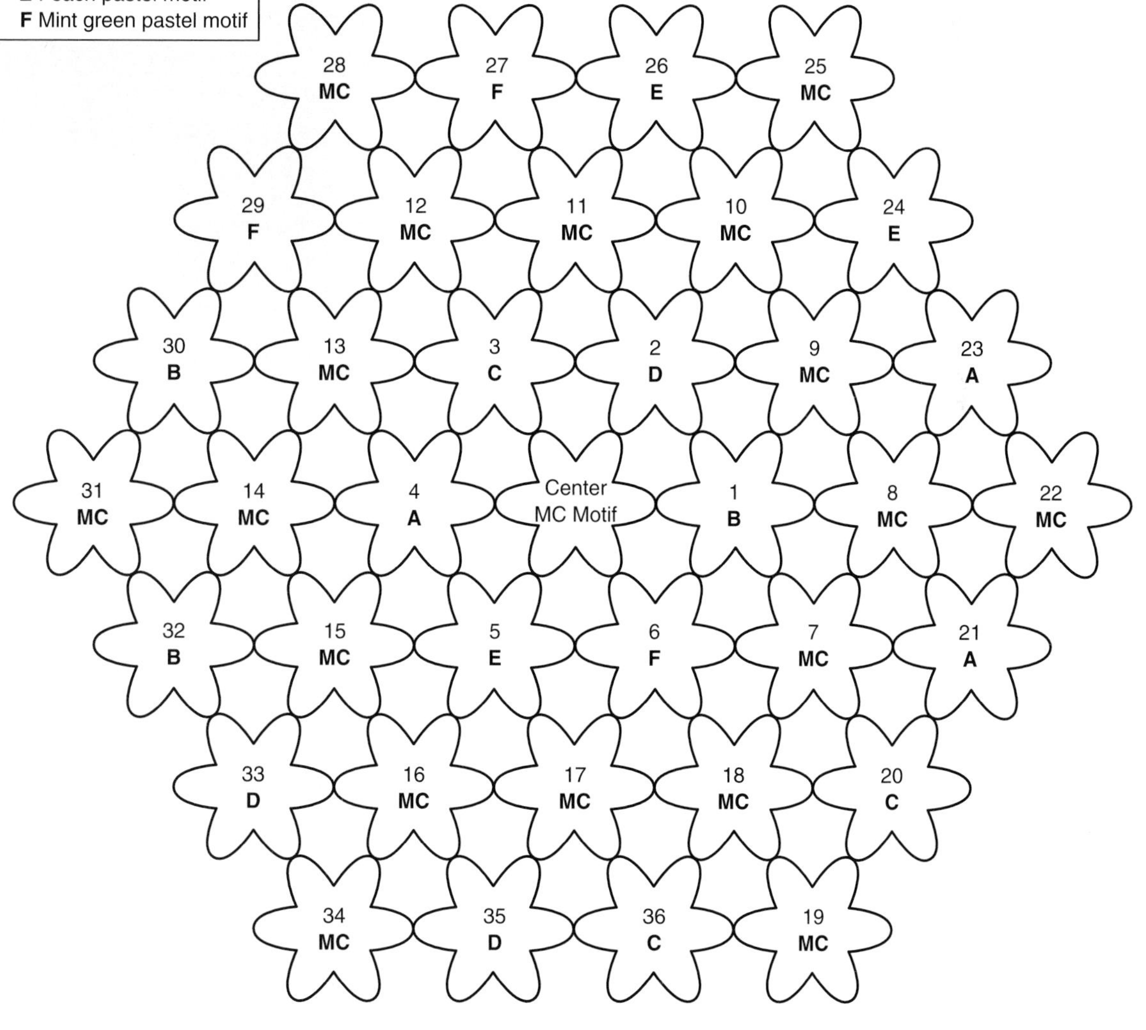

Joining Diagram

Loves Me, Loves Me Not

Designs by Maggie Petsch Chasalow

The answer always comes back, "He loves me," with these seven-petaled daisies. And why shouldn't he, when you set a cheery table and a lighthearted mood with these colorful daisy place mats?

Let's Begin!

Experience Level: Beginner

Finished Measurements

Place Mat: Approximately 11½" x 16" including border

Napkin Ring: Approximately 1½" in diameter x 2" wide including border

Materials

- J. & P. Coats Speed-Cro-Sheen crochet cotton size 3 (100 yds per ball): 1 ball white #001 (MC), 61 yds Spanish red #126 (C), and approximately 50 yds each hunter green #48 (A) and canary yellow #10A (B)
- J. & P. Coats Knit-Cro-Sheen crochet cotton size 10 (150 yds per ball): small amount each white #1 (D), canary yellow #10A (E) and Spanish red #126 (F)
- Size D/3 crochet hook or size needed to obtain gauge
- Size 7 steel crochet hook
- Tapestry needle
- Sewing needle
- Sewing thread: red and white
- Safety pin or other marker

Gauge: 16 sts and 18 rows = 3" in sc

To save time, take time to check gauge.

Pattern Notes

Join rnds with a sl st unless otherwise stated.

To change color in sc, work last sc before color change as follows: Insert hook in indicated st, yo with working color, draw up a lp, drop working color to WS, yo with next color, complete sc.

To join with next color, insert hook in indicated st, yo with next color, complete sl st.

Place Mat

CC Block (make 3 each A, B & C)

Row 1 (RS): With larger hook, ch 17, sc in 2nd ch from hook and in each rem ch across, ch 1, turn. (16 sc)

Rows 2–16: Sc in each sc across, ch 1, turn. (16 sc)

Rnd 17: Sc in each sc across to last sc of last row, 3 sc in last st, *work 14 sc evenly sp over row ends to next corner *, 3 sc in first rem lp of foundation ch, sc in each of next 14 rem lps of foundation ch, 3 sc in last st, rep from * to *, 2 sc in same st as beg sc, join in beg sc, fasten off.

MC Block (make 3)

Rows 1–16: With MC and larger hook, rep Rows 1–16 of CC block, changing to C in last st of Row 16; fasten off MC; ch 1, turn.

Rnd 17: Rep Rnd 17 of CC block.

Border & Joining

Block 1

Rnd 1: With larger hook and RS facing, attach MC with a sl st in first sc to the right of corner sc in upper left corner of block 1 on joining diagram, *ch 7, sk corner sc, sl st in next sc, [ch 5, sk 2 sc, sl st in next sc] 5 times, rep from around, ending with sl st in same st as beg sl st, fasten off.

Block 2

Rnd 1: With larger hook and RS facing, attach MC with a sl st in first sc to the right of corner sc in upper left corner of block 2 on joining diagram, *ch 3, sl st in corresponding corner ch-7 lp on

previous block, ch 3, sk corner sc on working block, sl st in next sc *, [ch 2, sl st in next ch-5 lp on previous block, ch 2, sk next 2 sc on working block, sl st in next sc] 5 times, rep from * to * (1 side joined), continue around as for Rnd 1 of border for block 1.

Rem blocks

Following joining diagram for color placement, join rem blocks as for block 2, joining as many sides as are indicated on joining diagram.

Daisy (make 6)

Rnd 1: With smaller hook and E, ch 2, 7 sc in 2nd ch from hook; do not join; mark first st of rnd with safety pin or other small marker. (7 sc)

Rnd 2: 2 sc in each sc around, join in beg sc with D. (14 sc)

Rnd 3: Ch 8, sc in 2nd ch from hook, dc in each of next 6 chs, sk next st on last rnd, sl st in next st] 7 times, fasten off. (7 petals)

Heart (make 3 each D & F)

Dc ch: With smaller hook, [ch 5, dc in 5th ch from hook] 14 times, fasten off.

Finishing

With sewing needle and white sewing thread, sew daisy to center of blocks 1, 3, 6, 8, 9 and 11. Sew red dc chs on MC blocks in heart shape; sew white dc chs on red blocks in heart shape. Wash mat; starch lightly. Pin out to dry.

Napkin Ring

Cut 36" length of C and set aside.

Row 1 (RS): With larger hook and A, ch 9, sc in 2nd ch from hook and in each rem ch across, ch 1, turn. (8 sc)

Rows 2–6: Sc in each sc across, ch 1, turn; at end of Row 6, change to ball of C, fasten off A, ch 1, turn.

Row 7: Sc in each sc across, ch 1, turn.

Row 8: Sc in first sc with C, changing to MC, sc in each of

Continued on page 41

Angelfish Pillow

Design by Connie L. Folse

Add this marine motif to a favorite sofa or armchair in your beach house. No beach house? Place this pillow in a bedroom or den at home to help evoke special memories of a vacation at the seaside.

Let's Begin!

Experience Level: Beginner

Finished Measurements: Approximately 17" long x 10" wide

Materials

- Worsted weight yarn: 5 oz white (MC), 3 oz turquoise (A) and 2 oz black (B)
- Size F/5 crochet hook or size needed to obtain gauge
- Polyester fiberfill
- Safety pin or other small marker
- Tapestry needle

Gauge: 7 sc = 2"

To save time, take time to check gauge.

Pattern Notes

Join rnds with a sl st unless otherwise stated.

To change color in sc, insert hook in indicated st, yo with working color, draw up a lp, drop working color to WS, yo with next color, complete sc.

To change color in sc dec, draw up a lp in each of next 2 indicated sts with working color, drop working color to WS, yo with next color, complete sc dec.

Front

Row 1 (RS): With A, ch 36, sc in 2nd ch from hook and in each rem ch across, ch 1, turn. (35 sc)

Row 2: Sc in each st across, ch 1, turn.

Row 3: Rep Row 2. (35 sc)

Row 4: Sc dec, sc across to last 2 sts, sc dec, ch 1, turn. (33 sts)

Row 5: Rep Row 2, changing to B in last st, fasten off A, ch 1, turn.

Rows 6 & 7: Rep Row 2.

Row 8: Rep Row 4. (31 sts)

Row 9: Rep Row 2.

Row 10: Rep Row 2, changing to A in last st, fasten off B, ch 1, turn.

Rows 11 & 12: Rep Row 2.

Row 13: Rep Row 4. (29 sts)

Row 14: Rep Row 2.

Row 15: Rep Row 5.

Rows 16–35: Rep Rows 6–15 alternately twice. (21 sts on each of last 3 rows)

Row 36: Rep Row 2.

Row 37: [Sc dec] twice, sc across to last 4 sts, [sc dec] twice, ch 1, turn. (17 sts)

Row 38: Rep Row 2.

Row 39: Rep Row 37. (13 sts)

Row 40: Rep Row 10.

Row 41: Rep Row 2.

Row 42: Rep Row 4. (11 sts)

Row 43: Rep Row 2.

Row 44: Rep Row 4. (9 sts)

Row 45: Rep Row 5.

Row 46: Rep Row 37. (5 sts)

Rows 47 & 48: Rep Row 2.

Row 49: Rep Row 4, changing to A in last st, ch 1, do not turn, fasten off B. (3 sts)

Rnd 50: With RS facing, sc evenly sp over ends of rows across to Row 1; working in rem lps across foundation ch, [sl st, ch 5, dtr] in first st, dtr in each of next 2 sts, tr in each of next 3 sts, dc in each of next 3 sts, hdc in each of next 3 sts, sc in each of next 8 sts (mark last sc made with safety pin or other small marker), sc in each of next 3 sts, hdc in each of next 3 sts, dc in each of next 3 sts, tr in each of next 3 sts, dtr in each of next 2 sts, [dtr, ch 5, sl st] in last rem lp, sc evenly sp across row ends to Row 49, sc in first st of Row 49, [dc, tr, dc] in center st, sc in last st, join in beg sc, fasten off.

Tail

Row 1: With WS facing, attach A with a sl st in marked sc on Rnd 50, ch 1, sc in same st and in each of next 4 sts, turn. (5 sc)

Row 2: Ch 2 (counts as first hdc throughout), hdc in each of next 4 sts, turn. (5 hdc)

Rows 3 & 4: Ch 2, hdc in first st, hdc in each st across to last st, 2 hdc in last st, turn. (9 hdc at end of Row 4)

Row 5: Ch 2, hdc in each rem st across, turn. (9 hdc)

Row 6: Ch 3 (counts as first dc throughout), dc in same st, dc in each st across to last st, 2 dc in last st, turn. (11 dc)

Row 7: Ch 3, dc in same st, hdc in each of next 2 sts, sc in each of next 5 sts, hdc in each of next 2 sts, 2 dc in last st, fasten off.

Back

Row 1–Rnd 50: With MC only, rep Row 1–Rnd 50 of front; do not change colors.

Tail

Rows 1–7: With MC only, rep Rows 1–7 of tail front.

Assembly

With WS of front and back held tog, front facing you, working through both thicknesses and stuffing with polyester fiberfill as work progresses, attach A with a sl st in beg sc of Rnd 50, ch 1, beg in same st, sc in each sc around, working 4 sc over each ch-5 sp on Rnd 50, and 2 sc over side of each dc and 1 sc over side of each hdc on tail, join in beg sc, fasten off.

Eye

Rnd 1: With A, ch 2, 6 sc in 2nd ch from hook, join in beg sc, fasten off.

Rnd 2: Attach MC with a sl st in any sc of Rnd 1, ch 1, 2 sc in same st and in each rem st around, join in beg sc, fasten off, leaving length for sewing. (12 sc)

With tapestry needle, sew eye to front over Rows 36–40. ❤

Reversible Rag Rug

Design by Loa Ann Thaxton

Your feet will enjoy the sensation created by the little tassels worked on one side of this eye-catching throw rug.

Let's Begin!

Experience Level: Beginner

Finished Measurements: Approximately 26" x 36"

Materials

- Worsted weight yarn: approximately 30 oz total of assorted colors
- Size H/8 crochet hook or size needed to obtain gauge

Gauge: 6 sc = 2"

To save time, take time to check gauge.

Rug

Cut yarn to varying lengths. Picking colors randomly, tie ends tog using a plain knot, leaving 2" tails at each knot and winding yarn into balls as you tie.

Row 1: Ch 79, sc in 2nd ch from hook and in each rem ch across, ch 1, turn. (78 sc)

Row 2: Sc in each sc across, ch 1, turn.

Rep Row 2 until rug measures 36" or desired length, leaving all tied ends on same side of rug; do not work over tied ends; at end of last row, fasten off.

Fringe

Cut 1 (8") length of yarn for each st across each short edge. Fold 1 strand in half. Insert hook in first st on either short edge, pick up folded end of strand and draw through st to form lp. Pull free ends through lp and tighten. Rep for each st across both short edges. ❤

Scrap Fashions

Turn your love of crochet into eye-catching and fashionable garments to fill your wardrobe! This collection of sweaters, vests, slippers, hats and more for women, kids and even the family dog will give you many gift-giving ideas for family, friends and even yourself!

Zesty Zigzag Cardigan

Design by Melissa Leapman

Zip through this crisp-looking cardigan with its multihued stripes. The V-style neck makes it an ideal sweater to wear when fashion rather than warmth is your primary interest.

Let's Begin!

Experience Level: Intermediate

Size: Woman's small(medium)(large)(extra-large) Instructions are given for smallest size, with larger sizes in parentheses. When only 1 number is given, it applies to all sizes.

Finished Measurements: Bust: 36(40)(44)(48)"

Materials

- Patons Paradiso (100 grams per skein): 5(5)(6)(7) skeins ecru #6452 (MC) and 1 skein each carrot #6474 (A), loden #6477 (B), claret #6472 (C), sunshine #6475 (D), black #6466 (E), citrus green #6476 (F), tomato #6473 (G), spice #6459 (H) and henna #6471 (I)
- Size F/5 crochet hook or size needed to obtain gauge
- Size E/4 crochet hook
- 5 (¾") Equator style #90354 buttons by JHB International
- Tapestry needle

Gauge: 2 pairs of dc = 1" with larger hook in pattern st
To save time, take time to check gauge.

Pattern Notes

Join rnds with a sl st unless otherwise stated.

To change color in dc, work last dc before color change until last 2 lps before final yo rem on hook, drop working color to WS, yo with next color, complete dc.

Back

Row 1 (RS): With MC and larger hook, ch 75(83)(91)(99), 2 dc in 5th ch from hook, [sk next ch, 2 dc in next ch] rep across to last 2 chs, sk next ch, dc in last ch, changing to A, fasten off MC, turn. (72, 80, 88, 96 dc, counting last 3 chs of foundation ch as first dc)

Row 2: Ch 3 (counts as first dc throughout), 2 dc between 2nd and 3rd dc of last row, [sk next dc, 2 dc between next 2 dc] rep across to last 2 sts, ending with sk next dc, dc in 3rd ch of turning ch-3, changing to MC in last dc, fasten off A, turn. (72, 80, 88, 96 dc)

Rep Row 2 until back measures 11½(12)(12½)(13)" from beg, ending with a RS row, in the following color sequence: *2 rows MC, 1 row B, 2 rows MC, 1 row C, 2 rows MC, 1 row D, 2 rows MC, 1 row E, 2 rows MC, 1 row F, 2 rows MC, 1 row G, 2 rows MC, 1 row H, 2 rows MC, 1 row I, 2 rows MC, 1 row A, rep from * as necessary; at end of last row, ch 1, turn.

Shape armholes

Next row: Sl st in each of first 7 dc, ch 3, 2 dc between next 2 dc, [sk next dc, 2 dc between next 2 dc] 28(32)(36)(40) times, sk next dc, dc in next dc, changing to next color in established color sequence, turn. (60, 68, 76, 84 dc)

Work even on 60(68)(76)(84) sts in established color pattern until armhole measures 8½(9)(9½)(10)" from beg, fasten off.

Right Front

Row 1: With MC and larger hook, ch 37(41)(45)(49), rep Row 1 of back. (34, 38, 42, 46 dc, counting last 3 chs of foundation ch as first dc)

Row 2: Rep Row 2 of back in established color sequence until right front measures 11½(12)(12½)(13)" from beg, ending with a RS row; at end of last row, ch 1, turn.

Shape armhole

Next row: Sl st in each of first 7 dc, ch 3, 2 dc between next 2 dc, [sk next dc, 2 dc between next 2 dc] 12(14)(16)(18) times, sk next dc, dc in 3rd ch of turning ch-3, changing to next color in established color sequence, turn. (28, 32, 36, 40 dc)

Work even on 28(32)(36)(40) sts in established color pattern until armhole measures 1(1½)(2)(2½)" from beg, ending with a WS row.

Shape neck

Row 1: Ch 3, dc between 2nd and 3rd dc of last row, [sk next dc, 2 dc between next 2 dc] rep across to last 2 sts, sk next dc, dc in 3rd ch of turning ch-3, changing to next color in last dc, turn. (27, 31, 35, 39 dc)

Row 2: Ch 3, 2 dc between 2nd and 3rd dc of last row, [sk next dc, 2 dc between next 2 dc] rep

across to last 2 dc before turning ch-3, sk next dc, dc in next dc, changing to next color, leave turning ch-3 unworked, turn. (26, 30, 34, 38 dc)

Rows 3–8: Rep Rows 1 and 2 alternately 3 times. (20, 24, 28, 32 dc at end of Row 8)

Rows 9 & 10: Work even in established color sequence.

Row 11: Rep Row 1. (19, 23, 27, 31 dc)

Row 12: Rep Row 2. (18, 22, 26, 30 dc)

Rows 13 & 14: Work even in established color sequence.

Rows 15 & 16: Rep Rows 1 and 2. (16, 20, 24, 28 dc at end of Row 16)

Work even on 16(20)(24)(28) sts in established color sequence until right front measures same as back, fasten off.

Left Front

Rep instructions for right front, reversing shaping.

Sleeve (make 2)

Row 1: With larger hook and MC, ch 39, rep Row 1 of back across. (36 dc, counting last 3 chs of foundation ch as first dc)

Row 2 (inc row): Ch 3, 2 dc in first dc, 2 dc between next 2 dc, [sk next dc, 2 dc between next 2 dc] rep across to last 2 sts, sk next dc, 3 dc in 3rd ch of turning ch-3, changing to next color in last dc, turn. (40 dc)

Continue to work in pattern st in established color sequence, rep inc row every other row 0(0)(2)(4) times, then every 4th row 8(9)(8)(7) times. (72, 76, 80, 84 dc at end of last inc row)

Work even in pattern st in established color sequence until sleeve measures 19" from beg, fasten off.

Finishing

Sew shoulder seams. Set in sleeves. Sew sleeve and side seams.

Front, bottom & neck band

Rnd 1: With RS facing, using smaller hook, attach MC with a sl st at bottom side seam, ch 1, sc in same st, sc evenly sp around entire cardigan, working 3 sc at each corner and dec as necessary at inside neck corners to keep work flat, join in beg sc.

Rnd 2: Ch 1, sc in same st as joining and in each sc around, working 3 sc in each corner sc and dec as necessary at inside neck corners to keep work flat, join in beg sc.

Rep Rnd 2 until band measures ½"; do not fasten off. Placing first and last markers ½" from beg of neck shaping and from bottom, place 5 markers for buttonholes on right front band.

Buttonhole rnd: Ch 1, sc in same st as joining, [sc in each sc across to buttonhole marker, ch 2, sk 2 sc] 5 times, continue around in sc, working incs and decs as established, join in beg sc.

Next rnd: Ch 1, sc in same st as joining, sc in each rem sc around, working incs and decs as established, and working 3 sc in each ch-2 sp, join in beg sc.

Rep Rnd 2 until band measures 1"; fasten off.

Sleeve band

Rnd 1: With RS facing, using smaller hook, attach MC with a sl st at seam on lower edge of sleeve, ch 1, sc in same st, sc evenly sp around, join in beg sc.

Rnd 2: Ch 1, sc in same st as joining and in each rem sc around, join in beg sc.

Rep Rnd 2 until band measures 1"; fasten off.

Sew buttons on left front band opposite buttonholes. ❤

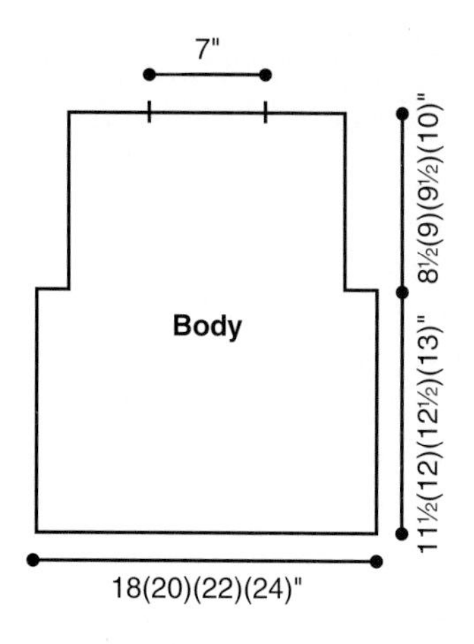

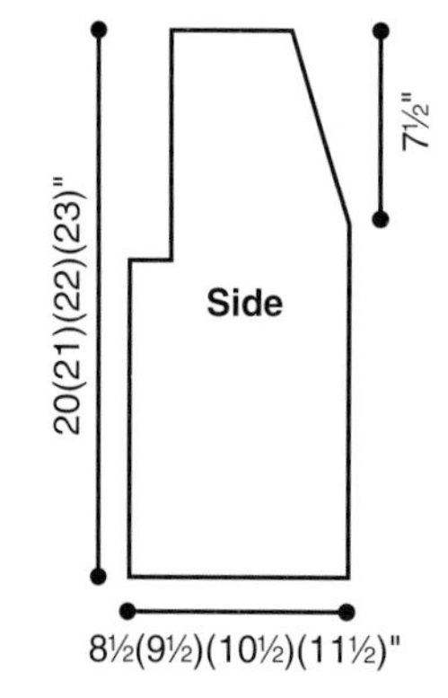

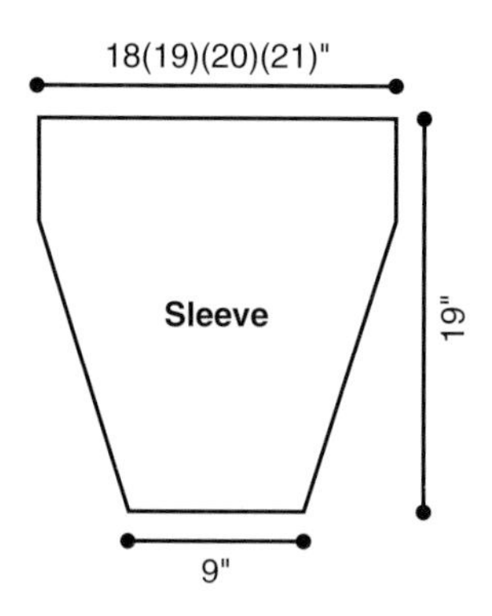

String of Clusters Pullover

Design by Melissa Leapman

Bold! Vivid! Versatile! These are a few of the words to describe this super cotton sweater for summer. You'll find that many slacks, skirts and accessories may be worn with this colorful sweater.

Let's Begin!

Experience Level: Intermediate

Size: Ladies small(medium)(large)(extra-large) Instructions are given for smallest size, with larger sizes in parentheses. When only 1 number is given, it applies to all sizes.

Finished Measurements: Chest: 34(39)(45)(47)"

Length: 18(19)(20)(21)"

Materials

- Coats & Clark South Maid Cotton 8 sport weight cotton yarn (2½ oz per skein): 6(6)(7)(8) skeins black #802 (MC) and 1 skein each white #801 (A), red #805 (B), yellow #808 (C), royal #819 (D), bright pink #809 (E) and jade #820 (F)
- Size F/5 crochet hook or size needed to obtain gauge

Gauge: 18 dc = 4"

To save time, take time to check gauge.

Pattern Notes

Join rnds with a sl st unless otherwise stated.

To change color in dc, work last dc before color change in working color until last 2 lps before final yo rem on hook, drop working color to WS, yo with next color, complete dc.

To change color in sc, insert hook in indicated st, yo with working color, draw up a lp, drop working color to WS, yo with next color, complete sc.

Pattern Stitch

Cl: Holding back on hook last lp of each st, work 5 dc in indicated st, yo, draw through all 6 lps on hook.

Back

Foundation row: With MC, ch 79(91)(103)(109), dc in 4th ch from hook and in each rem ch across, changing to A in last st, fasten off MC, ch 1, turn. (77, 89, 101, 107 dc, counting last 3 chs of foundation ch as first dc)

Row 1 (WS): Sc in each of first 5 dc, [cl, sc in each of next 5 sts] rep across, changing to MC in last st, fasten off A, turn.

Row 2: Ch 3 (counts as first dc throughout), dc in each rem st across, ch 1, turn. (77, 89, 101, 107 dc)

Row 3: Sc in each st across, turn. (77, 89, 101, 107 sc)

Row 4: Rep Row 2, changing to B in last st, fasten off MC, ch 1, turn.

Row 5: Sc in each of first 2 sts, [cl, sc in each of next 5 sts] rep across to last 3 sts, cl in next st, sc in each of last 2 sts, changing to MC in last st, fasten off B, ch 1, turn.

Rows 6–8: Rep Rows 2–4, changing to C in last st of Row 8, ch 1, turn.

Rep Rows 1–8 until piece measures 10½(11)(11½)(12)" from beg, changing to each CC in alphabetical order and ending with a RS row; at end of last row, do not ch 1; fasten off.

Shape armholes

Next row: With WS facing, sk first 6 sts, attach yarn with a sl st in next st, ch 1, beg in same st, work in pattern across to last 6 sts, leave rem sts unworked. (65, 77, 89, 95 sts)

Continue in established pattern until piece measures 6½(7)(7½)(8)" from beg of armhole shaping.

Shape neck

First shoulder

Next row: Work in pattern across first 13(19)(25)(28) sts, leave rem sts unworked, turn.

Work in pattern across 13(19)(25)(28) sts until piece measures 7½(8)(8½)(9)" from beg of armhole shaping, fasten off.

Second shoulder

Sk next 39 unworked sts on last row before neck shaping, attach yarn with a sl st in next st, beg in same st, work in pattern across last 13(19)(25)(28) sts, turn.

Complete as for first shoulder.

Front

Work same as back until piece measures 4½(5)(5½)(6)" from beg of armhole shaping.

Shape neck

First shoulder

Next row: Work in pattern across first 21(27)(33)(36) sts, leave rem sts unworked.

Continue to work in pattern, dec 1 st at neck edge every row 8

times. Work even on 13(19)(25)(28) sts until piece measures 7½(8)(8½)(9)" from beg of armhole shaping, fasten off.

Second shoulder

Sk next 23 unworked sts on last row before neck shaping, attach yarn with a sl st in next st, beg in same st, work in pattern across last 21(27)(33)(36) sts, turn.

Complete as for first shoulder for front.

Sleeve (make 2)

Foundation row: With MC, ch 55(55)(61)(67), dc in 4th ch from hook and in each rem ch across, changing to A in last st, fasten off MC, ch 1, turn. (53, 53, 59, 65 dc, counting last 3 chs of foundation ch as first dc)

Rep Rows 1–8 of back alternately, changing to each CC color in alphabetical order and inc 1 st at each end of every row twice and at end of every other row 5(8)(7)(6) times. (67, 73, 77, 81 sts)

Work even in pattern until sleeve measures 6½" from beg, fasten off.

Finishing

Sew shoulder seams.

Neck edging

Rnd 1: With RS facing, attach MC with a sl st at either shoulder, ch 1, beg in same st, sc evenly sp around neck opening, join in beg sc.

Rnd 2: Ch 1, beg in same st as joining, work reverse sc around, join in beg reverse sc, fasten off.

Set in sleeves. Sew sleeve and side seams.

Bottom edging

Rnd 1: With RS facing, attach MC with a sl st at either side seam, ch 1, beg in same st, sc evenly sp around bottom, join in beg sc.

Rnd 2: Rep Rnd 2 of neck edging.

Sleeve edging

Rnd 1: With RS facing, attach MC with a sl st at sleeve seam, ch 1, beg in same st, sc evenly sp around sleeve opening, join in beg sc.

Rnd 2: Rep Rnd 2 of neck edging. ♥

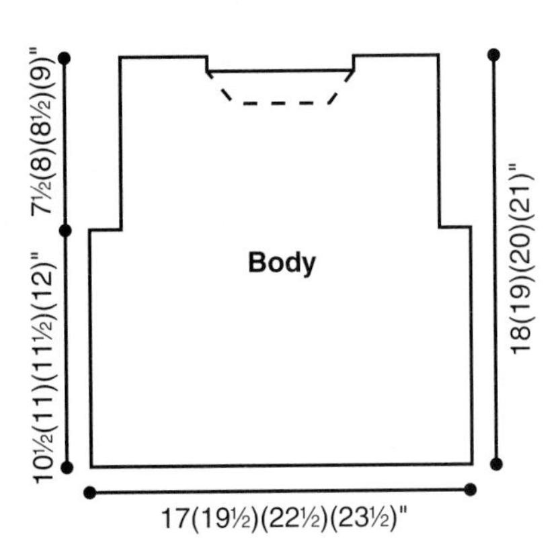

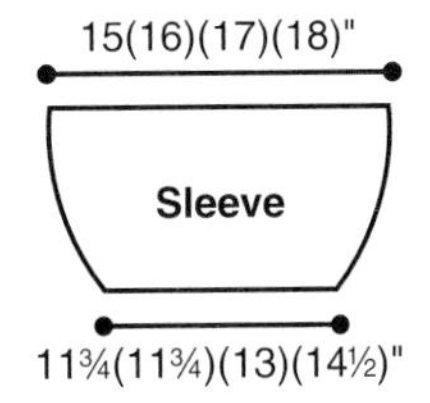

Finishing Techniques

By Jocelyn Sass

These hints may be used to ensure a neat, finished look.

When a pattern calls for using cardboard to line crochet pieces, use readily available plastic canvas, which stiffens better and can be washed.

Use enough polyester fiberfill to stuff firmly, yet do not use so much that the stuffing shows through your work. For small items, try using scraps of the same color yarn to stuff. This works very well when crocheting with darker colors where the fiberfill may more easily show through.

Make sure you use care when applying any finishing touches to your crochet project. Tie bows and apply laces and trims neatly. Glue materials on carefully and remember to remove any unsightly hot-glue strings.

If we put a little extra effort into finishing our crochet creations, they will be admired and will reflect our love of crochet.

Flower Garden Bolero

Design by Sue Childress

Flower child wannabes will love the retro colors in this '70s-style vest. You'll love the feel of the cotton yarn as you crochet with it and later wear it.

Let's Begin!

Experience Level: Intermediate

Size: Ladies small(medium)(large) Instructions are given for smallest size, with larger sizes in parentheses. When only 1 number is given, it applies to all sizes.

Finished Measurements: Chest: 40(48)(56)"
Length: 24(28)(32)"

Materials

- Worsted weight cotton yarn (50 grams/121 yds per skein): 3(4)(5) skeins MC and 1(2)(2) skeins each of 6 assorted CCs
- Size F/5 crochet hook or size needed to obtain gauge
- 4(5)(5) ⅞" buttons
- Sewing needle and thread to match MC

Gauge: Motif = 3½" between opposite points
To save time, take time to check gauge.

Pattern Note

Join rnds with a sl st unless otherwise stated.

Motif

Rnd 1 (RS): With any CC, ch 6, join to form a ring, ch 1, 12 sc in ring, join in beg sc. (12 sc)

Rnd 2: Ch 1, sc in same st as joining, ch 6, [sk next sc, sc in next sc, ch 6] 5 times, sk last sc, join in beg sc. (6 ch-6 lps)

Rnd 3: Ch 1, sc in same st as joining, 10 hdc in next ch-6 lp, [sc in next sc, 10 hdc in next ch-6 lp] 5 times, join in beg sc, fasten off. (6 petals)

Make a total of 56(80)(106) motifs in desired CCs.

Joining Motifs in Rows

Row 1

Rnd 1: With RS facing, using joining diagram as a guide, attach MC with a sl st between 5th and 6th hdc on any petal of any motif; working across top half of motif, ch 1, 2 sc in same sp, *[ch 5, 2 sc in next sc on same motif, ch 5, 2 sc between 5th and 6th hdc on next petal of same motif] 3 times **; with RS facing, working across top half of next motif, 2 sc between 5th and 6th hdc of any petal on next motif, rep from * across until last motif for size being worked has been joined, ending last rep at **; working across opposite half of each motif on row, [ch 5, 2 sc in next sc on same motif, ch 5, 2 sc between 5th and 6th hdc on next petal of same motif] twice, ch 5, 2 sc in next sc on same motif, †ch 5, 2 sc over joined sts between motifs, ch 5, 2 sc in next sc on next motif, [ch 5, 2 sc between 5th and 6th hdc on same motif, ch 5, 2 sc in next sc on same motif] twice, rep from † across, ending with ch 5, join in beg sc, fasten off.

Rows 2–6(7)(8)

Rnd 1: Rep Rnd 1 of Row 1, joining as many motifs as are indicated on joining diagram for desired size. Rows 5(5)(6)–6(7)(8) will each have 3 separate sections to divide for right front, back and left front.

Joining rows

Rows 1 & 2: With RS facing, beg at right-hand edge, attach MC with a sl st in ch-5 lp on first motif of Row 2 at point A indicated on Diagram A, ch 1, 2 sc in same lp, ch 2, 2 sc in next ch-5 lp on first motif of Row 1 at point B indicated on Diagram A; continue across, following Diagram A, until all motifs on Row 2 have been joined to Row 1, fasten off.

Continuing in established pattern, join rem rows.

Shoulder Seams

Matching points indicated on joining diagram, join shoulder seams in established pattern for joining rows.

Vest Edging

With RS facing, attach MC with a sl st in any ch-5 sp at center back neck opening, ch 1, beg in same sp, 6 sc in each ch-5 sp and 2 sc in each ch-2 sp around entire outer edge of vest, join in beg sc, fasten off.

Armhole Edging

With RS facing, attach MC with a sl st in any ch-5 sp on either armhole, ch 1, beg in same sp, 6 sc in each ch-5 sp and 2 sc in each

ch-2 sp around, join in beg sc, fasten off.

Rep on rem armhole.

Buttonhole Band

With RS facing, attach MC with a sl st in 3rd sc of 6-sc group over ch-5 lp at bottom of right front opening at point indicated on Diagram A, ch 1, sc in same st and in each of next 8 sc, [ch 5, sk next sc, sc in each of next 25 sc] 3(4)(4) times, ch 5, sk next sc, sc in each of next 12 sc, sl st in next st, fasten off.

Finishing

Sew buttons on left front opening opposite buttonholes. Using joining diagram as a guide, fold 1 motif at top corner of each front opening in half to WS; tack in place with sewing needle and sewing thread. ❤

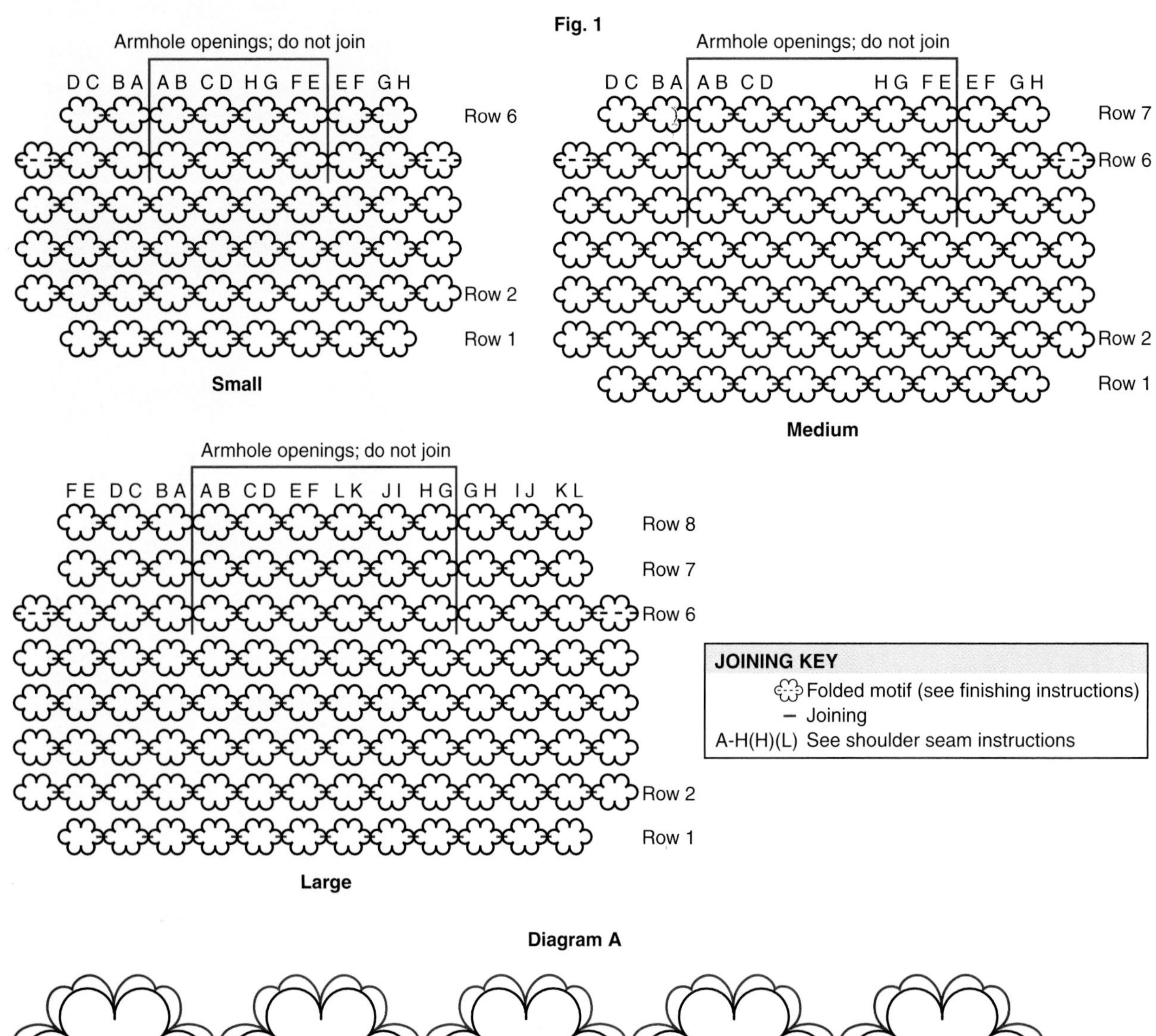

Windowpane Tunic

Design by Maureen Egan Emlet for Solutia's Designs for America Program

Indulge yourself by making this voluptuous sweater crocheted with soft, velvety chenille yarn. The jeweltone colors will make you feel like a queen when you wear this beautiful sweater.

Let's Begin!

Experience Level: Intermediate

Size: Woman's small(medium)(large) Instructions are given for smallest size, with larger sizes in parentheses. When only 1 number is given, it applies to all sizes.

Finished Measurements: Bust: 36(42)(48)"

Length: 27½"

Materials

- Lion Brand Chenille 100 percent Solutia acrylic worsted weight yarn (87 yds per skein): 8(9)(11) skeins antique white #098 (MC) and 2 skeins each midnight blue #110 (A), teal #178 (B), forest green #131 (C), black #153 (D), mulberry #142 (E), garnet #113 (F), raspberry #140 (G) and denim blue #111 (H)
- Size G/6 crochet hook or size needed to obtain gauge
- Size E/4 crochet hook
- 2 (½") white buttons
- Yarn needle and small amount off-white worsted weight yarn for sewing seams

Gauge: 23 sts = 6" and 16 rows = 4½" with larger hook in pattern st
To save time, take time to check gauge.

Pattern Notes

Join rnds with a sl st unless otherwise stated.

To change color in sc, insert hook in indicated st, yo with working color, draw up a lp, drop working color to WS, yo with next color, complete sc.

To change color in dc, work last dc before color change until last 2 lps before final yo rem on hook, drop working color to WS, yo with next color, complete dc.

Sweater is worked in 1 piece beg at bottom front and working up to shoulder and down to bottom back, adding sts for sleeves and an opening for neck.

For color sequence, alternate 2 rows of each CC in alphabetical order with 2 rows of MC.

Front

Row 1 (RS): With larger hook and MC, ch 71(83)(95), sc in 2nd ch from hook and in each sc across, ch 1, turn. (70, 82, 94 sc)

Row 2: Sc in each st across, changing to CC in last sc, turn.

Row 3: Ch 3 (counts as first dc throughout), dc in next st, hdc in next st, sc in next st, *ch 2, sk 2 sts, sc in next st, hdc in next st, dc in each of next 2 sts **, tr in each of next 2 sts, dc in each of next 2 sts, hdc in next st, sc in next st, rep from * across, ending last rep at **, turn.

Row 4: Ch 3, dc in next st, hdc in next st, sc in next st, *ch 2, sc in next sc, hdc in next st, dc in each of next 2 sts **, tr in each of next 2 sts, dc in each of next 2 sts, hdc in next st, sc in next st, rep from * across, ending last rep at **, changing to MC in last st, ch 1, turn.

Row 5: Sc in each of first 4 sts, *working over ch-2 sps, sc in each of next 2 unworked sc in last MC row **, sc in each of next 10 sts, rep from * across to last 4 sts, ending last rep at **, sc in each of last 4 sts, ch 1, turn.

Row 6: Sc in each sc across, changing to next CC in last sc, ch 1, turn.

Row 7: Sc in first st, *hdc in next st, dc in each of next 2 sts, tr in each of next 2 sts, dc in each of next 2 sts, hdc in next st, sc in next st **, ch 2, sk 2 sts, sc in next st, rep from * across, ending last rep at **, ch 1, turn.

Row 8: Sc in first st, *hdc in next st, dc in each of next 2 sts, tr in each of next 2 sts, dc in each of next 2 sts, hdc in next st, sc in next st **, ch 2, sc in next sc, rep from * across, ending last rep at ** and changing to MC in last sc, ch 1, turn.

Row 9: Sc in each of first 10 sts, *working over ch-2 sps, sc in each of next 2 unworked sc on last MC row, sc in each of next 10 sts, rep from * across, ch 1, turn.

Rows 10–64: Rep Rows 2–9 alternately, ending with a Row 8; at end of Row 64, change to MC in last st, ch 61 with MC, turn.

Front Sleeves

Row 65: Sc in 2nd ch from hook and in each of next 59 chs, rep Row 9 across body, ch 61, turn.

Row 66: Sc in 2nd ch from hook and in each rem ch across, rep Row 2 across body and next sleeve. (190, 202, 214 sts)

Rows 67–93: Work even in pattern st in color sequence established, ending with a Row 5.

Shape Neck

Right side

Row 94: Rep Row 6 across first 82(87)(92) sts.

Rows 95 & 96: Continue to work in pattern st across 82(87)(92) sts; at end of Row 96, do not change to MC; fasten off.

Left side

Row 94: Sk next 26(28)(30) unworked sts on Row 93; with larger hook, attach MC with a sl st in next st, ch 1, beg in same st, rep Row 6 across rem 82(87)(92) sts.

Rows 95 & 96: Rep Rows 95 and 96 of right side, changing to MC at end of Row 96; ch 1, turn.

Back Sleeves

Row 97: Work in pattern st across first 82(87)(92) sts, ch 26(28)(30), work in pattern st across rem sts, ch 1, turn. (190, 202, 214 sts)

Rows 98–129: Work even in pattern st, beg first CC row with same CC used for last 2 CC rows and reversing established color pattern, ending with a Row 9; at end of Row 9, do not ch 1; fasten off, turn.

Back

Row 130: Sk first 60 sts; with larger hook, attach MC with a sl st in next st, ch 1, beg in same st, rep Row 2 across next 70(82)(94) sts, leave rem 60 sts unworked.

Rows 131–194: Work even in pattern st on 70(82)(94) sts, ending with a Row 2; at end of Row 194, do not change to CC; fasten off.

Cuff

Row 1: With smaller hook and RS facing, attach MC with a sl st at right-hand edge of either sleeve bottom, ch 1, beg in same st, work 37(40)(43) sc evenly sp across sleeve, ch 1, turn.

Row 2: Sc in first st, [sc dec, sc in next st] rep across, turn. (25, 27, 29 sts)

Row 3: Ch 13, sc in 2nd ch from hook, sc in each of next 11 chs, sl st in each of first 2 sts on Row 2, ch 1, turn; *working in back lps only, sk 2 sl sts, sc in each of next 12 sc, ch 1, turn; working in back lps only, sc in each of next 12 sc **, sl st in each of next 2 unworked sts on Row 2, ch 1, turn, rep from * across, ending last rep at **, sl st in last st on Row 2, fasten off.

Rep on bottom of opposite sleeve.

Collar

Row 1: With smaller hook and MC, ch 17, sc in 2nd ch from hook and in each rem ch across, ch 1, turn. (16 sc)

Row 2: Working in back lps only, sc in each sc across, ch 1, turn. (16 sc)

Rows 3–64(66)(70): Rep Row 2; at end of Row 64(66)(70), do not fasten off; ch 1, turn.

Fold collar in half so first and last rows are parallel; working through both thicknesses, sl st in each of first 3 sts, turn collar so that sl st seam is on inside; working in front layer only, sc in next st, ch 3, sk next 2 sts, sc in each of next 6 sts, ch 3, sk next 2 sts, sc in each of last 2 sts, ch 1, turn; sc in each of first 2 sc, 4 sc in ch-3 sp, sc in each of next 6 sc, 4 sc in next ch-3 sp, sc in last sc, sl st in seam, fasten off.

Button Cover (make 2)

Rnd 1 (RS): With smaller hook and MC, ch 2, 10 sc in 2nd ch from hook, do not join.

Rnd 2: Working in back lps only, sc in each of next 10 sc, do not join.

Rnd 3: Place button on WS of work, sk next sc, [sc dec, sk next sc] 3 times, join in beg sc dec, fasten off, leaving a length for sewing.

Finishing

With yarn needle and off-white worsted weight yarn, sew underarm and side seams. Pin collar to neck opening with seam at left front shoulder and buttonholes in front. Sew in place, using small sts and leaving enough give to fit over head. Sew buttons to collar, opposite buttonholes.

Bottom edging

With smaller hook and RS facing, attach MC with a sl st at either side seam on bottom of sweater, ch 1, beg in same st, work 1 rnd reverse sc, join in beg reverse sc, fasten off.

Lay sweater flat to shape and spray lightly with water bottle. Allow to dry completely.

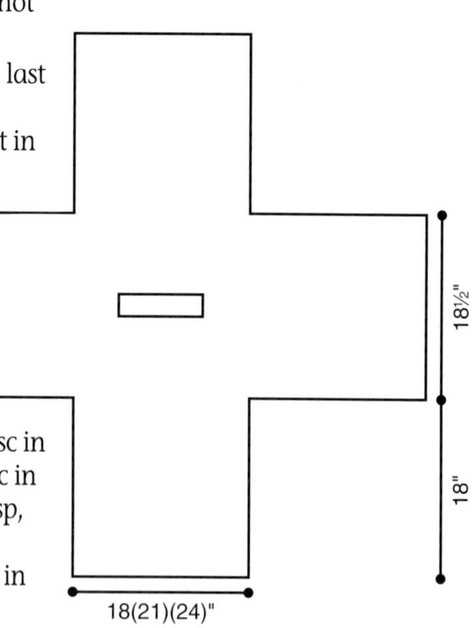

Mini-Entrelacs for Kids

Design by Hélène Rush

Dazzle your young darling with this bright, multicolored cardigan. With so many colors of yarns and buttons, this sweater will complement several back-to-school outfits worn by your youngster.

Let's Begin!

Experience Level: Intermediate

Size: Child's 4–6(8)(10–12) Instructions are given for smallest size, with larger sizes in parentheses. When only 1 number is given, it applies to all sizes.

Finished Measurements: Chest: 29(33)(37)"

Length: 14(16)(18)"

Materials

- Spinrite Bernat Berella "4" worsted weight yarn (100 yds per skein): 1(2)(2) skeins pretty purple #8708 (A) and 1 skein each aquamarine #8702 (B), mega magenta #8707 (C), kiwi #8705 (D), watermelon #8703 (E) and tangelo #8704 (F) *or* Lily Sugar 'n' Cream worsted weight cotton yarn (2.5 oz/120 yds per ball): 1(2)(2) balls grape #71 (A) and 1 ball each blueberry #74 (B), plum #76 (C), lime #70 (D), persimmon #33 (E) and orange #72 (F)
- Size J/10 crochet hook or size needed to obtain gauge
- 6 (11/16") buttons
- Tapestry needle
- Sewing needle and thread

Gauge: 4 squares and 8 rows = 4" in pattern st

To save time, take time to check gauge.

Pattern Notes

Join rnds with a sl st unless otherwise stated.

To change color in dc, work last dc before color change until last 2 lps before final yo rem on hook, drop working color to WS, yo with next color, complete dc.

To change color in sl st, insert hook in indicated st or sp, yo with next color, complete sl st.

Back

Row 1 (RS): With A, ch 60(68)(76) (foundation ch), ch 4 more (turning ch), dc in 8th ch from hook, *ch 3, work 3 dc over side of last dc made, sk next 3 chs, dc in next ch, rep from * across, changing to B in last dc, turn. (14, 16, 18 squares)

Row 2: Ch 4, *[sl st, ch 3, 3 dc] in next ch-3 sp, rep from * across, ending with sl st in turning ch-4 sp, changing to C, turn. (14, 16, 18 squares)

Rep Row 2 for pattern st until back measures 13(15)(17)" from beg, changing colors at end of each row in the following sequence: D, E, F, A, B and C.

Shoulder shaping

Last row: Ch 4, *[sl st, sc, hdc, dc] in next ch sp **, dc in next dc, hdc in next dc, sc in next dc, rep from * across, ending last rep at **, sl st in turning ch-4 sp, fasten off.

Left Front

Row 1 (RS): With A ch 32(36)(40) (foundation ch), ch 4 more (turning ch), rep Row 1 of back. (7, 8, 9 squares)

Row 2: Rep Row 2 of back. (7, 8, 9 squares)

Rep Row 2 until left front measures 11(14)(16)" from beg, ending with a RS row.

Neck shaping

Next row: Ch 4, [{sl st, sc, hdc, dc} in next ch-3 sp, dc in next dc, hdc in next dc, sc in next dc] 3 times, rep Row 2 of back from * across, changing to next color in last st. (4, 5, 6 squares)

Next row: Rep Row 2 of back across, ending with sl st in last sc of last row, changing to next color in established sequence, turn. (4, 5, 6 squares)

Work even in pattern st on 4(5)(6) squares until left front measures same as back to shoulder shaping. Rep last row for shoulder shaping. Fasten off.

Right Front

Rep instructions for left front (pattern st is reversible).

Sleeve (make 2)

Row 1 (RS): With A, ch 44(48)(52) (foundation ch), ch 4 more (turning ch), rep Row 1 of back. (10, 11, 12 squares)

Row 2: Rep Row 2 of back across to turning ch-4, ending with [sl st, ch 3, 3 dc] in turning ch-4, changing to next color in last dc, turn. (11, 12, 13 squares)

Row 3: Rep Row 2. (12, 13, 14 squares)

Work even in pattern st on 12(13)(14) squares until sleeve measures 9½(12)(13½)" from beg.

Next 2 rows: Rep Row 2 twice, fasten off at end of 2nd row. (14, 15, 16 squares at end of last row)

Finishing

Sew shoulder seams. Measure 7½(8)(8½)" down from shoulder seam on fronts and back; place marker at armhole edge. Set in sleeves between markers, stretching slightly to fit. Sew underarm and side seams.

Neck, front & bottom band

Rnd 1: With RS facing, attach A with a sl st at side seam, ch 1, sc in same st, sc evenly sp around entire cardigan, working 3 sc at each corner and dec as necessary at inside neck corners to keep work flat, join in beg sc.

Rnd 2: Ch 1, sc in same st as joining and in each sc around, working 3 sc at each corner and dec as necessary at inside neck corners to keep work flat, join in beg sc.

Rep Rnd 2 until band measures ½"; do not fasten off.

Placing first and last markers ½" from top and bottom, place 6 markers for buttonholes on right front band.

Buttonhole rnd: Ch 1, sc in same st as joining, [sc in each sc across to buttonhole marker, ch 2, sk 2 sc] 6 times, continue around in sc, working incs and decs as established, join in beg sc.

Next rnd: Ch 1, sc in same st as joining, sc in each rem sc around, working incs and decs as established, and working 2 sc in each ch-2 sp, join in beg sc.

Rep Rnd 2 until band measures 1"; fasten off.

Sleeve band

Rnd 1: With RS facing, attach A with a sl st at seam on lower edge of sleeve, ch 1, beg in same st, work 28(30)(32) sc evenly sp around, join in beg sc.

Rnd 2: Ch 1, sc in same st as joining and in each rem sc around, join in beg sc.

Rep Rnd 2 until sleeve band measures 1"; fasten off.

Sew buttons to left front band opposite buttonholes. ♥

Country Warmth Set

Designs by Sandra Abbate

Add sunshine brightness to a cold winter day with this hat, scarf and mitten set crocheted in bright primary colors. Overcast stitches worked on the color changes add a unique home-stitched look.

Let's Begin!

Experience Level
Beginner

Size
Child's small/2–3 years (medium/4–5 years) Instructions given are for smaller size, with larger size in parentheses. When only 1 number is given, it applies to both sizes.

Materials
- Coats & Clark Red Heart Super Saver worsted weight yarn (3 oz per skein): 1 skein each skipper blue #0384 (A), pale yellow #0322 (B), hot red #0390 (C) and jade #0369 (D)
- Size F/5 crochet hook
- Size G/6(H/8) crochet hook or size needed to obtain gauge
- Yarn needle
- 4" square piece of cardboard

Gauge: 15(13) dc = 4" with size G/6(H/8) hook

To save time, take time to check gauge.

Pattern Notes
Join rnds with a sl st unless otherwise stated.

To change color in sc, insert hook in indicated st, yo with working color, draw up a lp, drop working color to WS, yo with next color, complete sc.

To change color in dc, work last dc before color change with working color until last 2 lps before final yo rem on hook, drop working color to WS, yo with next color, complete dc.

To change color in sc dec, draw up a lp in each of next 2 sts with working color, drop working color to WS, yo with next color, complete sc dec.

Mitten

Make 2

Ribbing

Row 1 (WS): With smaller hook and A, ch 13, sc in 2nd ch from hook and in each rem ch across, ch 1, turn. (12 sc)

Rows 2–24: Working in back lps only, sc in each sc across, ch 1, turn; at end of Row 24, change to B in last st, fasten off A, ch 1, do not turn.

Body

Row 1 (RS): With larger hook, working across long edge, sc over end st of each row across, ch 1, turn. (24 sc)

Rows 2–4: Sc in each sc across, ch 1, turn. (24 sc)

Row 5: Sc in each of first 11 sts, sc inc in each of next 2 sts, sc in each of last 11 sts, changing to C in last st, fasten off B, ch 1, turn. (26 sc)

Row 6: Sc in each of first 11 sts, sc inc, sc in each of next 2 sts, sc inc, sc in each of last 11 sts, ch 1, turn. (28 sc)

Row 7: Sc in each of first 11 sts, sc inc, sc in each of next 4 sts, sc inc, sc in each of last 11 sts, ch 1, turn. (30 sc)

Row 8: Sc in each of first 10 sts, sc inc, sk next 8 sts for thumb opening, sc inc in next st, sc in each of last 10 sts, ch 1, turn.

Row 9: Sc in each sc across, ch 1, turn. (24 sc)

Row 10: Sc in each sc across, changing to D in last st, fasten off C, ch 1, turn. (24 sc)

Rows 11–15: Sc in each sc across, ch 1, turn; at end of Row 15, change to A in last st, fasten off D, ch 1, turn.

Rows 16–18: Sc in each sc across, ch 1, turn.

Mitten Tip

First side

Row 19: Sc in first st, [sc dec, sc in each of next 2 sts] twice, sc dec, sc in next st, leave rem sts unworked, ch 1, turn. (9 sts)

Row 20: Sc in first st, sc dec, sc in each of next 3 sts, sc dec, sc in last st, ch 1, turn. (7 sts)

Row 21: Sc in first st, [sc dec, sc in next st] twice, fasten off. (5 sts)

Second side

Row 19: With RS facing, attach A with a sl st in next unworked sc of Row 18, ch 1, sc in same st, [sc dec, sc in each of next 2 sts] twice, sc dec, sc in next st, ch 1, turn. (9 sts)

Rows 20 & 21: Rep Rows 20 and 21 of first side of mitten tip.

With yarn needle, using photo as a guide, work half-cross sts as follows: with D, slanting from left to right, over Rows 5 and 6; with B, slanting from right to left, over Rows 10 and 11; and with C, slanting from left to right, over Rows 15 and 16.

With RS tog, sew tip and side seam on mitten. Turn RS out.

Thumb

Rnd 1: Attach C with a sl st at thumb opening, ch 1, beg in same st, work 10 sc evenly sp around, join in beg sc. (10 sc)

Rnd 2: Ch 1, sc in same st as joining and in each rem sc around, changing to D in last st, join in beg sc, fasten off C. (10 sc)

Rnds 3–6: Ch 1, sc in same st as joining, sc in each rem sc around, join in beg sc; do not fasten off at end of Rnd 6. (10 sc)

With yarn needle, work half-cross sts with B, slanting from right to left, over Rnds 2 and 3.

Rnd 7: Ch 1, beg in same st as joining, [sc dec] 5 times, join in beg sc dec, fasten off, leaving 12" end.

Thread yarn needle with 12" end, weave yarn through tops of sts of last rnd, pull tightly to close, fasten off.

Tie

With smaller hook and C, ch 70 or desired length, fasten off. Beg at center back, weave ch through ends of rows of ribbing at base of Row 1 of mitten body. Knot each end of ch. Tie ch into bow.

Hat

Brim

Row 1: With A and larger hook, ch 10, sc in 2nd ch from hook and in each of next 2 chs, hdc in each of next 3 chs, dc in each of last 3 chs, turn. (9 sts)

Row 2 (RS): Ch 3 (counts as first dc throughout), working in back lps only, dc in each of next 2 dc, hdc in each of next 3 hdc, sc in each of next 3 sc, ch 1, turn. (9 sts)

Row 3: Working in back lps only, sc in each of first 3 sc, hdc in each of next 3 hdc, dc in each of last 3 dc, turn. (9 sts)

Rows 4–60: Rep Rows 2 and 3 alternately, ending with a Row 2; do not fasten off; turn.

Row 61: With RS tog, working through both thicknesses of last row and rem lps of foundation ch at once, sl st in each st across, fasten off.

Turn brim RS out.

Crown

Rnd 1: With RS facing, using larger hook and working over row ends around sc edge of brim, attach B with a sl st over last sc of any row, ch 1, beg in same st, sc over each end st around, join in front lp only of beg sc. (60 sc)

Rnd 2: Working in front lps only this round, ch 1, sc in same st as joining and in each rem sc around, join in beg sc. (60 sc)

Rnds 3–5: Ch 1, sc in same st as joining and in each rem sc around, join in beg sc; at end of Rnd 5, change to C in last st, fasten off B, join in beg sc. (60 sc)

Rnds 6–10: Ch 1, sc in same st as joining and in each rem sc around, join in beg sc; at end of Rnd 10, change to D in last st, fasten off C, join in beg sc. (60 sc)

Rnds 11–14: Ch 1, sc in same st as joining and in each rem sc around, join in beg sc. (60 sc)

Rnd 15: Ch 1, sc in same st as joining and in each of next 2 sts, sc dec, [sc in each of next 3 sts, sc dec] rep around, changing to A in last st, fasten off D. (48 sts)

Rnd 16: Ch 1, sc in same st as joining and in each rem st around, join in beg sc. (48 sc)

Rnd 17: Ch 1, sc in same st as joining, sc in next st, sc dec, [sc in each of next 2 sts, sc dec] rep around, join in beg sc. (36 sts)

Rnd 18: Rep Rnd 16. (36 sc)

Rnd 19: Ch 1, sc in same st as joining, sc dec, [sc in next sc, sc dec] rep around, join in beg sc. (24 sts)

Rnd 20: Rep Rnd 16. (24 sc)

Rnd 21: Ch 1, beg in same st as joining, sc dec around, join in beg sc dec. (12 sts)

Rnd 22: Rep Rnd 16; fasten off, leaving a 12" end.

Thread yarn needle with 12" end, weave end through tops of sts of last round, pull tightly to close, fasten off.

With yarn needle, using photo as a guide, work half-cross sts as follows: with D, slanting from left to right, over Rnds 5 and 6; with B, slanting from right to left, over Rnds 10 and 11; with C, slanting from left to right, over Rnds 15 and 16.

First Earflap

Row 1: Working in rem lps of Rnd 1 of crown, using larger hook, attach A with a sl st in any rem lp of Rnd 1, ch 1, sc in same st and in each of next 9 sts, ch 1, turn. (10 sc)

Rows 2–6: Sc in each sc across, ch 1, turn. (10 sc)

Rows 7–9: Sc dec, sc across to last 2 sts, sc dec, ch 1, turn. (4 sts at end of Row 9)

Row 10: Draw up lp on hook to ½", insert hook in first st, draw up lp to ½", [insert hook in next st, draw up lp to ½"] 3 times, yo, draw through all lps on hook, fasten off.

Tie

With RS facing, using larger hook, attach A with a sl st over end st of Row 1 of earflap; working over ends of rows, sc over end st of each of next 8 rows, sc at center of last row, ch 36 for tie, sc in 2nd ch from hook and in each rem ch across, sl st in center of last row of earflap, sc over end st of each of next 8 rows, sl st over end st of Row 1, fasten off.

Second Earflap

Row 1: Sk next 20 unworked rem lps of Rnd 1 of crown, attach A with a sl st in next st, ch 1, sc in same st and in each of next 9 sts, ch 1, turn. (10 sc)

Rows 2–10: Rep Rows 2–10 of first earflap.

Tie

Rep instructions for first tie.

Pompom

Holding 1 strand of each color tog, wrap yarn 35 times around cardboard. Remove yarn from cardboard. Wrap a 12" length of double yarn tightly around center and tie. Cut both ends of pompom open and trim evenly. Attach pompom to top of hat.

Hatband

With smaller hook and C, ch 140 or desired length. Beg over either earflap, weave through row ends of brim at base of Rnd 1 of crown. Tie a knot at each end of ch. Tie ch into bow.

Scarf

Row 1 (RS): With A and larger hook, ch 27, dc in 4th ch from hook and in each rem ch across, turn. (25 dc)

Row 2: Ch 3 (counts as first dc throughout), dc in each rem st across, turn. (25 dc)

Rows 3–6: Rep Row 2; at end of Row 6, change to B in last st, fasten off A, turn. (25 dc)

Rows 7 & 8: Rep Row 2, changing to C in last st of Row 8, turn.

Rows 9 & 10: Rep Row 2, changing to D in last st of Row 10, turn.

Rows 11 & 12: Rep Row 2, changing to A in last st of Row 12, turn.

Rows 13–18: Rep Row 2, changing to B in last st of Row 18, turn.

Rows 19–66: Rep Rows 7–18; at end of Row 66, fasten off.

With yarn needle, using photo as a guide, work half-cross sts as follows: with C, slanting from left to right, over Rows 6 and 7; with D, slanting from right to left, over Rows 8 and 9; with B, slanting from left to right, over Rows 10 and 11; with C, slanting from right to left, over Rows 12 and 13. Rep in established pattern to opposite end of scarf.

Fringe

Cut 1 (16") length of each color. Holding all lengths tog, fold in half. Insert hook from WS to RS in first st of last row of scarf, draw folded end of strands through st on hook to form a lp, pull free ends through lp, pull to tighten. Rep 10 times evenly sp across last row. Work fringe on opposite short edge of scarf as for first edge. Trim fringe evenly. ❤

Strawberry Motifs

Design by Isabelle Wolters

A favorite of spring and summer meals, strawberries are reminders of how pretty, as well as delicious, natural food can be. The stems are three-dimensional and the seed stitches are prominent, making these mofits as appealing as real stawberries.

— Let's Begin! —

Experience Level: Beginner

Size: 1¼" x 1⅝"

Materials

- Crochet cotton size 10: small amount each red, black and green
- Size 7 steel crochet hook or size needed to obtain gauge
- Tapestry needle
- Sewing needle and thread

Gauge: 8 sts and 8 rows = 1" in sc

To save time, take time to check gauge.

Strawberry

Row 1 (RS): With red, ch 10, sc in 2nd ch from hook and in each rem ch across, ch 1, turn. (9 sc)

Rows 2 & 3: Sc in each sc across, ch 1, turn. (9 sc)

Row 4: Sc dec, sc in each st across to last 2 sts, sc dec, ch 1, turn. (7 sts)

Row 5: Rep Row 2. (7 sc)

Rows 6–9: Rep Rows 4 and 5 alternately; at end of Row 9, fasten off. (3 sc at end of Row 9)

Leaves

Working in rem lps across opposite side of strawberry foundation ch, with RS facing, sk first 2 sts, attach green with a sl st in next st, [ch 9, sl st] in same st, *ch 6, [sl st, ch 9, sl st] in next st, rep from * 3 times, leave rem sts unworked, fasten off.

Finishing

With tapestry needle and black, embroider straight sts over strawberry for seeds. Leaving leaves free, sew strawberries to desired surface with sewing needle and thread. ❤

Fluffy Slippers

Design by Jo Ann Burrington

Soothe your feet after a long day in these pretty, plush slippers. A foam rubber cushion wrapped up in a soft, comfortable yarn and embellished with fake fur make these slippers ones you'll want to wear at every opportunity.

Let's Begin!

Experience Level: Intermediate

Finished Measurements: 9¼" long

Materials

- Mohairlike worsted weight yarn: 3 oz lilac
- Sport weight cotton yarn: 3 oz white and small amount yellow
- Size G/6 crochet hook or size needed to obtain gauge
- Size D/3 crochet hook
- 28" x 3" piece white fur trim
- 1"-thick piece of foam rubber
- Yarn needle

Gauge

3 sts = 1" and 3 rows = 1¼" in dc with worsted weight yarn and larger hook

To save time, take time to check gauge.

Pattern Notes

Join rnds with a sl st unless otherwise stated.

To change color in dc, work last dc before color change until last 2 lps before final yo rem on hook, drop working color to WS, yo with next color, complete dc.

When working color pattern on slipper top, carry white loosely across WS of work when not in use, working over it with color in use; drop lilac to WS of work after last lilac st of row is worked and pick up when it is needed again on next row.

When working from chart, read all odd-numbered (RS) rows from right to left, all even-numbered (WS) rows from left to right.

Lower Sole (make 2)

Rnd 1 (RS): With lilac and larger hook, beg at heel, ch 20, 3 sc in 2nd ch from hook, sc in each of next 8 chs, dc in each of next 9 chs, 5 dc in last ch; working in rem lps across opposite side of foundation ch, dc in each of next 9 chs, sc in each of next 8 chs, 2 sc in same ch as beg sc, join in beg sc. (44 sts)

Rnd 2: Ch 1, 2 sc in same st as joining, 2 sc in each of next 3 sc, sc in each of next 7 sc, dc in each of next 8 dc, 2 dc in each of next 7 dc, dc in each of next 8 dc, sc in each of next 7 sc, 2 sc in each of next 3 sc, join in beg sc. (58 sts)

Rnd 3: Ch 1, 2 sc in same st as joining, 2 sc in each of next 3 sc, sc in each of next 11 sc, dc in each of next 13 dc, 2 dc in each of next 4 dc, dc in each of next 13 dc, sc in each of next 11 sc, 2 sc in each of next 2 sc, join in beg sc. (68 sts)

Rnd 4: Ch 1, sc in same st as joining and in each of next 18 sc, dc in each of next 11 dc, [2 dc in next dc, dc in next dc] 6 times, dc in each of next 11 dc, sc in each of next 15 sc, join in beg sc, fasten off. (74 sts)

Upper Sole (make 2)

Rnd 1 (RS): With white and smaller hook, beg at heel, ch 22, 3 sc in 2nd ch from hook, sc in each of next 9 chs, dc in each of next 10 chs, 7 dc in last ch; working in rem lps across opposite side of foundation ch, dc in each of next 10 chs, sc in each of next 9 chs, 2 sc in same ch as beg sc, join in beg sc. (50 sts)

Rnd 2: Ch 1, 2 sc in same st as joining, 2 sc in each of next 2 sc, sc in each of next 9 sc, dc in each of next 9 dc, 2 dc in each of next 9 dc, dc in each of next 9 dc, sc in each of next 9 sc, 2 sc in each of next 2 sc, join in beg sc. (64 sts)

Rnd 3: Ch 1, 2 sc in same st as joining, 2 sc in each of next 5 sc, sc in each of next 9 sc, dc in each of next 11 dc, 2 dc in each of next 14 dc, dc in each of next 11 dc, sc in each of next 9 sc, 2 sc in each of next 4 sc, join in beg sc. (88 sts)

Rnd 4: Ch 1, sc in same st as joining, sc in each of next 20 sc, dc in each of next 18 dc, 2 dc in each of next 14 dc, dc in each of next 18 dc, sc in each of next 17 sc, join in beg sc. (102 sts)

Rnds 5 & 6: Ch 1, beg in same st as joining, sc in each sc and dc in each dc around, join in beg sc; at end of Rnd 6, fasten off. (102 sts)

Using lower sole as a pattern, cut 2 pieces of foam rubber for lining.

Sides

Rnd 1: With larger hook, attach lilac with a sl st in back lp only at center of heel on Rnd 4 of either lower sole, ch 1, beg in same st and working in back lps only this rnd, sc in each st around, join in beg sc. (74 sts)

Rnd 2: Ch 1, sc in same st as joining and in each rem sc around, join in beg sc, fasten off.

Rep on rem lower sole.

Place 1 piece of foam rubber between 1 lower sole and 1 upper sole. With tapestry needle and lilac, sew upper sole to lower sole through back lps only of last rnd of side. Rep for rem lower sole and upper sole.

Edging

With larger hook, attach lilac with a sl st in rem lp of Rnd 2 of side at center of heel, ch 1, beg in same st, sc in each rem lp around, join in beg sc, fasten off. Rep on rem slipper.

Top (make 2)

Row 1 (RS): With smaller hook and white, beg at top edge and working toward toe, ch 29, dc in 4th ch from hook and in each rem ch across, turn. (27 dc, counting last 3 chs of foundation ch as first dc)

Row 2: Ch 3 (counts as first dc throughout), 2 dc in next dc, dc in next dc, 2 dc in next dc, dc in each dc across to last 4 dc, [2 dc in next dc, dc in next dc] twice, turn. (31 dc)

Rows 3 & 4: Ch 3, dc in each rem dc across, turn. (31 dc)

Rows 5–10: Work from Chart A.

Row 11: Ch 3, [dc dec] twice, work from Chart A across to last

5 sts, [dc dec] twice, dc in last st, turn. (27 sts)

Row 12: Ch 3, dc in next st, dc dec, [dc in each of next 2 sts, dc dec] rep across to last 3 sts, dc in each of last 3 sts, turn. (21 sts)

Row 13: Ch 3, *[dc dec, dc in next st] 3 times *, dc in each of next 2 dc, rep from * to *, fasten off. (15 sts)

Lining for Top (make 2)

Rows 1–4: Rep Rows 1–4 of top.

Rows 5–10: Rep Row 4 of top.

Rows 11–13: Rep Rows 11–13 of top; at end of Row 13, fasten off.

Joining Top & Lining for Top

With WS tog, place lining for top below top, matching top edges and toe edges. With RS facing, using smaller hook, attach white with a sl st at left-hand edge of top edge, ch 1, reverse sc across, fasten off. Rep across toe edge. Rep on rem top and lining for top pieces.

Beg in 6th dc from center front of lower sole, sew edge of lined top piece to side. Rep for opposite side. Rep on rem slipper.

Cut 2 (8") lengths of fake fur and 2 (6") lengths. With tapestry needle and white, sew 6" length across toe edge of top and 8" length across top edge of top. Rep for rem slipper. ♥

COLOR & STITCH KEY
- ☐ White dc
- ☒ Lilac dc
- ◎ Yellow dc

Chart A

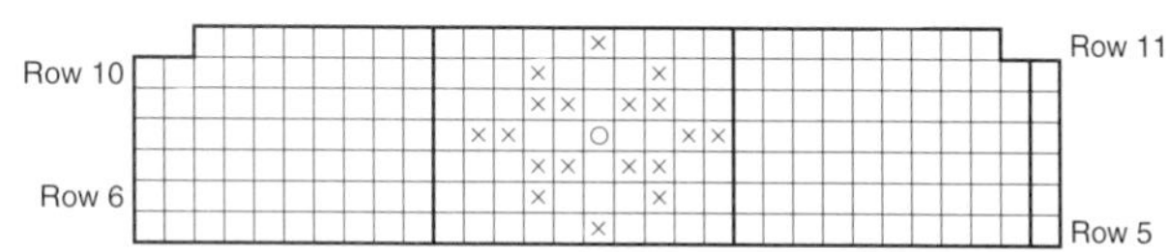

Fluttering Butterflies Motifs

Designs by Sue Collins-Ottinger

Gardeners who love attracting butterflies to their flower beds will appreciate these motifs. Three different patterns allow crocheters to use a variety of stitches while crocheting this trio of distinctive designs.

Let's Begin!

Experience Level: Intermediate

Size: Small Butterfly: 2⅛" x 2"

Medium Butterfly: 3" x 3"

Large Butterfly: 3¾" x 3¼"

Materials

- Crochet cotton size 10: small amount ecru or desired color
- Size 7 steel crochet hook

Gauge: Work evenly and consistently throughout

Pattern Stitch

P: Ch 3, sl st in 3rd ch from hook.

Small Butterfly

Body

Row 1: Ch 2, [sc, ch 1, sl st] in 2nd ch from hook to form head, ch 5, sl st in 3rd ch from hook to form ring, ch 5 (counts as first dc, ch-2), dc in ring, [ch 2, dc in ring] 3 times, ch 2, turn.

Row 2: [Hdc, 3 tr, ch 2, 3 tr, hdc] in first sp, ch 1, sl st in next dc, *ch 1, [3 dc, ch 2, 3 dc] in next sp, ch 1, sl st in next dc *, rep from * to *, ch 1, [hdc, 3 tr, ch 2, 3 tr, hdc, ch 1, sl st] in last sp, ch 1, turn.

Row 3: Sl st in ch-1 sp, **sl st in next hdc, sc in next tr, hdc in next st, 2 dc in next st, [2 dc, p, 2 dc] in next sp, 2 dc in next st, hdc in next st, sc in next st, sl st in next hdc **, *[sl st in next ch-1] twice, sc in next dc, hdc in next dc, dc in next dc, [tr, p, tr] in next sp, dc in next dc, hdc in next dc, sc in next dc *, rep from * to *, sl st in each of next 2 ch-1 sps, rep from ** to **, sl st in ch-1 sp, fasten off.

Antennae

Ch 6, sl st in top right corner of head, sl st in sc at center of head, sl st in top left corner of head, ch 6, fasten off.

Medium Butterfly

Body

Row 1: Ch 3, [hdc, ch 2, sl st] in 3rd ch from hook to form head, ch 5, sl st in 4th ch from hook to form ring, ch 6 (counts as first tr, ch-2), [2 tr in ring, ch 2] 3 times, tr in ring, turn.

Row 2: Ch 4 (counts as first tr), [2 tr, ch 2, 3 tr] in first sp, [{3 dc, ch 2, 3 dc} in next sp] twice, [3 tr, ch 2, 3 tr] in last sp, turn.

Row 3: **[4 tr, p, 4 tr] in next ch-2 sp **, sk next 2 tr, sl st between next tr and next dc, *[3 dc, ch 6, sl st in 3rd ch from hook, ch 3, 3 dc] in next ch-2 sp, sk next 2 dc *, sl st between next 2 dc, rep from * to *, sl st between next dc and next tr, rep from ** to **, sk 2 tr, sl st in next tr, fasten off.

Antennae

Ch 8, sl st in top right corner of head, sl st in hdc at center of head, sl st in top left corner of head, ch 8, fasten off.

Large Butterfly

Body

Rows 1 & 2: Rep Rows 1 and 2 of Medium Butterfly.

Row 3: [4 tr, ch 3, 4 tr] in next ch-2 sp, sk next 2 tr, sl st between next tr and next dc, *[3 dc, ch 3, 3 dc] in next ch-2 sp, sk next 2 dc *, sl st between next 2 dc, rep from * to *, sl st between next dc and next tr, [4 tr, ch 3, 4 tr] in last sp, sk 2 tr, sl st in top of last tr, turn.

Row 4: Sl st in first tr, **sc in next tr, hdc in next tr, dc in next tr, [3 dc, p, 3 dc] in next sp, dc in next tr, hdc in next tr, sc in next tr, sl st in next tr **, *sl st in next sl st, sc in next dc, hdc in next dc, dc in next dc, [3 dc, ch 6, sl st in 3rd ch from hook, ch 3, 3 dc] in next sp, dc in next dc, hdc in next dc, sc in next dc, rep from *, sl st in next sl st, sl st in next tr, rep from ** to **, fasten off.

Antennae

Ch 10, sl st in top right corner of head, sl st in hdc at center of head, sl st in top left corner of head, ch 10, fasten off. ❤

Accents in Blue Blouse Edging

Design by Alice Heim

Transform an ordinary white blouse into a special garment that shows your crochet interest and talent. Even beginner crocheters can complete the three flower motifs at the middle and sides of the back yoke and a scalloped edge along the collar.

Let's Begin!

Experience Level: Beginner

Size: Edging = 3/8" wide

Materials

- DMC Cebelia crochet cotton size 20 (50 grams per ball): 1 ball blue #799
- Size 10 steel crochet hook or size needed to obtain gauge
- Commercial fabric stiffener
- Plastic wrap
- Sheet of cardboard
- Cotton balls
- Rustproof straight pins
- Sewing needle

Gauge: Flower = 3/4" in diameter

To save time, take time to check gauge.

Pattern Stitch

P: Ch 3, sl st in 3rd ch from hook.

Collar Edging

Measure around edge of collar. Make a ch several inches longer than this measurement.

Row 1: Sc in 2nd ch from hook, *sk 2 chs, [3 dc, p, 3 dc] in next ch, sk 2 chs, sc in next ch, rep from * across until edging fits around edge of collar, fasten off. If necessary, untie slip knot and unravel excess chs.

Yoke Edging

Using photo as a guide, measure from outer edge of first shoulder seam at an angle to center back yoke and from center back yoke at an angle to outer edge of opposite shoulder seam. Make a ch several inches longer than this measurement, fasten off.

Row 1 (RS): Attach thread with a sl st in first ch, ch 1, sc in same st and in each rem ch across, fasten off, do not turn.

Row 2: With RS facing, attach thread with a sl st in first sc of last row, ch 1, sc in same st, *sk 2 sc, [3 dc, p, 3 dc] in next sc, sk 2 sc, sc in next sc, rep from * across until edging fits from shoulder to shoulder across back yoke, fasten off. If necessary, untie the slip knot and unravel excess scs and chs.

Pocket Edging

Measure across pocket. Make ch several inches longer than this measurement, fasten off.

Row 1: Rep Row 1 of yoke edging.

Row 2: Rep Row 2 of yoke edging until edging fits across pocket, fasten off. If necessary, untie the slip knot and unravel excess scs and chs.

Flower (make 3)

Ch 1 (center ch), [ch 3, dc, p, dc, ch 3, sl st] 5 times in center ch, fasten off. (5 petals)

Front Edging (make 2)

Measure front of blouse down inner edge of buttonhole band. Make ch several inches longer than this measurement.

Row 1: Rep Row 1 of collar edging until edging fits down front of blouse, fasten off. If necessary, untie the slip knot and unravel excess chs.

Finishing

Cover cardboard with plastic wrap and pin edgings to exact measurements. Pin flowers to board. Measure 1/8 teaspoon fabric stiffener into 1/3 cup of water and mix well. With cotton balls, apply mixture to edgings and flowers and allow to dry thoroughly.

Sew edgings to blouse with sewing needle and crochet cotton.

Using photo as a guide, sew 1 flower to each end of yoke edging and 1 at center back yoke. Work 3 French knots at the center of each flower.

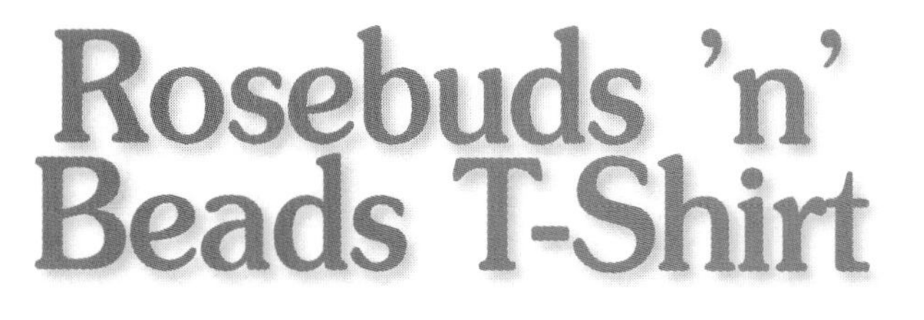

Design by Nazanin S. Fard

Crochet your own bouquet! Dress up any T-shirt with these dainty little roses, rosebuds and leaves. Add a little extra charm with the shiny beads. What a cute top to wear for summer outings!

Let's Begin!

Experience Level: Intermediate

Size: Rose: 1⅛" in diameter

Materials

- DMC #5 pearl cotton (48 yds per skein): 1 skein each rose #3687, pink #3689 and green #320
- Size 8 steel crochet hook or size needed to obtain gauge
- T-shirt
- 14 (⅛") gold beads (optional)
- Sewing needle and thread

Gauge: Rose = 1⅛" in diameter
To save time, take time to check gauge.

Pattern Note

Join rnds with a sl st unless otherwise stated.

Rose (make 2 pink & 1 rose)

Rnd 1: Ch 4, 9 dc in 4th ch from hook, join in 4th ch from hook of beg ch-4. (10 dc, counting last 3 chs of beg ch-4 as first dc)

Rnd 2: Ch 3, [sk next dc, sl st in next dc, ch 3] rep around, ending with ch 3, sk last dc, join in same st as joining st of Rnd 1. (5 ch-3 sps)

Rnd 3: Ch 1, [sc, hdc, 4 dc, hdc, sc] in each ch-3 sp around, do not join. (5 petals)

Rnd 4: Sl st in first unworked dc of Rnd 1, [ch 5, sl st in next unworked dc of Rnd 1] rep around, ending with ch 5, join in beg sl st. (5 ch-5 sps)

Rnd 5: Ch 1, [sc, hdc, 5 dc, hdc, sc] in each ch-5 sp around, join in beg sc, fasten off.

Rosebud (make 1 pink & 4 rose)

Ch 11, 3 dc in 4th ch from hook and in each rem ch across, fasten off.

Roll into rosebud shape and tack securely at bottom.

Leaf (make 7 green)

Ch 8, sc in 2nd ch from hook, hdc in next ch, dc in each of next 3 chs, hdc in next ch, 3 sc in last ch; working in rem lps across opposite side of foundation ch, hdc in next ch, dc in each of next 3 chs, hdc in next ch, sc in last ch, join in beg sc, fasten off.

Finishing

Using photo as a guide, position flowers, leaves and beads on T-shirt and sew in place with sewing needle and thread. ❤

Visually Impaired?

Visually impaired crocheters need not give up using their hands because their eyesight is impaired. Contact the National Braille Press, 88 St. Stephen St., Boston, MA 02115, or call toll-free, (800) 548-7323. Also you may telephone your local library and ask for the 800 number for your State Library Talking Book Program. This is a national free service for the blind. Visually impaired persons must register; the books will be delivered to their door, postage free. Please, help us spread the word to our sight-impaired friends, enabling them to enjoy the wonderful experience of crocheting.

Ponytail Elastics

Use the coated ponytail elastics (smaller size) as a base for skirts, dresses, shorts, etc. The elastics are just the waist size needed and will save you the time of sewing together regular round elastic. They come in many colors so you can color-coordinate them to your yarn or thread.

Dressed-Up Doggies

Designs by Vicki Blizzard

Dress up your "best friend" to go out to the beach or for a fancy night on the town with one or both of these fun projects.

Let's Begin!

Experience Level: Beginner

Finished Measurement: Neck: 12" (adjustable)

Materials

- Worsted weight yarn: 2 oz white and small amounts each red and royal blue for Sailor Collar; 2 oz desired color for Bow Tie
- Size H/8 crochet hook or size needed to obtain gauge
- Tapestry needle
- 1" square piece of hook-and-loop tape for each collar
- Sewing needle and thread
- 2 (5/8") red star-shaped buttons for Sailor Collar

Gauge: 4 sts and 4 rows = 1" in sc

To save time, take time to check gauge.

Bow Tie

Neck Band

Row 1: Ch 5, sc in 2nd ch from hook and in each rem ch across, ch 1, turn. (4 sc)

Row 2: Sc in each sc across, ch 1, turn.

Rep Row 2 until neck band wraps comfortably around dog's neck, allowing for a 2" overlap. At end of last row, do not ch 1; fasten off.

Sew hook piece of tape to 1 end of neck band. Sew loop piece to opposite side of opposite end of neck band.

Bow

Row 1: Rep Row 1 of neck band.

Rows 2–4: Rep Row 2 of neck band.

Row 5: Sc inc in first st, sc in each st across to last st, sc inc in last st, ch 1, turn. (6 sc)

Row 6: Rep Row 2 of neck band.

Rows 7–10: Rep Rows 5 and 6 alternately twice. (10 sc on each of last 2 rows)

Rows 11 & 12: Rep Row 6.

Row 13: Sc dec, sc in each st across to last 2 sts, sc dec, ch 1, turn. (8 sts)

Row 14: Rep Row 6.

Rows 15–18: Rep Rows 13 and 14 alternately twice. (4 sts on each of last 2 rows)

Rows 19–26: Rep Row 6.

Rows 27–44: Rep Rows 5–22; at end of Row 44, do not ch 1; fasten off, leaving a 12" length for sewing.

With tapestry needle and 12" length, whipstitch Rows 1 and 44 tog. Fold bow so that narrowest rows are at center and widest rows are at each end.

Knot

Row 1: Rep Row 1 of neck band.

Rows 2–10: Rep Row 2 of neck band; at end of Row 10, do not ch 1; fasten off, leaving a 12" length for sewing.

Wrap knot around center of bow. With tapestry needle and 12" length, whipstitch ends of knot tog.

Sew bow to end of neck band.

Sailor Collar

Neck Band

Row 1: With red, rep Row 1 of neck band for Bow Tie.

Row 2: Rep Row 2 of neck band for Bow Tie.

Rep Row 2 until neck band wraps comfortably around dog's neck, allowing for a 2" overlap. At end of last row, do not ch 1; fasten off.

Collar

Row 1 (RS): Working over ends of rows on neck band, attach white with a sl st over end of 11th row from center of neck band, ch 1, sc over end st of same row and each of next 21 rows, ch 1, turn. (22 sc)

Rows 2–4: Rep Row 2 of neck band for Bow Tie. (22 sc)

Row 5: Rep Row 5 of bow for Bow Tie. (24 sc)

Row 6: Rep Row 2 of neck band for Bow Tie. (24 sc)

Rows 7–19: Rep Rows 5 and 6 alternately, ending with a Row 5; at end of Row 19, fasten off. (38 sc on Row 19)

Border

Row 1: With RS facing, working around 3 edges of collar, attach royal blue with a sl st over end st of next unworked row on neck band, sc over end st of Row 1 of collar, sc over end st of each rem row across to corner, 3 sc in corner st, sc in each st across Row 19 to next corner, 3 sc in corner st, sc over end st of each row across to neck band, sl st over end st of next unworked row on neck band, fasten off.

Row 2: With RS facing, attach white with a sl st over end st of next unworked row on neck band after first sl st of Row 1 of border, sc in first sc of Row 1 of border and in each rem sc across, working 3 sc in each corner sc, ending with sl st in next unworked row on neck band, fasten off.

With sewing needle and thread, sew 1 button to each bottom corner of collar.

Bow

Row 1: With red, ch 2, sc in 2nd ch from hook, ch 1, turn. (1 sc)

Row 2: 2 sc in sc, ch 1, turn. (2 sc)

Row 3: 2 sc in each of 2 sc, ch 1, turn. (4 sc)

Rows 4–37: Rep Row 2 of neck band for Bow Tie. (4 sc)

Row 38: [Sc dec] twice, ch 1, turn. (2 sts)

Row 39: Sc dec, fasten off.

Tie loose overhand knot at center of bow to form knot with 2 ends hanging. With tapestry needle and red, sew bow to end of neck band. ❤

Storage Idea

Use large zip-lock bags to store small crochet projects in as you are working on them. The bags are large enough to hold your pattern as well as any other supplies you'll need to complete your project. They also help keep materials clean.

Out-of-Print Patterns

When searching for out-of-print patterns, be sure to contact Lynn Wohleber, c/o C.A.E. Library, Carnegie Office Park, Bldg. #1, 600 Bell Ave., Carnegie, PA 15106.

Help for Left-Handed Persons

Use a suction cup device to hold your crochet hook and act as your right hand. Wrap the yarn on your left fingers and let your left hand do all the work.

Coat Sweaters With a Flare

You can put a little flare in the back of a coat sweater by increasing midway on the left side in the middle, and midway on the right side. Depending on how much flare you want, a stitch or two probably would be sufficient if you start a few rows up from the bottom, and increase the number as you get to the bottom.

Remember, if you increase too few on a curve, it will buckle; if you increase too much it will ripple. It may take a couple of times experimenting to establish just the right number necessary, then you may make a permanent change to your pattern. Always write down such changes; you will have it for future reference.

Little Darlings

Cheery dolls, fluffy bunnies, soft booties and many more delightful darlings are at your fingertips in this colorful chapter! Crochet one and all to share with the special little people in your life!

Cutie Pie Clothespin Dolls

Design by Sue Childress

Clothespin dolls all fixed up with pretty hair and faces will look delightful in these fancy crocheted dresses, pinafores and frilly pantaloons.

Let's Begin!

Experience Level: Intermediate

Finished Measurement: Fits 4½"-tall clothespin doll

Materials

Each Doll

- Crochet cotton size 5: 11 yds each MC and CC
- Size B/1 crochet hook or size needed to obtain gauge
- 4½"-tall clothespin doll
- Mini-curl curly doll hair
- ½ yd ⅛"-wide satin ribbon in desired color
- 3 (⅜") shank buttons
- Tapestry needle
- Acrylic paint: black and lip color
- Liner paintbrush
- Fabric glue

Gauge: 7 hdc = 1"

To save time, take time to check gauge.

Pattern Note

Join rnds with a sl st unless otherwise stated.

Pattern Stitches

Shell: [2 dc, ch 2, 2 dc] in indicated st or sp.

Beg shell: [Ch 3, dc, ch 2, 2 dc] in indicated st or sp.

Doll Head

Referring to photo, glue hair on doll; paint on face. Lay aside to dry.

Panties

Row 1 (RS): With MC, ch 30, hdc in 3rd ch from hook and in each rem ch across to last ch, 2 hdc in last ch, turn. (30 hdc, counting last 2 chs of foundation ch as first hdc)

Row 2: Ch 2 (counts as first hdc throughout), hdc in each rem st across, turn. (30 hdc)

Rnd 3: Ch 2, hdc in each rem hdc around, join in 2nd ch of beg ch-2. (30 hdc)

Rnd 4: Rep Rnd 3.

First leg

Rnd 5: Ch 2, hdc in each of next 14 hdc, sk rem sts, join in 2nd ch of beg ch-2. (15 hdc)

Rnd 6: Rep Rnd 3. (15 hdc)

Rnd 7: Ch 1, sc in same st as joining, ch 3, [sc in next hdc, ch 3] rep around, join in beg sc. (15 ch-3 sps)

Rnd 8: Sl st in first sp, ch 1, beg in same sp, 3 sc in each ch-3 sp around, join in beg sc, fasten off.

Second leg

Rnd 5: With RS facing, attach MC with a sl st in next unworked hdc of Rnd 4, ch 2, hdc in each rem unworked st around, join in 2nd ch of beg ch-2. (15 hdc)

Rnds 6–8: Rep Rnds 6–8 of first leg.

Sew inseam. Weave short length of ribbon through sts of Row 1. Place panties on doll with opening at back and knot ribbon at waist. Weave short length of ribbon through sts of Rnd 6 on each pant leg; knot ribbon at outside of leg.

Sundress

Row 1 (WS): Beg at neck, with MC, ch 25, hdc in 3rd ch from hook, 2 hdc in each rem ch across, turn. (46 hdc, counting last 2 chs of foundation ch as first hdc)

Row 2: Ch 2, hdc in each of next 4 sts, 2 dc in each of next 13 sts, hdc in each of next 10 sts, 2 dc in each of next 13 sts, hdc in each of last 5 sts, turn. (72 sts)

Row 3: Ch 2, hdc in each of next 4 sts, *ch 2, sk next 26 dc for armhole *, hdc in each of next 10 hdc, rep from * to *, hdc in each of last 5 sts, turn. (20 sts; 2 ch-2 sps)

Row 4: Ch 3 (counts as first dc throughout), dc in each rem dc and ch st across, turn. (24 dc)

Row 5: Ch 3, [3 dc in next dc] rep across to last st, dc in last st, turn. (68 dc)

Rnd 6: Ch 3, dc in each rem dc around, join in 3rd ch of beg ch-3. (68 dc)

Rnd 7: Sl st in next dc, ch 3, 2 dc in same st, [sk 2 dc, 3 dc in next dc] rep around, join in 3rd ch of beg ch-3. (23 3-dc groups)

Rnd 8: Sl st in next dc, ch 3, 2 dc in same st, [3 dc in center dc of next 3-dc group] rep around, join in 3rd ch of beg ch-3. (23 3-dc groups)
Rnd 9: Sl st in next dc, ch 3, 4 dc in same st, sc between same 3-dc group and next 3-dc group, [5 dc in center dc of next 3-dc group, sc between same 3-dc group and next 3-dc group] rep around, join in 3rd ch of beg ch-3.
Rnd 10: Sl st in each of next 2 dc, ch 1, sc in same st, ch 3, sc in next sc, ch 3, [sc in center dc of next 5-dc group, ch 3, sc in next sc, ch 3] rep around, join in beg sc.
Rnd 11: Sl st into first ch-3 sp, ch 3, 4 dc in same sp, sc in next sp, [5 dc in next sp, sc in next sp] rep around, join in 3rd ch of beg ch-3, fasten off.

Placket

With RS facing, attach MC with a sl st at lower left back opening, ch 1, work 11 sc evenly sp over row ends to neck; working in rem lps across neck, [sc in each of next 2 sts, sk next st, sc in each of next 2 sts] rep across neck edge, adjusting number of sc worked at opposite end of neck edge, if necessary; working over row ends, work 11 sc evenly sp to bottom of back opening, ch 1, turn, sc in first sc, [ch 2, sk next 2 sc, sc in each of next 2 sc] twice, ch 2, sk 2 sc, sc in next sc, fasten off.

Sew buttons opposite buttonholes. Place dress on doll.

Pinafore

Bodice

Row 1: Beg at neck, with CC, ch 24, hdc in 3rd ch from hook, hdc in each of next 2 chs, [{2 dc, ch 2} twice in next ch] 4 times, hdc in each of next 7 chs, ch 2, [{2 dc, ch 2} twice in next ch] 3 times, shell in next ch, hdc in each of last 4 chs, turn. (47 sts, counting last 2 chs of foundation ch as first hdc; 16 ch-2 sps)
Row 2: Ch 2 (counts as first hdc throughout), hdc in each of next 3 sts, [shell in next ch-2 sp] 8 times, hdc in each of next 7 hdc, [shell in next ch-2 sp] 8 times, sk next 2 hdc, hdc in each of last 4 hdc, turn.
Row 3: Ch 2, hdc in each of next 3 sts, *ch 2, sk next 8 ch-2 sps for armhole *, hdc in each of next 7 hdc, rep from * to *, hdc in each of last 4 sts, turn. (15 hdc; 2 ch-2 sps)
Row 4: Ch 2, hdc in each rem hdc and ch st across, turn. (19 hdc)

Skirt

For less full skirt

Row 5: Ch 3 (counts as first dc throughout), dc in first st, [sk next st, shell in next st] rep across to last 2 sts, sk next st, 2 dc in last st, turn. (8 shells)

For fuller skirt

Row 5: Ch 3 (counts as first dc throughout), dc in first st, sk next

Continued on page 95

Bunny Delight

Design by Sue Childress

Any bunny would be delighted to have this beautiful ensemble as an Easter outfit! Crochet the lace slip, hat, booties and basket to complement the frilly pastel dress.

Let's Begin!

Experience Level: Intermediate

Finished Measurement: Fits 12"-tall soft-sculpture bunny

Materials

- Crochet cotton size 5 (200 yds per skein): 1 skein each blue, pink, yellow and green
- Size D/3 crochet hook or size needed to obtain gauge
- 12" soft-sculpture bunny by Wimpole Street Creations
- 1 yd ⅛"-wide off-white satin ribbon
- Scraps of green thread or yarn or small amount Easter grass
- Miniature colored eggs and carrot for basket
- Tapestry needle
- Craft glue

Gauge: 11 dc = 2"
To save time, take time to check gauge.

Pattern Note

Join rnds with a sl st unless otherwise stated.

Pattern Stitches

Shell: [2 dc, ch 2, 2 dc] in indicated sp or st.

Tr3tog: Holding back on hook last lp of each st, tr in each of next 3 sts, yo, draw through all 4 lps on hook.

Slip

Rnd 1: Beg at neck, with pink, ch 36, taking care not to twist ch, join to form a ring, ch 2 (counts as first hdc), hdc in each rem ch around, join in 2nd ch of beg ch-2. (36 hdc)

Rnd 2: Ch 2, hdc in same st as joining, 2 hdc in each of next 4 hdc, ch 8, sk next 9 hdc for first armhole, 2 hdc in each of next 9 hdc, ch 8, sk next 9 hdc for next armhole, 2 hdc in each of next 4 hdc, join in top of beg ch-2. (36 hdc; 2 ch-8 sps)

Rnd 3: Ch 3 (counts as first dc throughout), dc in same st as joining, dc in next st; working in each dc and in each ch st around, [2 dc in next st, dc in next st] rep around, join in 3rd ch of beg ch-3. (78 dc)

Rnds 4–15: Ch 3, dc in each rem dc around, join in 3rd ch of beg ch-3. (78 dc)

Rnd 16: Ch 3, dc in same st as joining, 2 dc in each rem dc around, join in 3rd ch of beg ch-3. (156 dc)

Rnd 17: Rep Rnd 4. (156 dc)

Rnd 18: Ch 1, sc in same st as joining, ch 3, [sk next dc, sc in next dc, ch 3] rep around, ending with sk last dc, join in beg sc, fasten off.

Put slip on bunny over head.

Dress

Bodice

Row 1 (RS): Beg at neck, with blue, ch 29, hdc in 3rd ch from hook and in each rem ch across, turn. (28 hdc, counting last 2 chs of foundation ch as first hdc)

Row 2: Ch 2 (counts as first hdc throughout), [2 hdc in next st, hdc in each of next 2 sts] rep across, turn. (37 hdc)

Row 3: Ch 3 (counts as first dc throughout), dc in each of next 5 sts, 3 dc in each of next 7 sts, dc in each of next 11 sts, 3 dc in each of next 7 sts, dc in each of last 6 sts, turn. (65 sts)

Row 4: Ch 2, hdc in first st, [hdc in next st, 2 hdc in next st] twice, hdc in next st, [dc in next st, ch 1] 20 times, dc in next st, [2 hdc in next st, hdc in next st] 5 times, hdc in next st, [dc in next st, ch 1] 20 times, dc in next st, [hdc in next st, 2 hdc in next st] 3 times, turn.

Row 5: Ch 2, hdc in each of next 8 sts, sk next 21 dc for first armhole, hdc in each of next 16 hdc, sk next 21 dc for next armhole, hdc in each of last 9 sts, turn. (34 hdc)

Row 6: Ch 2, [3 hdc in next st, sk next st] rep across to last 3 sts, 3 hdc in next st, sk next st, hdc in last st, turn. (50 hdc)

Row 7: Ch 3, 5 hdc in center hdc of each 3-hdc group across to last st, dc in last st, ch 1, do not fasten off, do not turn. (82 dc)

Placket

2 sc over end st of each of last 7 rows, sc in each rem lp of foundation ch across neck edge, 2 sc

over end st of each of next 7 rows, fasten off.

Skirt

Rnd 1: With RS facing, attach yellow with a sl st in last sc of placket, ch 1, sc in same st, [ch 3, sc in 2nd dc of next 5-dc group of Row 7, ch 3, sc in 4th dc of same 5-dc group] rep around to last 5-dc group, ch 3, sc in first sc of placket, join in beg sc. (33 ch-3 sps)

Rnd 2: Sl st in next ch-3 sp, ch 1, 3 sc in same sp, [5 dc in next sp, 3 sc in next sp] rep around, join in beg sc, fasten off yellow.

Rnd 3: With RS facing, attach pink with a sl st in center sc of first 3-sc group after joining st, ch 1, sc in same st, [ch 3, sc in 2nd dc of next 5-dc group, ch 3, sc in 4th dc of same 5-dc group, ch 3, sc in center sc of next 3-sc group] rep around to last 3-sc group, ch 3, join in beg sc. (49 ch-3 sps)

Rnd 4: Sl st into next ch-3 sp, ch 1, 3 sc in same sp, *5 dc in next ch-3 sp **, [3 sc in next ch-3 sp] twice, rep from * around to last 2 ch-3 sps, ending last rep at **, 3 sc in next sp, sl st in last sp, join in beg sc, fasten off pink.

Rnd 5: With RS facing, attach green with a sl st in center sc of first 3-sc group after joining st, ch 1, sc in same st, *ch 3, sc in 2nd dc of next 5-dc group, ch 3, sc in 4th dc of same 5-dc group **, [ch 3, sc in center sc of next 3-sc group] twice, rep from * around to last 5-dc group, ending last rep at **, ch 3, sc in last 3-sc group, ch 3, join in beg sc. (64 ch-3 sps)

Rnd 6: Sl st in next ch-3 sp, ch 1, 3 sc in same sp, [5 dc in next ch-3 sp, 3 sc in next ch-3 sp] rep around to last sp, 5 dc in last sp, join in beg sc, fasten off green.

Rnd 7: With RS facing, attach blue with a sl st in center dc of last 5-dc group made, ch 3, 4 dc in same st, shell in center sc of next 3-sc group, [5 dc in center dc of next 5-dc group, shell in center sc of next 3-sc group] rep around, join in 3rd ch of beg ch-3.

Rnds 8 & 9: Sl st in each of next 2 dc, ch 3, 4 dc in same st as last sl st, shell in next shell sp, [5 dc in center dc of next 5-dc group, shell in next shell sp] rep around, join in 3rd ch of beg ch-3.

Rnd 10: Sl st in each of next 2 dc, ch 3, 4 dc in same st, 5 dc in next shell sp, [5 dc in center dc of next 5-dc group, 5 dc in next shell sp] rep around, join in 3rd ch of beg ch-3. (64 5-dc groups)

Rnd 11: Ch 3, dc in next dc, 3 dc in next dc, dc in each of next 2 dc, [dc in each of next 2 dc, 3 dc in next dc, dc in each of next 2 dc] rep around, join in 3rd ch of beg ch-3, fasten off. (448 dc)

Row 12: With RS facing, attach yellow with a sl st in same st as joining, ch 1, sc in same st, ch 3, [sk next dc, sc in next dc, ch 3] rep around, ending with sk last dc, join in beg sc, fasten off. (224 ch-3 sps)

Rnd 13: With RS facing, attach pink with a sl st in first ch-3 sp, ch 1, sc in same sp, ch 3, [sc in next sp, ch 3] rep around, join in beg sc, fasten off.

Rnd 14: With green, rep Rnd 13, do not fasten off.

Rnd 15: Sl st into first ch-3 sp, ch 1, beg in same sp, 3 sc in each sp around, join in beg sc, fasten off.

Sleeve Edging

With RS facing, attach yellow with a sl st at bottom center of either armhole opening, ch 1, sc in same sp, ch 3, sc over side of next hdc, ch 3, [sc in next ch-1 sp, ch 3] rep around to opposite side of opening, sc over side of next hdc, ch 3, join in beg sc, fasten off.

Rep on rem armhole.

Place dress on bunny.

Beg at neck edge, weave a 20" length of ribbon through sc sts of back bodice opening; tie in bow at waist.

Hat

Rnd 1: With yellow, ch 1 (center ch), ch 2 more (counts as first hdc), 7 hdc in center ch, join in 2nd ch of beg ch-2. (8 hdc)

Rnd 2: Ch 2 (counts as first hdc throughout), hdc in same st as joining, 2 hdc in each rem hdc around, join in 2nd ch of beg ch-2. (16 hdc)

Rnd 3: Ch 1, sc in same st as joining, *sk next hdc, 5 dc in next hdc, sk next hdc **, sc in next hdc, rep from * around, ending last rep at **, join in beg sc.

Rnd 4: Ch 1, sc in same st as joining, *dc in each of next 2 dc, 3 dc in next dc, dc in each of next 2 dc **, sc in next sc, rep from * around, ending last rep at **, join in beg sc.

Rnd 5: Ch 1, sc in same st as joining, *ch 6, sc in center dc of next 7-dc group, ch 6 **, sc in next sc, rep from * around, ending last rep at **, join in beg sc. (8 ch-6 sps)

Rnd 6: Sl st in next ch-6 sp, ch 1, 8 sc in same sp for first ear hole, *[{dc, ch 1} 7 times in next ch-6 sp, dc in same sp] 3 times *, 8 sc in next sp for next ear hole, rep from * to *, join in beg sc, fasten off.

Tie rem length of ribbon to top of hat; tie into bow; trim ends to desired length.

Basket

Rnd 1: With yellow, ch 4, 11 dc in 4th ch from hook, join in 4th ch of beg ch-4. (12 dc, counting last 3 chs of beg ch-4 as first dc)

Rnd 2: Ch 3 (counts as first dc throughout), dc in same st as joining, 2 dc in each rem dc around, join in 3rd ch of beg ch-3. (24 dc)

Rnd 3: Ch 3, dc in same st as joining, 2 dc in each rem dc around, join in 3rd ch of beg ch-3. (48 dc)

Rnd 4: Ch 3, bpdc over each rem dc around, join in 3rd ch of beg ch-3. (48 sts)

Rnds 5–8: Ch 3, fpdc over next st, [bpdc over next st, fpdc over next st] rep around, join in 3rd ch of beg ch-3, fasten off at end of Rnd 8.

Handle

Row 1 (WS): With yellow, ch 5, dc in 4th ch from hook and in next ch, turn. (3 dc, counting last 3 chs of ch-5 as first dc)

Row 2: Ch 3 (counts as first dc throughout), fpdc over next st, dc in last st, turn.

Row 3: Ch 3, bpdc over next st, dc in last st, turn.

Rows 4–11: Rep Rows 2 and 3 alternately; at end of Row 11, fasten off.

Sew 1 end of handle to side of basket; sew opposite end to opposite side.

Fill basket with green yarn scraps or Easter grass. Glue miniature colored eggs and carrot on top.

Slippers

***Note:** Do not join rnds unless otherwise stated.*

Rnd 1: With blue, ch 10, hdc in 3rd ch from hook, hdc in each of next 6 chs, 5 dc in last ch; working in rem lps across opposite side of foundation ch, hdc in each of next 6 chs, 2 hdc in last ch. (21 sts, counting last 2 chs of foundation ch as first hdc)

Rnd 2: Sc in last ch of foundation ch, sc in next hdc, hdc in each of next 6 hdc, 2 dc in each of next 5 dc, hdc in each of next 6 hdc, sc in each of last 2 hdc. (26 sts)

Rnd 3: Dc in each of next 11 sts, 2 dc in each of next 4 sts, dc in each of next 11 sts. (30 sts)

Rnd 4: Dc in each st around. (30 dc)

Rnd 5: Dc in each of next 14 sts, tr3tog twice, dc in each of next 10 sts. (26 sts)

Rnd 6: Hdc in next st, sc in each of next 4 sts, *ch 30 for strap, sc in 2nd ch from hook and in each rem ch across *, sc in each of next 8 dc, draw up a lp in each of next 4 sts, yo, draw through all 5 lps on hook, sc in each of next 6 sts, rep from * to *, sc in each of last 3 sts, join in next st, fasten off. ♥

Fashion Doll Fun

Design by Dawn A. Kemp

Dress up a fashion doll in this easy-to-crochet outfit including a skirt, blouse and hat worked in crisp white and navy blue.

Let's Begin!

Experience Level: Intermediate

Finished Measurement: Fits 11½" fashion doll

Materials

- J. & P. Coats Knit-Cro-Sheen crochet cotton size 10: 50 yds dark blue (MC) and 30 yds white (CC)
- Size 2 steel crochet hook or size needed to obtain gauge
- 2 snaps
- Sewing needle and thread

Gauge: Skirt: 8 sts and 5 rows = 1"
To save time, take time to check gauge.

Pattern Notes

After Row 4, skirt is worked from back edge to back edge.

Join rnds with a sl st unless otherwise stated.

Skirt

Row 1: Beg at waist with MC, ch 23, sc in 2nd ch from hook and in each ch across, ch 23, turn. (22 sc)

Row 2: Sc in 2nd ch from hook, dc in next ch, [sc in next ch, dc in next ch] rep across, sl st in first sc of Row 1 (waistband), ch 1, turn. (22 sc)

Row 3: [Sc in next dc, dc in next sc] rep across, ch 1, turn.

Row 4: [Sc in next dc, dc in next sc] rep across, sl st in next sc of Row 1, ch 1, turn.

Rows 5–44: Rep Rows 3 and 4 alternately, at end of Row 44, ch 1, turn.

Edging

Rnd 1: Sc evenly around skirt, join in beg sc, fasten off.

Bottom Ruffle

Row 1: With RS facing, attach MC to bottom corner, ch 1, [sc, dc] in same st, rep between [] in each st across bottom, ch 1, turn.

Row 2: [Sc in next dc, dc in next sc] rep across, fasten off.

Finishing

Overlap right side of skirt over left side; sew snap to skirt, allowing extra room for blouse to be tucked in.

Blouse

Row 1: Beg at bottom with CC, ch 25, sc in 2nd ch from hook and in each ch across, ch 1, turn. (24 sc)

Row 2: Sc in each sc across, ch 1, turn.

Row 3: [Sc in next sc, 2 sc in next sc] rep across, ch 1, turn. (36 sc)

Rows 4–6: Rep Row 2.

Row 7: [Sc in each of next 2 sc, 2 sc in next sc] rep across, ch 1, turn. (48 sc)

Rows 8–14: Rep Row 2.

Right Front

Row 15: Sc in first sc, [sc dec] 7 times, ch 1, turn. (8 sts)

Row 16: Sc in each sc across, ch 1, turn.

Row 17: Sc dec, sc in each sc across, ch 1, turn. (7 sts)

Row 18: Rep Row 16.

Rows 19–24: Rep Rows 17 and 18 alternately, fasten off at end of Row 24. (4 sc at end of Row 24)

Back

Row 15: Sk next 2 sc of Row 14, attach CC in next sc, ch 1, sc in same sc and in each of next 13 sc, ch 1, turn. (14 sc)

Rows 16-24: Rep Row 16 of right front; do not ch 1 at end of Row 24; fasten off.

Continued on page 95

Itzy-Bitzy Bear

Design by Sandra Abbate

He may be small, but he's warm and snuggly in his bright stocking cap. Because he's jointed you can pose him standing by a pine tree or sitting on a sled.

Let's Begin!

Experience Level: Intermediate

Finished Measurement: 4" tall

Materials

- Crochet cotton size 10: approximately 100 yds maize (MC) and small amounts each blue (A) and green (B)
- Size 7 steel crochet hook or size needed to obtain gauge
- 2 yds brown 6-strand embroidery floss
- ½ yd ⅛"-wide red satin ribbon
- Tapestry needle
- Small amount polyester fiberfill
- Blusher

Gauge: 10 sts and 9 rows = 1" in sc
To save time, take time to check gauge.

Pattern Note

Join rnds with a sl st unless otherwise stated.

Head

Note: Do not join rnds unless otherwise stated; mark first st of each rnd with safety pin or other small marker.

Rnd 1: With MC, ch 2, 6 sc in 2nd ch from hook. (6 sc)

Rnd 2: 2 sc in each st around. (12 sc)

Rnd 3: [Sc in next st, 2 sc in next st] rep around. (18 sc)

Rnd 4: [Sc in each of next 2 sts, 2 sc in next st] rep around. (24 sc)

Rnds 5 & 6: Sc in each st around. (24 sc)

Rnd 7: 2 sc in each of first 4 sts, sc in each rem st around. (28 sc)

Rnds 8 & 9: Rep Rnds 5 and 6. (28 sc)

Rnd 10: [Sc dec] 4 times, sc in each rem st around. (24 sts)

Rnd 11: [Sc in each of next 2 sts, sc dec] rep around. (18 sts)

Rnd 12: [Sc in next st, sc dec] rep around. (12 sts)

Body

Rnds 13 & 14: Rep Rnds 3 and 4. (24 sc at end of Rnd 14)

Rnd 15: [Sc in each of next 3 sts, 2 sc in next st] rep around. (30 sc)

Rnds 16–22: Sc in each st around. (30 sc)

Rnd 23: [Sc in each of next 3 sts, sc dec] rep around. (24 sts)

Rnds 24 & 25: Rep Rnds 11 and 12. (12 sts at end of Rnd 25)

Stuff head and body.

Rnd 26: [Sc dec] rep around, join in beg sc dec, fasten off, leaving a 12" end.

Thread end into tapestry needle, weave through sts of last rnd, pull tightly to close and fasten off.

Arm (make 2)

Note: Do not join rnds unless otherwise stated; mark first st of each rnd with safety pin or other small marker.

Rnds 1 & 2: Beg at top of arm, rep Rnds 1 and 2 of head. (12 sc)

Rnds 3–12: Sc in each st around. (12 sc)

Stuff arm lightly.

Rnd 13: [Sc dec] rep around, join in beg sc, fasten off, leaving a 12" end.

Close opening as for body.

Leg (make 2)

Note: Do not join rnds unless otherwise stated; mark first st of each rnd with safety pin or other small marker.

Rnds 1–3: Beg at foot, rep Rnds 1–3 of head. (18 sc)

Rnds 4–6: Sc in each st around. (18 sc)

Rnd 7: [Sc dec] 4 times, sc in each rem st around. (14 sts)

Rnds 8–15: Sc in each st around. (14 sc)

Stuff leg lightly.

Rnd 16: [Sc dec] rep around, join in beg sc dec, fasten off, leaving a 12" end.

Close opening as for body.

Ear (make 2)

Row 1: With MC, ch 5, sc in 2nd ch from hook and in each of next 3 chs, ch 1, turn. (4 sc)

Row 2: 2 sc in first st, sc in each of next 2 sts, 2 sc in last st, ch 1, turn. (6 sc)

Row 3: Sc in each sc across, ch 1, turn. (6 sc)

Row 4: Sc dec, sc in each of next 2 sts, sc dec, fasten off.

Hat Ribbing

Row 1: With A, ch 6, sc in 2nd ch from hook and in each rem ch across, ch 1, turn. (5 sc)

Rows 2–24: Working in back lps only, sc in each sc across, ch 1 turn; at end of Row 24, do not turn, do not fasten off.

Crown

Row 1: Working across long edge, sc over end st of each row across, ch 1, turn. (24 sc)

Row 2: Ch 3 (counts as first dc throughout), dc in each of next 3 sts, ch 4, sk next 4 sts, dc in each of next 8 sts, ch 4, sk next 4 sts, dc in each of next 4 sts, turn.

Row 3: Ch 3, dc in each rem dc and 4 dc in each ch-4 sp across, turn. (24 dc)

Row 4: Ch 3, dc in each rem dc across, fasten off. (24 dc)

Thread tapestry needle with 20" length of A. Beg at bottom of hat, sew back seam to top, weave thread through sts of last row and pull tightly to close, fasten off.

Pompom

Wrap B 30 times around your thumb. Remove thread from thumb and tie securely at center with separate piece of B. Trim and tie to top of hat.

Finishing

Using photo as a guide, embroider face, paws and toes using 6 strands floss. Sew on ears, arms and legs.

Place hat on head and poke ears through holes. Apply blusher to cheeks, inside of ears, and bottoms of paws and feet. Cut satin ribbon in half; tie each length into bow around neck and ankle. ❤

Stuffed Toys

Use a size F crochet hook when crocheting toys because it gives the stitches a firmer surface and you'll be less like to see any stuffing material between stitches. You may have to add a few extra rows because of using a smaller hook. Use your hands to do the final shaping, and do not overstuff.

Sparkling Snowflakes

When crocheting snowflakes for your Christmas tree, add a strand of fine metallic thread to your crochet cotton. The lights from the tree will make your snowflakes sparkle and shimmer.

Crocheted Eyes

When crocheting toys for children, here's a substitute idea for plastic sew-on eyes: With black, ch 2, 6 sc in 2nd ch from hook, sl st in first sc or rnd to join, fasten off black. With white, work 2 sc in each st around, join, fasten off. These do not fall off and are safer for children under the age of 5.

Key Chain Combo

Designs by Jessica Caldwell

Girls will love having one of these cuties on their newly acquired set of keys. They make great favors for a 16-year-old's birthday party!

Let's Begin!

Experience Level: Intermediate

Finished Measurement: 2½" wide

Materials

Key Chain Cutie

- Size 10 crochet cotton: small amount each pink, golden yellow and white
- Pink chenille stem

Curlicue Key Chain

- Size 10 crochet cotton: small amount each lavender and purple
- Lavender chenille stem

Each Doll

- Kreinik Fine (#8) Braid: small amount
- Size 6 steel crochet hook or size needed to obtain gauge
- 50mm wooden bead
- Key chain
- Small amount polyester fiberfill
- Craft glue

Gauge: Rnds 1 and 2 of Key Chain Cutie hat = 1¼" in diameter
To save time, take time to check gauge.

Pattern Note

Join rnds with a sl st unless otherwise stated.

Key Chain Cutie

Hat

Rnd 1: With pink, ch 8, join to form a ring, ch 3 (counts as first dc throughout), 23 dc in ring, join in 3rd ch of beg ch-3. (24 dc)

Rnd 2: Ch 3, dc in same st as joining, dc in next st, [2 dc in next st, dc in next st] rep around, join in 3rd ch of beg ch-3. (36 dc)

Rnd 3: Rep Rnd 2. (54 dc)

Rnd 4: Ch 3, dc in each of next 3 sts, dc dec, [dc in each of next 4 sts, dc dec] rep around, join in 3rd ch of beg ch-3. (45 sts)

Rnd 5: Ch 3, dc dec, [dc in next st, dc dec] rep around, join in 3rd ch of beg ch-3. (30 sts)

Rnd 6: Rep Rnd 5. (20 sts)

Rnd 7: Ch 3, working in front lps only this rnd, dc in same st as joining, 2 dc in each rem st around, join in 3rd ch of beg ch-3, fasten off. (40 sts)

Rnd 8: Attach white with a sl st in same st as joining, ch 3, dc in same st, 2 dc in each rem st around, join in 3rd ch of beg ch-3, fasten off. (80 sts)

Rnd 9: Attach fine braid with a sl st in same st as joining, ch 1, sc in same st, ch 1, [sc in next st, ch 1] rep around, join in beg sc, fasten off.

Neck Ruffle

Rnd 1: With pink, ch 8, join in first ch to form a ring, ch 3 (counts as first dc throughout), 7 dc in same st as joining, turn, 8 dc in rem lp on opposite side of same st as joining, join in 3rd ch of beg ch-3. (16 dc on top of ch-8 lp)

Rnd 2: Ch 3, dc in same st as joining, 2 dc in each rem st around, join in 3rd ch of beg ch-3. (32 dc)

Rnd 3: Rep Rnd 2, fasten off. (64 dc)

Rnd 4: Attach white with a sl st in same st as joining, ch 3, dc in each rem st around, join in 3rd ch of beg ch-3, fasten off. (64 dc)

Rnd 5: Rep Rnd 9 of hat.

Finishing

Hair

Cut 36 (12") lengths of golden yellow. Holding 2 strands tog, fold in half, insert hook through any rem lp of Rnd 6 of hat, pull lp end of strands through st on hook, pull free ends through lp and tighten. Rep across next 17 rem lps of Rnd 6; leave last 2 rem lps unworked for front.

Assembly

Stuff hat with small amount of polyester fiberfill. Cut a 5" length of chenille stem and fold in half. Thread folded end up through bead and top of hat.

Attach small ring at bottom of key chain to lp. Lp the 2 free ends at bottom of stem through ch-8 lp on neck ruffle and tuck ends up into hole at bottom of bead. Secure with small amount of glue. Apply small amount of glue at top of bead to hold hat in place.

Divide strands of hair in half, crisscrossing 8 strands at each side of center back to cover back of bead. Make 2 braids. Tie each braid with small amount of pink and cut ends to desired length.

Curlicue Key Chain

Hat

Rnd 1: With purple, ch 1 (center ch), ch 3 more (counts as first dc), 15 dc in center ch, join in 3rd ch of beg ch-3. (16 dc)

Rnd 2: Ch 3, 2 dc in next st, [dc in next st, 2 dc in next st] rep around, join in 3rd ch of beg ch-3. (24 dc)

Rnd 3: Ch 1, sc in same st as joining, sc in next st, 3 sc in next st, [sc in each of next 2 sts, 3 sc in next st] rep around, join in beg sc, fasten off purple. (40 sc)

Rnd 4: Attach lavender with a sl st in center sc of any 3-sc group, ch 1, beg in same st, *3 sc in center sc of 3-sc group, sc in next st, sk 2 sts, sc in next st, rep from * around, join in beg sc, fasten off.

Rnd 5: With purple, rep Rnd 4, do not fasten off.

Rnd 6: Ch 1, sc in same st as joining, *3 sc in next st, sc in next st, sk each of next 2 sts **, sc in next st, rep from * around, ending last rep at **, join in beg sc, fasten off.

Rnd 7: Attach lavender with a sl st in front lp only of center sc of any 3-sc group, ch 1; working in front lps only this rnd and beg in same st as joining, [3 sc in center sc of 3-sc group, sc in each of next 4 sc] rep around, join in beg sc, fasten off.

Rnd 8: Attach purple with a sl st in center sc of any 3-sc group, ch 1, beg in same st, [3 sc in center sc of 3-sc group, sc in each of next 6 sc] rep around, join in beg sc.

Rnd 9: Ch 1, sc in same st as joining, *3 sc in center sc of any 3-sc group **, sc in each of next 8 sc, rep from * around to last 7 sts, ending last rep at **, sc in each of last 7 sts, join in beg sc, fasten off.

Rnd 10: Attach lavender with a sl st in center sc of any 3-sc group, ch 1, beg in same st, [3 sc in center sc of 3-sc group, sc in each of next 10 sc] rep around, join in beg sc, fasten off.

Rnd 11: Rep Rnd 9 of hat for Key Chain Cutie.

Neck Ruffle

Rnds 1 & 2: With purple, rep Rnds 1 and 2 of neck ruffle for Key Chain Cutie, fasten off at end of Rnd 2. (32 dc)

Rnd 3: Attach lavender with a sl st in same st as joining, ch 1, sc in same st and in each of next 2

Continued on page 96

Happy Hair Doll

Design by Isabelle Wolters

This comical character will remind you that bad hair adds a certain kind of charm to one's personality! This quick and easy project will bring smiles to all who see it.

Let's Begin!

Experience Level: Beginner

Finished Measurements: Approximately 7" x 9"

Materials

- Worsted weight yarn: small amount each red (MC), light variegated or light solid color (A) and dark variegated or dark solid color (B)
- Size F/5 crochet hook or size needed to obtain gauge
- 2" x 6" piece of cardboard
- Tapestry needle
- Polyester fiberfill
- Comb

Gauge: 4 sts and 4 rows = 1" in sc

To save time, take time to check gauge.

Pattern Note

Join rnds with a sl st unless otherwise stated.

Body (make 2)

Row 1 (WS): With MC, ch 2, 3 sc in 2nd ch from hook, ch 1, turn. (3 sc)

Row 2: 2 sc in first st, sc in next st, 2 sc in last st, ch 1, turn. (5 sc)

Row 3: 2 sc in first st, sc in each st across to last st, 2 sc in last st, ch 1, turn. (7 sc)

Rows 4–9: Rep Row 3. (19 sc at end of Row 9)

Row 10: Sc in each st across, ch 1, turn. (19 sc)

Row 11: Rep Row 3. (21 sc)

Row 12: Rep Row 10. (21 sc)

Row 13: Rep Row 3. (23 sc)

Rows 14–17: Rep Row 10. (23 sc)

Row 18: Sc in each of first 2 sc, *hdc in each of next 2 sc, dc in each of next 2 sc, hdc in each of next 2 sc, sc in each of next 2 sc *, sl st in each of next 3 sc, sc in each of next 2 sc, rep from * to *, ch 1, turn. (23 sts)

Row 19: Sc in each of first 2 sts, hdc in next st, 2 hdc in next st, 2 dc in each of next 2 sts, hdc in each of next 2 sts, sc in each of next 2 sts, sl st in each of next 3 sts, sc in each of next 2 sts, hdc in each of next 2 sts, 2 dc in each of next 2 sts, 2 hdc in next st, hdc in next st, sc in each of last 2 sts, ch 1, turn. (29 sts)

Row 20: Sc in each of first 2 sts, hdc in each of next 3 sts, dc in each of next 4 sts, hdc in each of next 2 sts, sc in each of next 2 sts, sl st in each of next 3 sts, sc in each of next 2 sts, hdc in each of next 2 sts, dc in each of next 4 sts, hdc in each of next 3 sts, sc in each of last 2 sts, ch 1, do not turn. (29 sts)

Continued on page 97

Yo-yo Bunny

Design by Sandra Abbate

Simple yo-yos in a variety of colors and sizes, combined with a sweet face and collar, make this bunny a true delight to crochet.

Let's Begin!

Experience Level: Beginner

Finished Measurement
Approximately 11" tall including ears

Materials

- Worsted weight yarn: 1 oz each off-white and black; 14 yds each red, rust, dark green, purple and tan; 8 yds each cranberry, forest green and lavender; 4 yds each country blue and violet; and 1 yd dark pink
- Crochet cotton size 10: small amount gold metallic
- Size G/6 crochet hook or size needed to obtain gauge
- Size 7 steel crochet hook
- 2 yds ⅛"-wide gold metallic ribbon
- 4 small red ribbon roses with leaves
- 2 (9mm) brown eyes with shank and disk
- Small amount polyester fiberfill
- Blusher
- Cotton swab
- Long yarn needle
- Craft glue

Gauge: 4 sc = 1" with larger hook and worsted weight yarn
To save time, take time to check gauge.

Pattern Note
Join rnds with a sl st unless otherwise stated.

Pattern Stitches
Cl: Holding back on hook last lp of each st, dc in each of next 3 sts, yo, draw through all 4 lps on hook.
Beg cl: Ch 2, holding back on hook last lp of each st, dc in each of next 2 sts, yo, draw through all 3 lps on hook.
Shell: [2 dc, ch 3, 2 dc] in indicated st or sp.
Beg shell: [Ch 3, dc, ch 3, 2 dc] in indicated st or sp.

Large Yo-yo
***Note:** Make 1 each red, rust, dark green, purple and tan.*
Rnd 1 (RS): With worsted weight yarn and larger hook, ch 3, join to form a ring, ch 3 (counts as first dc throughout), 15 dc in ring, join in 3rd ch of beg ch-3. (16 dc)
Rnd 2: Ch 3, dc in same st as joining, 2 dc in each rem dc around, join in 3rd ch of beg ch-3, fasten off. (32 dc)

Small Yo-yo
***Note:** Make 2 each country blue and violet and 4 each cranberry, dark green, purple, rust, red, forest green, lavender and tan.*
Rnd 1 (RS): Rep Rnd 1 of larger yo-yo, fasten off. (16 sc)

Boot (make 2)
Rnd 1: With black and large hook, ch 2, 9 sc in 2nd ch from hook, join in beg sc. (9 sc)
Rnd 2: Ch 1, sc in same st as joining, sc in next st, 2 sc in next st, [sc in each of next 2 sts, 2 sc in next st] rep around, join in beg sc. (12 sc)
Rnds 3–6: Ch 1, sc in same st as joining, sc in each rem sc around, join in beg sc. (12 sc)

Row 7: Ch 1, sc in same st as joining, sc in each of next 11 sc, ch 1, turn.

Rows 8–11: Sc in each st across, ch 1, turn; at end of Row 11, do not fasten off.

Fold last row in half. Working through both thicknesses, sl st first 6 sts tog, fasten off. Turn boot RS out.

Stuff boot lightly with polyester fiberfill. With larger hook and RS facing, attach black with a sl st at back seam, ch 1, work 12 sc evenly sp around, join in beg sc, fasten off, leaving a 20" end. Thread end into yarn needle, weave through sts of last rnd, pull tightly to close; secure, but do not fasten off. Set aside.

Head

Note: Do not join rnds unless otherwise stated; mark first st of each rnd with safety pin or other small marker.

Rnd 1: With larger hook and off-white, beg at front of head, ch 2, 6 sc in 2nd ch from hook. (6 sc)

Rnd 2: 2 sc in each st around. (12 sc)

Rnd 3: Sc in each st around. (12 sc)

Rnd 4: [Sc in each of next 2 sts, 2 sc in next st] rep around. (16 sc)

Rnd 5: Rep Rnd 3. (16 sc)

Rnd 6: [Sc in each of next 3 sts, 2 sc in next st] rep around. (20 sc)

Rnd 7: Rep Rnd 6. (25 sc)

Rnd 8: [Sc in each of next 4 sts, 2 sc in next st] rep around. (30 sc)

Rnds 9–11: Rep Rnd 3. (30 sc)

Rnd 12: [Sc in each of next 3 sts, sc dec] rep around, do not fasten off. (24 sts)

Using photo as a guide, sew on eyes over Rnd 7. With dark pink and yarn needle, embroider nose and mouth.

Rnd 13: Rep Rnd 3. (24 sc)

Rnd 14: [Sc in each of next 2 sts, sc dec] rep around. (18 sts)

Stuff head with polyester fiberfill.

Rnd 15: Rep Rnd 3. (18 sts)

Rnd 16: [Sc in next st, sc dec] rep around. (12 sts)

Rnd 17: [Sc dec] rep around, join in beg sc dec, fasten off, leaving a 12" end.

Thead yarn needle with 12" end, weave through sts of last rnd, pull tightly to close, fasten off.

Paw (make 2)

Note: Do not join rnds unless otherwise stated; mark first st of each rnd with safety pin or other small marker.

Rnds 1 & 2: Rep Rnds 1 and 2 of head. (12 sc at end of Rnd 2)

Rnds 3 & 4: Rep Rnd 3 of head. (12 sc)

Rnd 5: [Sc dec] rep around, join in beg sc dec, fasten off, leaving 12" end.

Stuff paw lightly and close opening as for head.

Ear (make 2)

Row 1: With larger hook and off-white, ch 5, sc in 2nd ch from hook, sc in each of next 3 chs, ch 1, turn. (4 sc)

Rows 2–10: Sc in each sc across, ch 1, turn. (4 sc)

Row 11: [Sc dec] twice, ch 1, turn. (2 sts)

Row 12: Sc dec, ch 1, do not turn, do not fasten off.

Rnd 13: Sc over end st of each of last 12 rows, sc in each rem lp across foundation ch, sc over end st of each of next 12 rows, join in beg sc, fasten off.

With cotton swab, apply blusher to inside of ear, leaving Rnd 13 white.

Sew ears to head over Rnd 12, approximately ¾" apart.

Collar

Rnd 1: With smaller hook and gold metallic crochet cotton, ch 1 (center ch), ch 3 more (counts as first dc), 35 dc in center ch, join in 3rd ch of beg ch-3. (36 dc)

Rnd 2: Beg cl, ch 7, [cl, ch 7] rep around, join in top of beg cl. (12 cls)

Rnd 3: Sl st in each of next 3 chs of first ch-7 sp, beg shell in same ch-7 sp, shell in next ch-7 sp, ch 5, [shell in each of next 2 ch-7 lps, ch 5] rep around, join in top of beg ch-3.

Rnd 4: Sl st in next dc and in shell sp, beg shell in same sp, shell in next sp, *ch 3, [sc, ch 3] twice in next ch-5 sp **, shell in each of next 2 shell sps, rep from * around, ending last rep at **, join in 3rd ch of beg ch-3, fasten off.

Assembly

Arms

Thread yarn needle with 20" length off-white yarn. With RS facing to the right, string small yo-yos in following color sequence: 1 cranberry, 1 dark green, 1 purple, 1 rust, 1 red, 1 forest green, 1 lavender and 1 tan for first arm; with RS facing to the left, string 8 more small yo-yos on same length of yarn in reverse color sequence. Set aside.

Leg (make 2)

Thread yarn needle with 20" end on boot. With RS facing toward boot, string small yo-yos in the following color sequence: 1 cranberry, 1 violet, 1 dark green, 1 country blue, 1 purple, 1 rust, 1 red, 1 forest green, 1 lavender and 1 tan. Do not cut yarn. Rep for 2nd leg with rem boot.

Body

Thread yarn needle with ends from both legs tog. String large yo-yos, RS facing down, in the following color sequence: 1 red, 1 rust, 1 dark green, 1 purple and 1 tan. Remove yarn needle and tie ends of black yarn securely at midpoint of white yarn between first and 2nd arm; do not cut yarn.

Head

Thread yarn needle with 1 end of black yarn from top of body. *Insert needle through center of collar, into bottom center of head and out through a sp between sts at top of head *. Thread yarn needle with rem end of black yarn and rep from * to *, entering bottom of head 1 st away from first end and coming out through same sp at top of head as first end. Pull both ends up tightly and tie securely tog. Thread yarn needle with both ends, insert needle down through same hole from which ends came up, and out bottom of head, pulling tightly. Cut ends close to head; ends will disappear into head.

Paws
Thread yarn needle with off-white yarn from either end of arms, insert into top center of last rnd of paw and out again 1 st away, insert needle through centers of yo-yos to midpoint between arms and tie securely. Push needle halfway down yo-yos of same arm; fasten off. Rep for 2nd arm, pulling tightly so arms are close to body.

Finishing
Thread yarn needle with small length of metallic ribbon, draw through st at top front of boot. Tie into bow. Rep for rem boot. Rep halfway down outer edge of left ear and on right front of collar. With double piece of ribbon, rep at bottom center front of right ear. Glue 1 red rose over each bow except for bow on left ear. Apply blusher to cheeks and tops of paws. ❤

Cutie Pie Clothespin Dolls

Continued from page 81

st, shell in next st, [ch 2, shell in next st] rep across to last st, ch 2, 2 dc in last st, turn. (16 shells)

For all skirts
Row 6: Ch 3, dc in first st, shell in each shell sp and in each ch-2 sp across, 2 dc in last st, turn. (8 shells for less full skirt/32 shells for fuller skirt)
Row 7: Ch 3, dc in first st, shell in each shell sp across, 2 dc in last st, turn. (8/32 shells)
Row 8: Beg shell in first st, shell in each shell sp across, shell in last st, ch 1, turn. (10/34 shells)
Row 9: Sc in first st, *ch 3, sc in next shell sp, ch 3 **, sc between same shell and next shell, rep from * across, ending last rep at **, sc in last dc of last shell, turn. (20/68 ch-3 sps)
Row 10: Sl st in first ch-3 sp, ch 3, 4 dc in same sp, sc in next ch-3 sp, [5 dc in next ch-3 sp, sc in next ch-3 sp] rep across, do not fasten off, do not turn.

Working over end sts of each row, [ch 3, sc over end st of next row] rep across to neck, ch 3, sc in first rem lp of foundation ch at neck edge, sc in each rem lp across neck, [ch 3, sc over end st of next row] rep across to bottom, ch 3, sc in last sc of Row 9, fasten off.

Decorate pinafore with ribbon or other small decorations. Place pinafore on doll over sundress; button through ch-3 lps at back opening to buttons on sundress. ❤

Fashion Doll Fun

Continued from page 85

Left Front
Row 15: Sk next 2 sc on Row 14, attach CC in next sc, ch 1, beg in same st, [sc dec] 7 times, sc in last sc, ch 1, turn. (8 sts)
Row 16: Sc in each sc across, ch 1, turn.
Row 17: Sc in each sc across to last 2 sc, sc dec, ch 1, turn. (7 sc)
Rows 18–24: Rep Rows 16 and 17 alternately, end with Row 16, fasten off at end of Row 24. (4 sc at end of Row 24)
Sew shoulder seams.

Armhole Trim
Rnd 1: Attach CC at center of underarm, ch 1, sc in same st, 18 sc evenly around armhole opening, join in beg sc, fasten off. (19 sc)
Rep for 2nd armhole.

Edging
Rnd 1: With RS facing, attach CC to either bottom corner, ch 1, sc around front openings, neck and bottom of blouse, join in beg sc, fasten off.

Collar
Row 1: With WS facing, attach MC with a sl st at beg of neck shaping on left front, ch 1, beg in same st, [sc, dc] in each st around neck edge to beg of right front neck shaping, ch 1, turn.
Row 2: [Sc in next dc, dc in next sc] rep across, fasten off.

Finishing
Sew snap to front opening at neck below collar.

Hat

Rnd 1: Beg at top center with CC, ch 2, 6 sc in 2nd ch from hook, join in beg sc, ch 1, turn. (6 sc)
Rnd 2: 2 sc in each sc around, join in beg sc, ch 1, turn. (12 sc)
Rnd 3: [Sc in next sc, 2 sc in next sc] rep around, join in beg sc, ch 1, turn. (18 sc)
Rnd 4: [Sc in each of next 2 sc, 2 sc in next sc] rep around, join in beg sc, ch 1, turn. (24 sc)
Rnd 5: [Sc in each of next 3 sc, 2 sc in next sc] rep around, join in beg sc, ch 1, turn. (30 sc)
Rnds 6–8: Sc in each sc around, join in beg sc, ch 1, turn, fasten off at end of Rnd 8, attach MC, ch 1, turn.

Brim
Rnd 9: [Sc, dc] in each sc around, join in beg sc, ch 1, turn. (60 sc)
Rnd 10: [Sc in next dc, dc in next sc] rep around, join in beg sc, fasten off. ❤

Key Chain Combo

Continued from page 89

sts, 3 sc in next st, [sc in each of next 3 sts, 3 sc in next st] rep around, join in beg sc.

Rnd 4: Ch 1, sc in same st as joining and in each of next 3 sts, 3 sc in next st, [sc in each of next 5 sts, 3 sc in next st] rep around to last st, sc in last st, join in beg sc, fasten off.

Rnd 5: Attach purple with a sl st in center sc of any 3-sc group, ch 1, beg in same st, [3 sc in center sc of 3-sc group, sc in each of next 7 sts] rep around, join in beg sc.

Rnd 6: Ch 1, sc in same st as joining, *3 sc in next st **, sc in each of next 9 sts, rep from * around to last 8 sts, ending last rep at **, sc in each of last 8 sts, join in beg sc, fasten off.

Rnd 7: Attach lavender with a sl st in center sc of any 3-sc group, ch 1, beg in same st, [3 sc in center sc of 3-sc group, sc in each of next 5 sts, sk next sc, sc in each of next 5 sts] rep around, join in beg sc.

Rnd 8: Ch 1, sc in same st as joining, *3 sc in next sc, sc in each of next 5 sts, sk 2 sc **, sc in each of next 5 sc, rep from * around to last 4 sts, ending last rep at **, sc in each of last 4 sts, join in beg sc, fasten off.

Rnd 9: Rep Rnd 9 of hat for Key Chain Cutie.

Finishing

Hair

Attach yellow with a sl st in rem lp of any st of Rnd 6 of hat, [ch 25, sc in 2nd ch from hook and in each of next 23 chs, allowing ch to curl, sk next 2 rem lps on Rnd 6, sl st in next st] 11 times, fasten off.

Assembly

Attach hat, key chain and neck ruffle as for Key Chain Cutie. ❤

Booties for Baby

Continued from page 91

Toe Straps

First strap

With Rnd 5 of sole pointing down and toe pointing to left, working in rem lps of Rnd 4 of sole, sk next 5 rem lps after left edge of first heel strap, attach red with a sl st in next st, ch 15, sk next 17 sts around front of sandal, sl st in next st, sk next st toward toe, sl st in next st, hdc in each of last 15 chs, sk next 13 sts around toe, sl st in next st, fasten off.

Second strap

With Rnd 5 of sole pointing down and toe pointing to left, working in rem lps of Rnd 4 of sole, sk next 2 rem lps after left edge of first toe strap, attach blue with a sl st in next st, ch 15, sk next 5 unworked rem lps toward toe after 2nd heel strap on opposite side of sandal, sl st in next rem lp and in each of next 2 rem lps toward toe, hdc in each of next 15 chs, sk next 8 unworked rem lps around front of sandal after front edge of first toe strap, sl st in next rem lp, fasten off.

Ankle Strap

With green, ch 40, hdc in 3rd ch from hook and in each rem ch across, fasten off.

Thread ankle strap through 2 heel lps, overlap slightly and sew button through both thicknesses to hold in place.

Toe Decoration

With purple, ch 5, join to form a ring, ch 1, 10 sc in ring, join in beg sc, fasten off. Using photo as a guide, place toe decoration at point where toe straps overlap; center button over decoration; sew in place through both straps. ❤

Tiny Pompoms

Here's a way to make tiny pompoms for doll clothes: Cut two strands of yarn each about 12" long. Place two ¼" washers together and wrap the strands of yarn around them, drawing the yarn through the centers of the washers with a small crochet hook until all the yarn is used. Cut yarn between washers along the outside edge.

Using about 6" of 3 strands of 6-strand embroidery floss, tie tightly in the center between washers which have been separated. For slightly larger pompoms, use ½" washers.

Embroidery Floss Trim

Embroidery floss makes a nice contrast trim for fashion doll clothes. The shine of the floss adds a very nice touch, and the floss comes in many lovely colors.

Adding Accessories

When crocheting fashion doll outfits for gift-giving, why not complete the dress or play wear with purchased accessories? Matching plastic shoes, tennis rackets, sunglasses, etc., are inexpensive and easily available in toy and department stores.

Roll, Don't Fold

Roll your cherished items instead of folding. Folding strains the fibers. Use only acid-free paper for storing. Never use blue tissue paper, because if any moisture whatsoever comes in contact with it, you'll have unremovable blue stains.

Happy Hair Doll

Continued from page 92

Rnd 21: Sc over end st of each of last 20 rows, 3 sc in rem lp of ch at base of Row 1, sc over end st of each of next 19 rows, 3 sc over end st of Row 20, sc in each st across Row 20, 2 sc in same st as beg sc, join in beg sc, fasten off.

Hand (make 2)

With either A or B, ch 2, 6 sc in 2nd ch from hook, join in beg sc, fasten off.

Arm (make 2)

Attach MC with a sl st in joining st of hand, ch 16, 2 sc in 2nd ch from hook, [sc in next ch, 2 sc in next ch] rep across, sl st in hand at base of ch-16, fasten off.

Foot (make 2)

Rep instructions for hand.

Leg (make 2)

Attach MC with a sl st in joining st of foot, ch 20, 2 sc in 2nd ch from hook, [sc in next ch, 2 sc in next ch] rep across, sl st in foot at base of ch-20, fasten off.

Socks

With tapestry needle and A, bring needle through ch-2 at center of foot; Overcast around foot until covered.

Eye (make 2)

Rep instructions for hand.

Assembly

Using photo as a guide, sew eyes to RS of 1 body piece. Embroider French knots at center of each eye with either CC. Embroider 3 eyelashes over each eye.

Embroider mouth.

Holding 2 body pieces with WS tog, sew 2 pieces tog with tapestry needle through back lps only, stuffing with polyester fiberfill before closing completely. Sew arms to sides of body at each end of Row 12. Sew legs to bottom of body approximately 1" from bottom center on each side.

Hair

Wind A in single layer around 2" side of cardboard until cardboard is completely covered. Cut through lps at 1 edge. Rep with B. Holding 1 strand each of A and B tog, fold in half, insert hook in any st at top of head, pull folded end of strands through st on hook to form lp, draw free ends through lp and tighten. Rep as desired across top of head. Comb through hair to frizz ends. Bring several strands at center front forward to form bangs. ❤

Teach Your Children Well

Every few years there is a rekindled interest in spool knitting. Spool knitting, rat-tail, mushroom and horse rein are all common names for a finger-crochet technique to create table mats, scatter rugs, belts, ties, trims, bracelets, berets, chair backs and seats, etc. The tool may be made in the shape of a rectangle and used to make two-layer scarves. The possibilities are endless, and it is a great way to get kids excited about learning a craft.

Basic instructions are as follows: Put the end of the yarn through the hole in the top of the spool, leaving at least a 4" tail. Working clockwise, wind the yarn around peg #1, then loop yarn around pegs #2, #3 and #4. Hold spool and yarn in left hand and crochet hook or knitting needle in right hand. Run yarn around the outside of peg #1, above the loop made previously. Slip the bottom loop over the top piece of yarn, dropping it off on the right side of the same peg. Occasionally, put on the tail or yarn at the bottom of the spool to keep stitches even.

When desired length has been reached, take the last loop made off the hook and put it on the peg to the left. Pick up the bottom loop, slip it over the top loop, and drop it right off the peg. Put the remaining loop from the peg on which you were working to the loop on the left.

Cut yarn 3" above the last loop and thread through the last loop on the spool. Take the loop right off the peg and pull the yarn tight, turning the last loop into a knot.

Crocheted Tongues

When making crocheted baby toys, such as animals, that require felt tongues, use red or pink crochet cotton and a small steel crochet hook to crochet the tongues instead. The crochet cotton lasts longer than the felt, and it doesn't pull off easily.

Boy or Girl?

When making sweaters for an expected baby, crochet buttonholes down both sides of the front opening of the garment. It will be easy enough to close the buttonholes on one side and sew on buttons on the correct side once you know if the baby is a boy or a girl.

Crocheted Toys

Stuff crocheted toys with nylon stockings instead of fiberfill.

Ovals

All ovals are designed by determining the length of the center chains. Take the width from the length and add 1". (i.e. to make a 6' x 9' rug you subtract 6' from 9' = 3' plus 1"; so beginning chain needs to be 37").

Kitchen Accents

As your family gathers around the kitchen table, treat them to pretty crocheted accents throughout the kitchen to make mealtime a feast for the eyes as well as the mouth!

Butterfly's Fancy Table Set

Designs by Maggie Petsch Chasalow

Invite a butterfly to your table for breakfast, lunch or dinner, and make every mealtime as pleasant as springtime.

Let's Begin!

Experience Level: Intermediate

Finished Measurements: Place Mat: 16" x 12½"

Napkin Ring: 2¼" wide

Materials

- J. & P. Coats Speed-Cro-Sheen crochet cotton size 3 (100 yds per ball): 1 ball white #001 and small amount each black #12, canary yellow #10A, hunter green #48 and mid rose #46A
- Size D/3 crochet hook or size needed to obtain gauge
- Tapestry needle

Gauge: Rnds 1 and 2 of head = 1¾" in diameter

To save time, take time to check gauge.

Pattern Note

Join rnds with a sl st unless otherwise stated.

Pattern Stitches

Joined lp: Ch 2, sl st in indicated lp, ch 2.

3-dc cl: Holding back on hook last lp of each st, 3 dc in indicated st, yo, draw through all 4 lps on hook.

Beg 3-tr cl: Ch 3, holding back on hook last lp of each st, 2 tr in same st, yo, draw through all 3 lps on hook.

3-tr cl: Holding back on hook last lp of each st, 3 tr in indicated st, yo, draw through all 4 lps on hook.

Beg 4-tr cl: Ch 3, holding back on hook last lp of each st, tr in same st, 2 tr in next st, yo, draw through all 4 lps on hook.

Tr cl: Holding back on hook last lp of each st, 2 tr in each of next 2 sts, yo, draw through all 5 lps on hook.

Place Mat

Head

Rnd 1: With black, ch 4, 11 dc in 4th ch from hook, join in 4th ch of beg ch-4. (12 dc, counting last 3 chs of beg ch-4 as first dc)

Rnd 2: Ch 3 (counts as first dc throughout), dc in same st as joining, 2 dc in each rem dc around, join in 3rd ch of beg ch-3; do not fasten off, do not turn. (24 dc)

Body

Row 1 (RS): Ch 3, 4 dc in same st as joining, turn. (5 dc)

Rows 2–34: Ch 2 (counts as first hdc), hdc in each of next 4 sts, turn. (5 hdc)

Row 35: Ch 2, holding back on hook last lp of each st, dc in each of next 4 sts, yo, draw through all 5 lps on hook, fasten off.

Upper Left Wing

Rnd 1 (RS): With white, ch 2, 6 sc in 2nd ch from hook, join in beg sc. (6 sc)

Rnd 2: Ch 1, 2 sc in same st as joining, 2 sc in each rem sc around, join in beg sc, fasten off. (12 sc)

Rnd 3: With RS facing, attach mid rose with a sl st in any sc, beg 4-tr cl, ch 7, [4-tr cl, ch 7] rep around, join in top of beg tr cl, fasten off.

Rnd 4: With RS facing, attach hunter green with a sl st in top of any 4-tr cl, beg 3-tr cl in same st, ch 3, *[3-dc cl, ch 3, 3-dc cl] in 4th ch of next ch-7, ch 3 **, 3-tr cl in next 4-tr cl, ch 3, rep from * around, ending last rep at **, join in top of beg 3-tr cl, fasten off.

Rnd 5: With RS facing, attach canary yellow with a sl st in any ch-3 sp, ch 6, [sl st in next sp, ch 6] rep around, join in same sp as beg sl st, fasten off.

Lower Left Wing

Rnds 1 & 2: Rep Rnds 1 and 2 of upper left wing; at end of Rnd 2, do not fasten off.

Rnd 3: Ch 1, sc in same st as joining, 2 sc in next sc, [sc in next sc, 2 sc in next sc] rep around, join in beg sc, fasten off. (18 sc)

Rnd 4: With RS facing, attach mid rose with a sl st in any sc, ch 1, sc in same st as joining, [sc in next sc of Rnd 1, sc in each of next 3 sc on working rnd] 5 times, sc in next sc of Rnd 1, sc in each of next 2 sc, join in beg sc. (24 sc)

Rnd 5: Ch 5, [sk next sc, sl st in next sc, ch 5] rep around, join in same st as joining st of Rnd 4, fasten off. (12 ch-5 lps)

Rnd 6: With RS facing, attach hunter green with a sl st in any ch-5 lp, ch 5, [sl st in next lp, ch

5] rep around, join in same lp as beg sl st, fasten off. (12 ch-5 lps)

Rnd 7: With RS facing, attach canary yellow with a sl st in any ch-5 lp, ch 6, [sl st in next lp, ch 6] rep around, join in same lp as beg sl st, fasten off. (12 ch-6 lps)

Joining Upper & Lower Left Wings

First Bruges lace band

Row 1 (WS): With white, ch 8, dc in 6th ch from hook and in each of next 2 chs, turn.

Row 2: With RS of upper left wing facing, joined lp in any ch-6 lp of upper left wing, dc in each of next 3 dc, turn.

Row 3: Ch 5, dc in each of next 3 dc, turn.

Row 4: With RS of upper left wing facing, joined lp in next ch-6 lp of upper left wing, dc in each of next 3 dc, turn.

Row 5: Rep Row 3.

Rows 6–9: Rep Rows 4 and 5 alternately twice.

Row 10: With RS of upper left wing facing, joined lp in same ch-6 lp of upper left wing as joined lp of row before last, dc in each of next 3 dc, turn.

Rows 11–17: Rep Rows 3 and 4 alternately, ending with a Row 3.

Row 18: Rep Row 10.

Rows 19–42: Rep Rows 11–18 alternately 3 times.

Rows 43 & 44: Rep Rows 3 and 4.

Rows 45–47: Rep Row 3.

Row 48: With RS facing, joined lp in rem lp of foundation ch at base of center dc of Row 1 3-dc group, dc in each of next 3 dc, turn.

Rows 49–53: Rep Row 3.

Row 54: With RS of lower left wing facing, joined lp in any ch-6 lp of lower left wing, dc in each of next 3 dc, turn.

Row 55: Rep Row 3.

Row 56: With RS of lower left wing facing, joined lp in next ch-6 lp of lower left wing, dc in each of next 3 dc, turn.

Rows 57 & 58: Rep Rows 55 and 56.

Row 59: Rep Row 55.

Row 60: With RS of lower left wing facing, joined lp in same ch-6 lp of lower left wing as joined lp of row before last, dc in each of next 3 dc, turn.

Rows 61–64: Rep Rows 57–60.

Rows 65–70: Rep Rows 55–60.

Rows 71–80: Rep Rows 61–70.

Rows 81 & 82: Rep Rows 55 and 56.

Row 83: With WS facing, joined lp in ch-5 lp of Row 7, dc in each of next 3 dc, turn.

Row 84: Rep Row 56.

Row 85: With WS facing, joined lp in ch-5 lp of Row 5, dc in each of next 3 dc, turn.

Row 86: Rep Row 60.

Row 87: With WS facing, joined lp in ch-5 lp of Row 3, dc in each of next 3 dc, turn.

Row 88: Rep Row 56.

Row 89: With WS facing, joined lp in ch-5 lp of Row 1, sl st in ch-5 lp of Row 50, dc in each of next 3 dc, ch 2, sl st in ch-5 lp of Row 52, fasten off.

Border for Left Wing

Rnd 1: With RS facing, attach mid rose with a sl st in ch-5 lp on Row 9 of first Bruges lace band, [ch 3, sl st] in same lp, ch 6, sl st in next joined lp, ch 3, sl st in next joined lp, *ch 6, [sl st, ch 3, sl st] in next lp, rep from * around, ending with ch 6, join in beg sl st, fasten off.

Joining Left Wing to Body

Rnd 1: With RS facing, attach black with a sl st in first ch-6 lp of Rnd 1 of border for left wing, ch 3, sl st in next ch-6 lp, ch 6, *[sl st, ch 3, sl st] in next ch-6 lp, ch 4, sl st in 2nd ch from hook for p, ch 3 *, rep from * to * 9 times, sl st

in next ch-6 lp, ch 3, sl st over end st of Row 32 of body, [ch 3, sl st in next ch-6 lp on border, ch 3, sk next 2 rows on body, sl st over end st of next row] 9 times, ch 3, sl st in next ch-6 lp on border, ch 4, sl st in 2nd ch from hook for p, ch 3, rep from * to * around, ending with [sl st, ch 3, sl st] in last

ch-6 lp, ch 6, join in beg sl st, fasten off.

Upper Right Wing

Rnds 1–5: Rep Rnds 1–5 of upper left wing.

Lower Right Wing

Rnds 1–7: Rep Rnds 1–7 of lower left wing.

Joining Upper & Lower Right Wings

Second Bruges lace band

Row 1 (RS): Rep Row 1 of first Bruges lace band.

Row 2: With WS of upper right wing facing, joined lp in any ch-6 lp of upper right wing, dc in each of next 3 dc, turn.

Row 3: Rep Row 3 of first Bruges lace band.

Row 4: With WS of upper right wing facing, joined lp in next ch-6 lp of upper right wing, dc in each of next 3 dc, turn.

Row 5: Rep Row 3.

Rows 6–9: Rep Rows 4 and 5 alternately twice.

Row 10: With WS of upper right wing facing, joined lp in same ch-6 lp as joined lp of row before last, dc in each of next 3 dc, turn.

Rows 11–17: Rep Rows 3 and 4 alternately, ending with a Row 3.

Row 18: Rep Row 10.

Rows 19–42: Rep Rows 11–18 alternately 3 times.

Rows 43 & 44: Rep Rows 3 and 4.

Rows 45–47: Rep Row 3.

Row 48: With WS facing, joined lp in rem lp of foundation ch at base of center dc of Row 1 3-dc group, dc in each of next 3 dc, turn.

Rows 49–53: Rep Row 3.

Row 54: With WS of lower right wing facing, joined lp in any ch-6 lp of lower right wing, dc in each of next 3 dc, turn.

Row 55: Rep Row 3.

Row 56: With WS of lower right wing facing, joined lp in next ch-6 lp of lower right wing, dc in each of next 3 dc, turn.

Rows 57 & 58: Rep Rows 55 and 56.

Row 59: Rep Row 55.

Row 60: With WS of lower right wing facing, joined lp in same ch-6 lp of lower right wing as joined lp of row before last, dc in each of next 3 dc, turn.

Rows 61–64: Rep Rows 57–60.

Rows 65–70: Rep Rows 55–60.

Rows 71–80: Rep Rows 61–70.

Rows 81 & 82: Rep Rows 55 and 56.

Row 83: With RS facing, joined lp in ch-5 lp of Row 7, dc in each of next 3 dc, turn.

Row 84: Rep Row 56.

Row 85: With RS facing, joined lp in ch-5 lp of Row 5, dc in each of next 3 dc, turn.

Row 86: Rep Row 60.

Row 87: With RS facing, joined lp in ch-5 lp of Row 3, dc in each of next 3 dc, turn.

Row 88: Rep Row 56.

Row 89: With RS facing, joined lp in ch-5 lp of Row 1, sl st in ch-5 lp of Row 50, dc in each of next 3 dc, ch 2, sl st in ch-5 lp of Row 52, fasten off.

Border for Right Wing

Rnd 1: With RS facing, attach mid rose with a sl st in ch-5 lp on Row 81 of Bruges lace band, rep Rnd 1 of border for left wing.

Joining Right Wing to Body

Rnd 1: With RS facing, attach black with a sl st in first ch-6 lp of Rnd 1 of border for right wing, ch 3, sl st in next ch-6 lp, ch 6, *[sl st, ch 3, sl st] in next ch-6 lp, ch 4, sl st in 2nd ch from hook for p, ch 3 *, rep from * to * 14 times, sl st in next ch-6 lp, ch 3, sl st over end st of Row 5 of body, [ch-3, sl st in next ch-6 lp on border, ch 3, sk next 2 rows of body, sl st over end st of next row] 9 times, ch 3, sl st in next ch-6 lp on border, ch 4, sl st in 2nd ch from hook for p, ch 3, rep from * to * around, ending with [sl st, ch 3, sl st] in last ch-6 lp, ch 6, join in beg sl st, fasten off.

Antennae

Row 1: With WS facing, attach black with a sl st in 4th p from last joining of wing and body at top right-hand side of butterfly wing, ch 15, sl st in 11th unworked sc from Row 1 of body on right-hand side of Rnd 2 of head, sl st in each of next 2 sc, ch 15, sl st in corresponding p at top left-hand side of opposite butterfly wing, ch 1, turn.

Row 2: Sl st in each of next 15 chs, sk next sl st, sl st in next sl st, sk next sl st, sl st in each of last 15 chs, sl st in same st on butterfly wing as beg of sl st of Row 1, fasten off.

Napkin Ring

Row 1: With white, rep Row 1 of first Bruges lace band.

Rows 2–16: Rep Row 3 of first Bruges lace band; fasten off at end of Row 16, leaving length for sewing.

With tapestry needle, sew top of each of last 3 dc of last row to rem lp of foundation ch at base of each of 3 dc of first row.

Border

First edge

Rnd 1: With RS facing, attach mid rose with a sl st in any ch-5 lp on either edge of napkin ring, ch 5, [sl st in next ch-5 lp, ch 5] rep around, join in beg sl st, fasten off.

Rnd 2: With black, rep Rnd 1.

Second edge

Rnd 1: With hunter green, rep Rnd 1 of first edge.

Rnd 2: With canary yellow, rep Rnd 2 of first edge.

Finishing

Wash place mat and napkin ring. Starch lightly. When dry, steam-press place mat lightly on WS. ❤

Butterfly Magnets

Designs by Tammy Hildebrand

These double-winged beauties with their large coiled bodies have special visual appeal! Place important reminders on your fridge held securely in place by colorful butterfly magnets.

Let's Begin!

Experience Level
Intermediate

Finished Measurements
4" x 4½"

Materials

- Worsted weight yarn: 15 yds each ombre (MC) and solid color (CC)
- Size G/6 crochet hook or size needed to obtain gauge
- 2 chenille stems in complementary color
- Pencil
- Small magnetic strip
- Craft glue or hot-glue gun

Gauge: Rnd 1 = 1¾" in diameter

To save time, take time to check gauge.

Pattern Note

Join rnds with a sl st unless otherwise stated.

Butterfly

Rnd 1: With MC, ch 6, join to form a ring, ch 3 (counts as first dc throughout), [2 dc, ch 3, {3 dc, ch 3} 7 times] in ring, join in 3rd ch of beg ch-3. (8 ch-3 sps)

Rnd 2: Sl st in each of next 2 dc and in ch-3 sp, [ch 3, 2 dc, ch 3, 3 dc] in same sp, [3 dc, ch 3, 3 dc]

Continued on page 105

Jute Jar Lid Covers

Designs by Janet Giese

Identify your strawberry preserves and grape jam with jar lid covers that depict the contents. When giving canned goods as a gift, your friend will have a remembrance of you long after the goodies inside the jar are gone!

Let's Begin!

Experience Level: Intermediate

Finished Measurements: 3¾" in diameter x 1½" deep

Materials

- Jute twine: 2 balls
- #5 pearl cotton: 7 yds each purple (A) and rust (B) and 5 yds green (C)
- 6-strand embroidery floss: small amount each light blue (D) and gold (E)
- Size F/5 crochet hook or size needed to obtain gauge
- Size B/1 crochet hook
- Yarn needle
- Embroidery needle

Gauge: Rnds 1–3 of jar lid cover = 2½" in diameter

To save time, take time to check gauge.

Pattern Notes

Join rnds with a sl st unless otherwise stated.

When working fpdc, do not work into top of same st over which fpdc was worked.

Pattern Stitch

P: Ch 1, sl st in top of last sc or last dc made.

Jar Lid Cover

Note: Do not join Rnds 1 and 2; mark first st of each rnd with safety pin or other small marker.

Rnd 1: With jute twine and larger hook, ch 6, join to form a ring, ch 1, 12 sc in ring. (12 sc)

Rnd 2: Working in back lps only, 2 sc in each st around. (24 sc)

Rnd 3: Working in back lps only, [2 sc in next st, sc in next st] rep around, join in back lp only of beg sc. (36 sc)

Rnd 4: Working in back lps only, ch 3 (counts as first dc throughout), dc in each of next 2 sts, 2 dc in next st, [dc in each of next 3 sts, 2 dc in next st] rep around, join in 3rd ch of beg ch-3. (45 dc)

Rnd 5: Working in back lps only, ch 3, dc in each rem dc around, join in 3rd ch of beg ch-3. (45 dc)

Rnd 6: Ch 3, dc in each rem dc around, join in 3rd ch of beg ch-3. (45 dc)

Rnd 7: Ch 2, hdc in back lp only of next st, [2 fpdc over next st, hdc in back lp only of each of next 2 sts] rep around to last st, 2 fpdc over last st, join in 2nd ch of beg ch-2, fasten off.

Tie

With jute twine and larger hook, ch 90, fasten off. With WS of ch up, wrap ch around jar lid cover between Rnds 5 and 6, tie ends into bow and fray edges. With yarn needle, sew ch to jar lid cover.

Strawberry (make 3)

Row 1: With B and smaller hook, ch 2, 2 sc in 2nd ch from hook, ch 1, turn. (2 sc)

Row 2: 2 sc in each sc across, ch 1, turn. (4 sc)

Row 3: 2 sc in first st, sc in each of next 2 sts, 2 sc in last st, ch 1, turn. (6 sc)

Rows 4–7: Sc in each sc across, ch 1, turn. (6 sc)

Row 8: Sc dec, sc in each of next 2 sts, sc dec, fasten off. (4 sts)

Leaf (make 2)

Rnd 1: With smaller hook and C, ch 11, dc in 4th ch from hook, dc in each of next 2 sts, sl st in next st, sc in each of next 3 sts, sl st in last st; working in rem lps on opposite side of foundation ch, sc in each of next 3 sts, sl st in next st, dc in each of next 3 sts, join in last ch of foundation ch, fasten off.

With embroidery needle and 3 strands E, using photo as a guide, embroider seeds randomly on strawberries with small straight sts. With embroidery needle and C, using photo as a guide, beg in center top of strawberry, embroider 2 ch sts diagonally from center toward left edge, 2 ch sts from center straight down, and 2 ch sts diagonally from center toward right edge for each strawberry.

Sew berries and leaves to top of jar lid cover.

With embroidery needle and 1 strand B and 1 strand C held tog, whipstitch around rem lps of Rnd 4 of jar lid cover.

Grape (make 7)

Rnd 1 (WS): With A and smaller hook, ch 4, 11 dc in 4th ch from hook, join in 4th ch of beg ch-4, fasten off.

Leaf

With C and smaller hook, ch 15, dc in 4th ch from hook, p, [dc in each of next 2 sts, p] twice, [sc in each of next 2 sts, p] twice, sl st in each of next 2 sts, [sl st, ch 1, sl st] in last st; working in rem lps on opposite side of foundation ch, sl st in each of next 2 sts, sc in next st, p, sc in each of next 2 sts, p, sc in next st, dc in next st, p, [dc in each of next 2 sts, p] twice, ch 3, sl st in same ch as last dc, ch 5 for stem, fasten off.

With embroidery needle and D, embroider 1 highlight on each grape with straight st.

Using photo as a guide, sew grapes on jar lid cover. Fold tip of leaf under. Sew stem and lower edge of leaf only to top of jar lid cover.

With embroidery needle and 1 strand A and C held tog, whipstitch around rem lps of Rnd 4 of jar lid cover. ❤

Piggyback

Design by Michele Wilcox

Fry some bacon and eggs for a good country breakfast. Once the kitchen is cleaned up, crochet this whimsical farm-friendly decorator item.

Let's Begin!

Experience Level: Intermediate

Finished Measurements: 8½" x 9½"

Materials

- Worsted weight yarn: 3 oz peach and small amount each white, cranberry, gold and black
- Size F/5 crochet hook or size needed to obtain gauge
- Polyester fiberfill
- Tapestry needle

Gauge: Rnds 1–3 of snout = 1½" in diameter

To save time, take time to check gauge.

Pattern Note

Join rnds with a sl st unless otherwise stated.

Pig

Body

Note: Do not join rnds unless otherwise stated; mark first st of each rnd with safety pin or other small marker.

Rnd 1: With peach, beg at tail end, ch 2, 6 sc in 2nd ch from hook. (6 sc)

Rnd 2: 2 sc in each sc around. (12 sc)

Rnd 3: [Sc in next sc, 2 sc in next sc] rep around. (18 sc)

Rnd 4: [Sc in each of next 2 sc, 2 sc in next sc] rep around. (24 sc)

Rnd 5: [Sc in each of next 3 sc, 2 sc in next sc] rep around. (30 sc)

Rnd 6: [Sc in each of next 4 sc, 2 sc in next sc] rep around. (36 sc)

Rnd 7: [Sc in each of next 5 sc, 2 sc in next sc] rep around. (42 sc)

Rnds 8–26: Sc in each sc around. (42)

Rnd 27: [Sc in each of next 5 sc, sc dec] rep around. (36 sts)

Rnd 28: [Sc in each of next 4 sts, sc dec] rep around. (30 sts)

Rnd 29: [Sc in each of next 3 sts, sc dec] rep around. (24 sts)

Rnd 30: [Sc in each of next 2 sts, sc dec] rep around. (18 sts)

Stuff body with polyester fiberfill.

Rnd 31: [Sc in next st, sc dec] rep around. (12 sts)

Rnd 32: Sc dec around, join in beg sc dec; fasten off, leaving short length for sewing. (6 sts)

With tapestry needle, draw rem short length through tops of sts of last rnd, pull tightly to close, fasten off.

Head

Note: Do not join rnds unless otherwise stated; mark first st of each rnd with safety pin or other small marker.

Rnds 1–6: Beg at snout end, rep Rnds 1–6 of body. (36 sc)

Rnds 7–12: Sc in each sc around. (36 sc)

Rnds 13–17: Rep Rnds 28–32 of body.

Close opening as for body.

Snout

Rnds 1–3: Rep Rnds 1–3 of body. (18 sc)

Rnd 4: Working in back lps only this rnd, sc in each sc around. (18 sc)

Rnds 5 & 6: Sc in each sc around; at end of Rnd 6, join in beg sc, fasten off.

With tapestry needle, sew snout to front of head, stuffing lightly before closing.

With tapestry needle, sew head to body, pushing head to flatten slightly and stitching where flattened edge meets body.

Ear (make 2)

Row 1: With peach, ch 5, sc in 2nd ch from hook and in each of next 2 chs, 3 sc in last ch; working in rem lps on opposite side of foundation ch, sc in each of next 3 chs, ch 1, turn. (9 sc)

Row 2: Sc in each of first 4 sc, 3 sc in next sc, sc in each of last 4 sc, fasten off, leaving short length for sewing.

With tapestry needle, using photo as a guide, sew ears to top of head.

With tapestry needle and black, satin-st eyes on head.

Tail

With peach, ch 10, 3 sc in 2nd ch from hook and in each rem ch across, fasten off. Sew tail in place.

Leg (make 4)

Rnds 1–6: Rep Rnds 1–6 of snout; at end of Rnd 6, do not join, do not fasten off. (18 sc)

Rnds 7–11: Sc in each sc around; at end of Rnd 11, join in beg sc, fasten off, leaving a short length for sewing.

Stuff leg with polyester fiberfill. Sew in place.

Continued on page 134

Granny's Scrap Bag Apron

Design by Tammy Hildebrand

Delight your granny with this apron crocheted with a rainbow of color. The ample neck opening and drawstring waist make this an apron that will fit grannies of all ages and sizes.

Let's Begin!

Experience Level: Beginner

Finished Measurements: 19" x 31"

Materials

- Worsted weight yarn: 5 oz off-white (MC) and small amount each assorted colors to total 5 oz (CC)
- Size I/9 crochet hook or size needed to obtain gauge
- Size G/6 crochet hook
- Tapestry needle

Gauge: Motif = 2¾" square with larger hook

To save time, take time to check gauge.

Pattern Note

Join rnds with a sl st unless otherwise stated.

Pattern Stitches

Shell: [3 dc, ch 3, 3 dc] in indicated sp or st.

Beg shell: [Ch 3, 2 dc, ch 3, 3 dc] in indicated sp or st.

Motif (make 59)

Rnd 1 (RS): With larger hook and any CC, ch 3, join to form a ring, ch 3 (counts as first dc), [3 dc, ch 2, {4 dc, ch 2} 3 times] in ring, join in 3rd ch of beg ch-3, fasten off. (16 dc)

Rnd 2: With RS facing, using larger hook, attach MC with a sl st in any ch-2 sp, beg shell in same sp, [shell in next ch-2 sp] rep around, join in 3rd ch of beg ch-3, fasten off.

With tapestry needle and MC, whipstitch 35 motifs tog through back lps only in 5 rows of 7 motifs each to form skirt.

Waistband

With RS facing, using larger hook, attach MC with a sl st in center ch at upper right corner of either longer edge, ch 5 (counts as first dc, ch-2), *[sk next dc, dc in next dc, ch 2] 3 times **, dc in seam between motifs, ch 2, rep from * across to next corner, ending last rep at **, dc in center ch of 7th motif, fasten off.

With tapestry needle and MC, following joining diagram, whipstitch rem motifs tog through back lps only to form bib. Whipstitch bottom of bib to top of waistband.

Belt

Row 1: With smaller hook and any CC color, ch 4, sc in 2nd ch from hook and in each of next 2 chs, ch 1, turn. (3 sc)

Row 2: Working in back lps only, sc in each sc across, ch 1, turn.

Rep Row 2 until belt measures approximately 80" or desired length, fasten off.

Weave belt through ch-2 sps of waistband.

Neck Edging

Rnd 1: With RS facing, using smaller hook, attach MC with a sl st in any st around inner neck opening, ch 1, sc in same st, sc in each rem st, seam and corner sp around, join in beg sc, fasten off.

Rnd 2: With RS facing, using smaller hook, attach same CC as used for belt with a sl st in any sc of last rnd, ch 1, [sl st, ch 1] in each rem st around, join in beg sl st, fasten off.

Border

Rnd 1: With RS facing, using smaller hook, attach MC with a sl st in ch-3 sp of motif at upper right corner of bib, ch 1, 5 sc in same sp, sc in each st and seam across to next corner, 5 sc in corner sp, sc in each st, sp, and seam to waistband, 2 sc in each ch-2 sp and sc in each dc across waistband to next corner sp, 5 sc in corner sp, continue around in established pattern, join in beg sc, fasten off.

Rnd 2: Rep Rnd 2 of neck edging. ❤

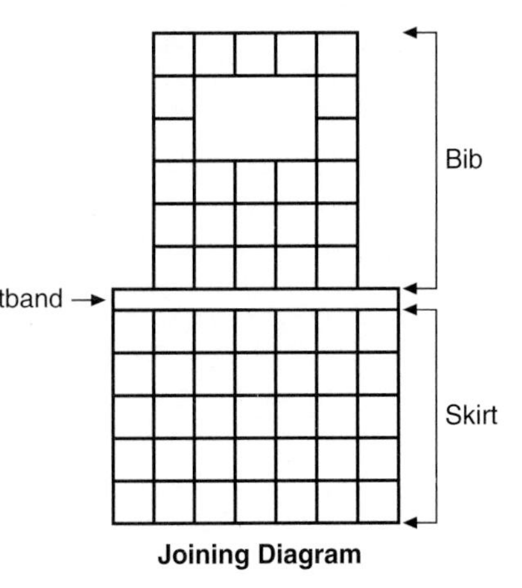

Joining Diagram

Confetti Place Mat

Design by Shirley Patterson

Celebrate with balloons, candles, shiny paper and these brightly colored place mats. The zigzag design and tasseled corners give this place mat the festive look you'll want for your parties!

Let's Begin!

Experience Level: Intermediate

Finished Measurements: 13" x 17½"

Materials

- Worsted weight yarn (3½-oz skeins): 2 skeins MC and small amount each assorted CCs
- Size G/6 crochet hook or size needed to obtain gauge
- 3" square piece of cardboard

Gauge: 19 sts and 20 rows = 4" in sc

To save time, take time to check gauge.

Place Mat

Row 1 (RS): With MC, ch 58, sc in 2nd ch from hook, sc in each rem ch across, ch 1, turn. (57 sc)

Row 2: Sc in each sc across, ch 1, turn. (57 sc)

Row 3: Rep Row 2; at end of row, do not ch 1, do not turn; pull last lp up to approximately 2" so it will not unravel; remove hook from lp. (57 sc)

Row 4: With RS facing, attach any CC with a sl st in first rem lp of foundation ch; working in rem lps of foundation ch across, ch 1, sc in same st, [ch 9, sk next 7 sts, sc in next st] rep across, fasten off CC; pick up dropped lp at end of last MC row, ch 1, turn. (7 ch-9 lps)

Row 5 (WS): Sc in each of first 4 sts, sc in next st and through first ch-9 lp at the same time, [sc in each of next 7 sts, sc in next st and through next ch-9 lp at the same time] twice, sc in each of next 6 sts, sc in next st and through next ch-9 lp at the same time, sc in next st, sc in next st and through same ch-9 lp as next-to-last sc at the same time, sc in each of next 6 sts, [sc in next st and next ch-9 lp at the same time, sc in each of next 7 sts] twice, sc in next st and next ch-9 lp at the same time, sc in each of last 4 sts, ch 1, turn.

Row 6: Sc in back lp only of first sc, [sc in both lps of each of next 7 sc, sc in back lp only of next st] rep across, do not ch 1, do not turn; pull last lp up to approximately 2" so it will not unravel; remove hook from lp. (57 sc)

Row 7: With RS facing, attach next CC with a sl st in first rem lp of row before last; working in rem lps across, rep Row 4.

Rows 8 & 9: Rep Row 2.

Row 10: Rep Row 5.

Rows 11–110: Rep Rows 6–10 alternately.

Row 111: Rep Row 2; fasten off.

With RS facing, attach MC with a sl st in first rem lp on opposite side of foundation ch, ch 1, sc in same st and in each rem st across, fasten off. (57 sc)

Edging

First edge

With RS facing, attach any CC with a sl st over side of last sc of Row 111, ch 2 (counts as first hdc), hdc over end st of next row, [ch 3, hdc over end st of next row into which CC row was worked] rep across to next corner, hdc in end st of first row, fasten off.

Second edge

With RS facing, attach same CC as was used for first edge over end st of Row 1 on opposite long edge, rep instructions for first edge, ending with ch 3, hdc over end st of each of last 2 rows, fasten off.

Edging chain (make 2)

Hold 1 strand of MC and 1 strand of same CC used for edging tog; leaving a 6" length at beg, ch 70, fasten off, leaving a 6" length at end. Weave 1 ch through ch-3 sps of edging on each side.

Tassel (make 4)

Wrap 6–8 strands of each CC 6 times around cardboard. Cut along 1 edge. Holding all strands tog, tie tightly around center with 6" length at any corner of place mat. Cut an 8" length of CC. Fold tassel in half and tie with 8" length approximately 1" from top of tassel. Trim ends evenly.

HAPPY BIRTHDAY

Sitting Pretty Table Set

Designs by Sandra Abbate

Invite springtime into your home with this lovely pastel table set. Place mat, coaster and napkin ring all have dainty little flowers and pretty ruffled edges in soft colors to help make any meal a pleasant experience.

Let's Begin!

Experience Level: Intermediate

Finished Measurements: Place Mat: 12½" x 17½"

Coaster: 6" square

Napkin Ring: 4½" wide

Materials

- Worsted weight yarn: 3 oz mint green (MC)
- Pompadour baby yarn: 3 oz pink (A) and small amount each lavender (B), blue (C), peach (D) and yellow (E)
- Size G/6 crochet hook or size needed to obtain gauge
- Size B/1 crochet hook
- 2 yds ¼"-wide yellow picot ribbon
- 3½ yds 1"-wide white eyelet
- Yarn needle
- Sewing needle and white sewing thread

Gauge

[{Sc, shell} twice, sc] = 2⅜" with MC and larger hook

To save time, take time to check gauge.

Pattern Note

Join rnds with a sl st unless otherwise stated.

Pattern Stitches

Shell: 3 dc in indicated st or sp.

P: Ch 3, sc in 3rd ch from hook.

P shell: [{Dc, p} 5 times, dc] in indicated st or sp.

Beg p shell: [Ch 6, sc in 3rd ch from hook (counts as first dc, p), {dc, p} 4 times, dc] in indicated st or sp.

Place Mat

Row 1 (RS): With larger hook and MC, ch 66, sc in 2nd ch from hook and in each rem ch across, ch 1, turn. (65 sc)

Row 2: Sc in first st, [ch 4, sk 3 sts, sc in next st] rep across, turn. (16 ch-4 sps)

Row 3: Ch 3 (counts as first dc throughout), dc in first sc, sc in next ch-4 sp, [ch 4, sc in next ch-4 sp] 3 times, *shell in next sc, sc in next ch-4 sp, [ch 4, sc in next ch-4 sp] 3 times, rep from * across to last sc, 2 dc in last sc, ch 1, turn.

Row 4: Sc in first dc, sk next dc, shell in next sc, *sc in next ch-4 sp, [ch 4, sc in next ch-4 sp] twice, shell in next sc **, sc in center dc

of next shell, shell in next sc, rep from * across, ending last rep at **, sk last dc, sc in 3rd ch of turning ch-3, turn.

Row 5: Ch 3, dc in first sc, *sc in center dc of next shell, ch 4, sc in next ch-4 sp, shell in next sc, sc in next ch-4 sp, ch 4, sc in center dc of next shell **, shell in next sc, rep from * across, ending last rep at **, 2 dc in last sc, ch 1, turn.

Row 6: Sc in first dc, *ch 4, sc in next ch-4 sp, shell in next sc, sc in center dc of next shell, shell in next sc, sc in next ch-4 sp, ch 4 **, sc in center dc of next shell, rep from * across, ending last rep at **, sc in 3rd ch of turning ch-3, turn.

Row 7: Ch 3, dc in first sc, *sc in next ch-4 sp, ch 4, sc in center dc of next shell, shell in next sc, sc in center dc of next shell, ch 4, sc in next ch-4 sp **, shell in next sc, rep from * across, ending last rep at **, 2 dc in last sc, ch 1, turn.

Row 8: Sc in first dc, *shell in next sc, sc in next ch-4 sp, ch 4, sc in center dc of next shell, ch 4, sc in next ch-4 sp, shell in next sc **, sc in center dc of next shell, rep from * across, ending last rep at **, sc in 3rd ch of turning ch-3, turn.

Rows 9–28: Reps Rows 5–8 alternately 5 times.

Row 29: Ch 3, dc in first st, *sc in center dc of next shell, [ch 4, sc in next ch-4 sp] twice, ch 4, sc in center dc of next shell **, shell in next sc, rep from * across, ending last rep at **, 2 dc in last sc, ch 1, turn.

Row 30: Sc in first dc, *[ch 3, sc in next ch-4 sp] 3 times, ch 3 **, sc in center dc of next shell, rep from * across, ending last rep at **, sc in 3rd ch of turning ch-3, ch 1, turn. (16 ch-3 sps)

Row 31: Work 65 sc evenly sp across, fasten off.

Side Edging

With RS facing, using larger hook, attach MC with a sl st over end st of first row at right-hand edge of either side edge, ch 1, beg in same st, work 46 sc evenly sp over end sts of rows across to next corner, fasten off.

Rep on opposite side edge.

Ruffle

With RS facing, using smaller hook, attach A with a sl st in front lp only of any corner st, beg p shell in same st; working in front lps only around, sc in next st, [p shell in next st, sc in next st] rep around, join with a sl st in 3rd ch of beg ch-6, fasten off.

Large Rose

Rnd 1: With smaller hook and A, ch 2, [sc, ch 3] 5 times in 2nd ch from hook, join in beg sc. (5 ch-3 sps)

Rnd 2 (WS): [Sc, hdc, 5 dc, hdc, sc] in each ch-3 sp around, do not join. (5 petals)

Rnd 3: Working in front of petals of last rnd, sc in first sc of Rnd 1, ch 4, [sc in next unworked sc of Rnd 1, ch 4] rep around, join in beg sc. (5 ch-4 sps)

Rnd 4: [Sc, hdc, 7 dc, hdc, sc] in each ch-4 sp around, do not join. (5 petals)

Rnd 5: Working in front of petals of last rnd, sc in first sc of Rnd 3, ch 5, [sc in next unworked sc of Rnd 3, ch 5] rep around, join in beg sc. (5 ch-5 sps)

Rnd 6: [Sc, hdc, 9 dc, hdc, sc] in each ch-5 sp around, join in beg sc, fasten off. (5 petals)

Center

Pinch ends of 1 petal on Rnd 2 tog to form circle and tack in place at center of rose.

Small Flower

Note: Make 2 each B, C and D.

Ch 2, [sc, ch 3] 6 times in 2nd ch from hook, join in beg sc, fasten off.

With yarn needle and E, work French knot in center.

Finishing

Using photo as a guide, tie a 19" length of yellow ribbon into a bow through a st at upper right-hand corner of place mat, leaving 8" streamer at each end. Tack large rose over center of bow. Sew 1 small flower of each color on each side of large rose, looping streamers slightly between flowers.

Sew eyelet behind ruffle around place mat, gathering slightly at each corner.

Coaster

Row 1 (RS): With larger hook and MC, ch 18, sc in 2nd ch from hook and in each rem ch across, ch 1, turn. (17 sc)

Row 2: Sc in first sc, [ch 4, sk next 3 sts, sc in next st] rep across, turn. (4 ch-4 sps)

Row 3: Ch 4 (counts as first dc, ch-1), sc in next ch-4 sp, [ch 4, sc in next ch-4 sp] 3 times, ch 1, dc in last sc, ch 1, turn.

Row 4: Sc in first dc, ch 4, [sc in next ch-4 sp, ch 4] 3 times, sc in 3rd ch of turning ch-4, ch 1, turn. (4 ch-4 sps)

Row 5: Ch 4 (counts as first dc, ch-1), sc in first ch-4 sp, ch 4, sc in next ch-4 sp, shell in next sc, sc in next ch-4 sp, ch 4, sc in next ch-4 sp, ch 1, dc in last sc, ch 1, turn.

Row 6: Sc in first dc, ch 4, sc in next ch-4 sp, shell in next sc, sc in center dc of next shell, shell in next sc, sc in next ch-4 sp, ch 4, sc in 3rd ch of turning ch-4, turn.

Row 7: Ch 4 (counts as first dc, ch-1), sc in first ch-4 sp, ch 4, sc in center dc of next shell, shell in next sc, sc in center dc of next shell, ch 4, sc in next ch-4 sp, ch 1, dc in last sc, ch 1, turn.

Row 8: Sc in first dc, ch 4, sc in first ch-4 sp, ch 4, sc in center dc of next shell, ch 4, sc in next ch-4 sp, ch 4, sc in 3rd ch of turning ch-4, turn.

Row 9: Rep Row 3.

Row 10: Sc in first dc, [ch 3, sc in next ch-4 sp] 3 times, ch 3, sc in 3rd ch of turning ch-4, ch 1, turn. (4 ch-3 sps)

Row 11: Work 17 sc evenly sp across, fasten off.

Side Edging

With RS facing, using larger hook, attach MC with a sl st over end st of first row at right-hand edge of either side edge, ch 1, beg in same st, work 17 sc evenly sp over end sts of rows across to next corner, fasten off.

Rep on opposite side edge.

Ruffle

Rep instructions for ruffle for Place Mat.

Small Flower

Note: Make 1 each B, C and D.

Rep instructions for small flower for Place Mat.

Finishing

Tie a 12" length of yellow ribbon into a bow through a st at upper right-hand corner of coaster. Tack 1 small flower of each color over center of bow.

Sew eyelet around coaster as for Place Mat.

Napkin Ring

Row 1 (RS): With larger hook and MC, ch 26, sc in 2nd ch from hook and in each rem ch across, ch 1, turn. (25 sc)

Row 2: Sc in first sc, [ch 4, sk 3 sc, sc in next sc] rep across, ch 1, turn. (6 ch-4 sps)

Row 3: Ch 4 (counts as first dc, ch-1), sc in first ch-4 sp, [ch 4, sc in next ch-4 sp] twice, shell in next sc, sc in next ch-4 sp, [ch 4, sc in next ch-4 sp] twice, ch 1, dc in last sc, ch 1, turn.

Row 4: Sc in first dc, [ch 4, sc in next ch-4 sp] twice, shell in next sc, sc in center dc of next shell, shell in next sc, sc in next ch-4 sp, ch 4, sc in next ch-4 sp, ch 4, sc in 3rd ch of turning ch-4, turn.

Row 5: Ch 4 (counts as first dc, ch-1), sc in first ch-4 sp, ch 4, sc in next ch-4 sp, ch 4, sc in center dc of next shell, shell in next sc, sc in center dc of next shell, [ch 4, sc in next ch-4 sp] twice, ch 1, dc in last sc, ch 1, turn.

Row 6: Sc in first dc, [ch 3, sc in next ch-4 sp] twice, ch 3, sc in center dc of next shell, [ch 3, sc in next ch-4 sp] twice, ch 3, sc in 3rd ch of turning ch-4, ch 1, turn.

Row 7: Work 25 sc evenly sp across, fasten off.

Side Edging

With RS facing, using larger hook, attach MC with a sl st over end st of first row at right-hand edge of either side edge, ch 1, beg in same st, work 10 sc evenly sp over end sts of rows across to corner, fasten off.

Rep on opposite side edge.

Ruffle

Row 1: With RS facing, using smaller hook, attach A with a sl st in front lp only of first st of Row 7 at right-hand edge; working in front lps only across, sc in same st, [p shell in next st, sc in next st] rep across, fasten off.

Rep Row 1 in rem lps of foundation ch across opposite edge.

Small Rose

Rnds 1–4: Rep Rnds 1–4 of large rose for Place Mat, fasten off at end of Rnd 4.

Center

Rep instructions for center for large rose.

Small Flower

***Note:** Make 1 each B, C and D.*

Rep instructions for small flower for Place Mat.

Finishing

Tie a 12" length of yellow ribbon into a bow through a st at center of napkin ring. Tack small rose over center of bow. Tack 1 small flower of each color under small rose. Sew length of eyelet across top and bottom of napkin ring behind ruffle. Pull 1 end of rem length of yellow ribbon through center sc at either side of napkin ring; pull rem end through center sc on opposite side of napkin ring. Tie into bow. ❤

Thread Guide

Threads are sold according to size, by number. The higher the number, the finer the thread. Tatting usually requires size 70 or 80 thread. Sewing threads are usually around size 50. Bedspread weight cotton is usually considered around size 10. Some threads labeled "bedspread weight" are close to size 20, rather than 10. That is why it is very important to always work out a sample swatch to determine your exact gauge before beginning any project.

There are also some beautiful sizes 3 and 5 threads available. These may be used for fashion crochet or even holiday ornaments. They may also be used for numerous embroidery techniques, such as Teneriffe embroidery, twilling and candlewicking.

Mercerized cotton is threaded cotton with a sheen to it. Mercerized cotton wears far better than untreated cotton.

When purchasing thread, carefully check to make certain you are getting fresh stock and the same dye-lot. Sometimes thread collects dust on store shelves, so gently push aside the outer layers with your thumbnail to see if the color is consistent underneath. This is important for ecru and white thread as well as dyed ones.

Always wash your hands before working on any thread project. Even if your hands seem clean, you have oil on you skin that will discolor your thread.

Daisy in the Sun Doily

Design by Sandra Abbate

Show your love for bright and cheerful daisies by crocheting this colorful little doily. Overlapping arches surround the daisy center to give added interest and dimension.

Let's Begin!

Experience Level: Intermediate

Finished Measurement: 6½" in diameter

Materials

- Crochet cotton size 10: small amount each yellow (A), white (B) and light blue (C)
- Size 8 steel crochet hook or size needed to obtain gauge

Gauge: Rnds 1 and 2 = 2¼" in diameter

To save time, take time to check gauge.

Pattern Note

Join rnds with a sl st unless otherwise stated.

Doily

Rnd 1 (RS): With A, ch 8, join to form a ring, ch 1, [sc in ring, ch 5] 12 times, join in beg sc, fasten off. (12 ch-5 sps)

Rnd 2: With RS facing, attach B with a sl st in any ch-5 sp, ch 1, beg in same sp, [sc, ch 9, hdc in 4th ch from hook, hdc in next ch, dc in each of next 4 chs] in each ch-5 sp around, join in beg sc, fasten off. (12 petals)

Rnd 3: With RS facing, attach C with a sl st in ch-3 sp at tip of any petal, ch 1, sc in same sp, ch 6, [sc in sp at tip of next petal, ch 6] rep around, join in beg sc. (12 ch-6 sps)

Rnd 4: Sl st in first ch-6 sp, ch 3 (counts as first dc throughout), 7 dc in same sp, 8 dc in each rem sp around, join in 3rd ch of beg ch-3. (96 dc)

Rnd 5: Ch 1, sc in same st as joining, ch 5, [sc in each of next 3 sts, ch 5] rep around to last 2 sts, sc in each of last 2 sts, join in beg sc. (32 ch-5 sps)

Rnd 6: Sl st in first ch-5 sp, ch 1, sc in same sp, *ch 25, sk next 2 ch-5 sps, sc in next sp, ch 4 **, sc in next sp, rep from * around, ending last rep at **, join in beg sc.

Rnd 7: Sl st in ch-25 sp, [ch 3, 17 dc, ch 3, 18 dc] in same sp, [18 dc, ch 3, 18 dc] in each rem ch-25 sp around, join in 3rd ch of beg ch-3, fasten off.

Rnd 8: With RS facing, working behind ch-25 sps of Rnd 6, attach A with a sl st in first unworked ch-5 sp to the left of any pair of unworked ch-5 sps on Rnd 5, ch 1, sc in same sp, *ch 25, sc in next unworked ch-5 sp, ch 4 **, sc in next unworked ch-5 sp, rep from * around, ending last rep at **, join in beg sc.

Rnd 9: Rep Rnd 7.

Rnd 10: With RS facing, attach A with a sl st in ch-3 sp at tip of any point, ch 1, [sc, ch 3, sc] in same sp, *ch 6, holding same point and next point tog and working through both thicknesses at the same time, [sc, ch 3, sc] in 7th dc from ch-3 sps at tips of points, ch 6 **, [sc, ch 3, sc] in ch-3 sp at tip of next point, rep from * around, ending last rep at **, join in beg sc, fasten off. ♥

Needle Me On Pincushion

Design by Debra Caldwell

Make your sewing room even more distinctive with this charming little porcelain doll. Her full crocheted skirt will hold your pins and needles in style. Add buttons or charms near her scalloped hem to define her interest and yours!

Let's Begin!

Experience Level
Intermediate

Finished Measurements
5" wide x 6" tall

Materials

- Crochet cotton size 10 (230 yds per ball): 1 ball blue (A) and approximately 65 yds bright yellow (B)
- Kreinik Fine (#8) Braid (11 yds per spool): 2 spools red #003
- Size 6 steel crochet hook or size needed to obtain gauge
- 50mm porcelain lady head and hands
- 9"-long x 5"-diameter (at center) foam football
- Chenille stem
- 6" ¼"-diameter dowel
- Hot-glue gun
- Assorted charms or buttons
- Tapestry needle
- Sewing needle and yellow sewing thread

Gauge: Rnds 1–5 of bottom 2½" in diameter
To save time, take time to check gauge.

Rosebud Hair Accent

Design by Nazanin S. Fard

Sweep up your hair, gently twist it into place and hold it securely and beautifully with this dainty floral piece. Rayon floss gives this project a soft appearance sure to complement your hair.

Let's Begin!

Experience Level: Intermediate

Finished Measurement: To fit 1¾"-wide x 4"-long oval hair accessory

Materials

- DMC rayon floss: small amount each ecru #30746, pink #33689 and green #30700
- Size 0 steel crochet hook or size needed to obtain gauge
- 1¾"-wide ecru Hair Hook Up hair accessory
- Small white flower beads
- Low-temperature glue gun
- Tapestry needle

Gauge: 5 dc = 1"
To save time, take time to check gauge.

Pattern Note

Join rnds with a sl st unless otherwise stated.

Rose

Rnd 1: With ecru, ch 4, 9 dc in 4th ch from hook, join in 3rd ch of beg ch-3. (10 dc, counting last 3 chs of ch-4 as first dc)

Rnd 2: Ch 3, [sk next dc, sl st in next dc, ch 3] rep around, join in same st as beg sl st. (5 ch-3 sps)

Rnd 3: [Sc, hdc, 4 dc, hdc, sc] in each ch-3 sp around, do not join. (5 petals)

Rnd 4: Working behind petals of last rnd, sl st in first unworked dc of Rnd 1, ch 5, [sl st in next unworked dc of Rnd 1, ch 5] rep around, join in beg sl st. (5 ch-5 sps)

Rnd 5: [Sc, hdc, 5 dc, hdc, sc] in each sp around, join in beg sc, fasten off.

Rosebud

Note: Make 1 ecru and 2 pink.

Row 1: Ch 9, 3 dc in 4th ch from hook, 3 dc in each rem ch across, fasten off, leaving 6" length for finishing.

Leaf (make 4)

Row 1: With green, ch 8, sc in 2nd ch from hook, hdc in next ch, dc in each of next 3 chs, hdc in next ch, 3 sc in last ch; working in rem lps across opposite side of foundation ch, hdc in next st, dc in each of next 3 sts, hdc in next st, sc in last st, fasten off.

Finishing

With tapestry needle and 6" length, sew ecru rosebud to center of rose. Using photo as a guide, glue rose to center of hair accessory and 1 pink rosebud on each side. Glue leaves in place. Glue small white flower beads randomly on leaves and rem sps on hair accessory. ❤

Forget-Me-Not Trinket Box

Design by Nazanin S. Fard

Add a decorator touch to a small trinket box with charming little forget-me-not crocheted flowers. It makes a special gift sure to be treasured.

— Let's Begin! —

Experience Level
Intermediate

Finished Measurements
To fit 2" x 3¾" trinket box

Materials

- #8 pearl cotton: small amount each blue, yellow and green
- Size 10 steel crochet hook or size needed to obtain gauge
- 2" x 3¾" trinket box
- 6 (1") gold seed beads
- Commercial fabric stiffener
- Hot-glue gun

Gauge: 10 dc = 1"
To save time, take time to check gauge.

Pattern Note
Join rnds with a sl st unless otherwise stated.

Pattern Stitch
Cl: Holding back on hook last lp of each st, 3 tr in indicated st, yo, draw through all 4 lps on hook.

Flower (make 8)
Rnd 1: With yellow, ch 2, 10 sc in 2nd ch from hook, join in beg sc, fasten off. (10 sc)

Rnd 2: Attach blue with a sl st in any sc, [ch 4, cl, ch 4, sl st] in same st, sk next st, *[sl st, ch 4, cl, ch 4, sl st] in next st, sk next st, rep from * around, join in beg sl st, fasten off. (5 petals)

Leaf (make 2)
Row 1: With green, ch 15, sc in 2nd ch from hook, sc in each rem ch across, ch 1, turn. (14 sc)

Row 2: Sc in each of first 3 sts, hdc in each of next 2 sts, dc in each of next 2 sts, tr in each of next 3 sts, dc in each of next 2 sts, hdc in next st, sc in last st, do not turn. (14 sts)

Row 3: Working in rem lps on opposite side of foundation ch, sc in first st, hdc in next st, dc in each of next 2 sts, tr in each of next 3 sts, dc in each of next 2 sts, hdc in each of next 2 sts, sc in each of next 3 sts, fasten off.

Finishing
Stiffen flowers and leaves with commercial fabric stiffener, shaping as they dry. Using photo as a guide, place beads and flowers on box top and glue in place.

Brimming With Roses Hat

Design by Debra Caldwell

Decorate this wide-brimmed hat with roses, accent flowers and Spanish moss to create a lovely spring arrangement. The open shells make this a project that is quick to crochet and pleasant to view.

Let's Begin!

Experience Level: Beginner
Finished Measurement: 7½" in diameter

Materials

- Crochet cotton size 10: small amount ecru
- Size 7 steel crochet hook or size needed to obtain gauge
- Small pink artificial rosebuds
- Small white artificial flowers
- Small amount Spanish moss
- 2½" Styrofoam plastic-foam ball
- Plastic wrap
- Rustproof pins
- Commercial fabric stiffener
- Craft glue
- Piece of cardboard

Gauge: Rnds 1–3 = 2" in diameter
To save time, take time to check gauge.

Pattern Note

Join rnds with a sl st unless otherwise stated.

Pattern Stitches

Open shell: [{Dc, ch 2} 3 times, dc] in indicated st or sp.

Beg open shell: [Ch 5, {dc, ch 2} twice, dc] in indicated st or sp.

V-st: [Dc, ch 2, dc] in indicated sp or st.

Crown

Rnd 1: Ch 5, join to form a ring, ch 4 (counts as first dc, ch-1), [dc in ring, ch 1] 11 times, join in 3rd ch of beg ch-4. (12 ch-1 sps)

Rnd 2: Sl st in first sp, ch 5 (counts as first dc, ch-2 throughout), [dc in next sp, ch 2] rep around, join in 3rd ch of beg ch-5. (12 ch-2 sps)

Rnd 3: Ch 5, dc in next sp, ch 2, [dc in next dc, ch 2, dc in next sp, ch 2] rep around, join in 3rd ch of beg ch-5. (24 ch-2 sps)

Rnds 4–9: Ch 5, [dc in next dc, ch 2] rep around, join in 3rd ch of beg ch-5. (24 ch-2 sps)

Brim

Rnd 10: Beg open shell in same st as joining, sk next dc, [open shell in next dc, sk next dc] rep around, join in 3rd ch of beg ch-5. (12 open shells)

Rnd 11: Sl st in each of next 2 chs, in next dc and in next sp, beg open shell in same sp as last sl st, [dc, ch 1, dc] between same open shell and next open shell, [open shell in center ch-2 sp of next open shell, {dc, ch 1, dc} between same open shell and next open shell] rep around, join in 3rd ch of beg ch-5.

Rnd 12: Sl st in each of next 2 chs, in next dc and in next sp, beg open shell in same sp as last sl st, V-st in next ch-1 sp, [open shell in center ch-2 sp of next open shell, V-st in next ch-1 sp] rep around, join in 3rd ch of beg ch-5.

Rnd 13: Sl st in each of next 2 chs, in next dc and in next sp, beg open shell in same sp as last sl st, V-st in next V-st sp, [open shell in center ch-2 sp of next open shell, V-st in next V-st sp] rep around, join in 3rd ch of beg ch-5.

Rnd 14: Sl st in each of next 2 chs, in next dc and in next sp, beg open shell in same sp as last

sl st, open shell in next V-st sp, [open shell in center ch-2 sp of next open shell, open shell in next V-st sp] rep around, join in 3rd ch of beg ch-5. (24 open shells)

Rnd 15: Sl st in each of next 2 chs, in next dc and in next sp, beg open shell in same sp as last sl st, open shell in center ch-2 sp of each open shell around, join in 3rd ch of beg ch-5, fasten off. (24 open shells)

Finishing

Cut plastic-foam ball in half. Wrap half of ball and piece of cardboard with plastic wrap. Saturate hat in fabric stiffener; squeeze out excess. Shape crown of hat over rounded side of plastic-wrapped ball. Place hat on cardboard and pin out brim. Allow to dry thoroughly. Using photo as a guide, glue flowers and Spanish moss around brim of hat. ♥

Tresses Trio

Designs by Maggie Petsch Chasalow

Add a touch of class to your favorite swept-up hairdo. The pearl filament crocheted into these beautiful barrettes helps to create an elegant look you will appreciate when dressing up for a special occasion.

Let's Begin!

Barrette #1

Experience Level Intermediate

Finished Measurements: 4½" x 1⅞"

Materials

- Crochet cotton size 10: small amount white
- Kreinik Blending Filament (55 yds per spool): 1 spool pearl #032-BF
- Size 7 steel crochet hook or size needed to obtain gauge
- ½"-wide hairpin frame
- 3⅞" x 1½" white matte barrette plate
- 3" silver barrette back
- 3 (3/16") white pearls
- 6 (⅛") white pearls
- Tapestry needle
- Sewing needle and white sewing thread
- Hot-glue gun

Gauge: Center flower = 1½" in diameter

To save time, take time to check gauge.

Pattern Notes

Join rnds with a sl st unless otherwise stated.

Work with 1 strand crochet cotton and 1 strand blending filament held tog throughout.

Pattern Stitch

Dc cl: [Ch 3, 5 dc] in indicated st or sp, remove lp from hook, insert hook in 3rd ch of ch-3, pick up dropped lp and draw through st on hook.

Center Flower

Rnd 1 (RS): Ch 1 (center ch), ch 4 more (counts as first hdc, ch-2), [hdc in center ch, ch 2] 5 times, join in 2nd ch of beg ch-4. (6 ch-2 sps)

Rnd 2: [Sc, 3 dc, sc] in each ch-2 sp around, do not join. (6 petals)

Rnd 3: Working behind petals of last rnd, sc in 2nd ch of beg ch-4 of Rnd 1, ch 3, [sc in next unworked hdc of Rnd 1, ch 3] rep around, join in beg sc. (6 ch-3 sps)

Rnd 4: [Sc, 5 dc, sc] in each ch-3 sp around, do not join. (6 petals)

Rnd 5: *Sl st in first sc of next petal, [ch 3, sk next st, sl st in next st] 3 times, rep from * around, join in beg sl st, fasten off.

Side Flower (make 2)

Rnd 1 (RS): Ch 1 (center ch), ch 3 more (counts as first hdc, ch-1), [hdc in center ch, ch 1] 5 times, join in 2nd ch of beg ch-3. (6 ch-1 sps)

Rnd 2: Sl st in first ch-1 sp, [dc cl, ch 3, sl st] in first ch-1 sp, [sl st, dc cl, ch 3, sl st] in each rem ch-1 sp around, join in beg ch-1 sp, fasten off.

Edging

Make a ½"-wide strip of hairpin lace with 54 lps on each side, fasten off, leaving short end for sewing.

Inner edge

Keeping twist in lps, attach thread and blending filament with a sl st in top of any lp on either edge of hairpin lace strip, ch 1, sc in same lp, [ch 1, sc in next lp] 10 times, sc next 5 lps tog, sc in next lp, [ch 1, sc in next lp] 21 times, sc next 5 lps tog, sc in next lp, ch 1, [sc in next lp, ch 1] 10 times, join in beg sc, fasten off.

With tapestry needle, sew ends of spine tog.

Finishing

With sewing needle and white thread, sew 1 (3/16") pearl in center of center flower and in center of each side flower. Sew 1 (⅛") pearl over each ch-2 sp of center flower.

Glue edging around edge of barrette plate. Glue center flower at center of barrette and 1 side flower on each side of center flower. Glue barrette back to back of barrette plate.

Barrette #1
Barrette #2
Barrette #3

Barrette #2

Experience Level
Intermediate

Finished Measurements
4¼" x 2"

Materials

- Crochet cotton size 10: small amount white
- Kreinik Blending Filament (55 yds per spool): 1 spool pearl #032-BF
- Size 7 steel crochet hook or size needed to obtain gauge
- 3⅞" x 1½" white matte barrette plate
- 3" silver barrette back
- 36 (⅛") white pearls
- Sewing needle and white sewing thread
- Hot-glue gun

Gauge: Center flower = 1⅝" in diameter

To save time, take time to check gauge.

Pattern Notes

Join rnds with a sl st unless otherwise stated.

Work with 1 strand crochet cotton and 1 strand blending filament held tog throughout.

Pattern Stitch

Beaded ch (bch): Slide bead up against hook, ch 1.

Center Flower

Rnds 1–4: Rep Rnds 1–4 of center flower for Barrette #1.

Rnd 5: Working behind petals of last rnd, sc in beg sc of Rnd 3, ch 4, [sc in next unworked sc of Rnd 3, ch 4] rep around, join in beg sc. (6 ch-4 sps)

Rnd 6: [Sc, dc, 5 tr, dc, sc] in each ch-4 sp around, do not join. (6 petals)

Rnd 7: *Sl st in first sc of next petal, [ch 3, sk next st, sl st in next st] 4 times, rep from * around, join in beg sl st, fasten off.

Rnd 8: With RS facing, attach thread and blending filament with a sl st in first sc of any petal on Rnd 4, *[ch 3, sk next st, sl st in next st] 3 times **, sl st in first sc of next petal, rep from * around, ending last rep at **, join in beg sl st, fasten off.

Center

Leaving 4" end, ch 4; holding back on hook last lp of each st, 4 tr in 4th ch from hook, yo, draw through all lps on hook, sl st tightly in first ch of beg ch-4, fasten off, leaving 4" end. Tie center to center flower through ch-2 sps of Rnd 1.

Side Flower (make 2)

Rnds 1–5: Rep Rnds 1–5 of center flower for Barrette #1.

Center

Rep instructions for center flower center. Tie 1 center to center of each side flower through ch-2 sps of Rnd 1.

Edging

String 36 pearls on blending filament only.

Rnd 1 (RS): With 1 strand cotton and 1 strand beaded blending filament held tog, ch 72, taking care not to twist, join to form a ring, ch 1, sc in same st as joining, sc in each rem ch around, join in beg sc, turn. (72 sc)

Rnd 2: [Ch 2, bch, ch 2, sk next st, sl st in next st] rep around, ending with sk next st, join in joining st of Rnd 1, fasten off.

Finishing

Glue edging around edge of barrette plate. Glue center flower to center of barrette plate and 1 side flower on each side of center flower. Glue barrette back to back of barrette plate.

Barrette #3

Experience Level
Intermediate

Finished Measurements
4⅛" x 1½"

Materials

- Crochet cotton size 10: small amount white
- Kreinik Blending Filament (55 yds per spool): 1 spool pearl #032-BF
- Size 7 steel crochet hook or size needed to obtain gauge
- 3⅞" x 1½" white matte barrette plate
- 3" silver barrette back
- 28 (⅛") white pearls
- Sewing needle and white sewing thread
- Hot-glue gun

Gauge: Flower = 1" in diameter

To save time, take time to check gauge.

Pattern Notes

Join rnds with a sl st unless otherwise stated.

Work with 1 strand crochet cotton and 1 strand blending filament held tog throughout.

Pattern Stitch

Tr cl: 5 tr in indicated st or sp, remove lp from hook, insert hook from RS to WS in top of first tr, pick up dropped lp, draw through st on hook.

Flower (make 4)

Rnd 1: Ch 1 (center ch), ch 3 more (counts as first hdc, ch-1), [hdc in center ch, ch 1] 5 times, join in 2nd ch of beg ch-3. (6 ch-1 sps)

Rnd 2: [Sl st in next ch-1 sp, ch 4, tr cl, ch 4, sl st in same sp] rep around, join in same sp as beg sl st, fasten off.

Edging

[Ch 3, sc in 2nd ch from hook, dc in next ch] 25 times (25 points

Continued on page 150

Wild Rose Sachet

Design by Laura Gebhardt

Fragrant closets and dresser drawers will add a pleasing touch to your boudoir with these pretty sachets. Fill them with your favorite potpourri to appeal to several of your senses.

Let's Begin!

Experience Level
Intermediate

Finished Measurement
4" square

Materials

- Crochet cotton size 10: 47 yds cream, 21 yds jade green and 20 yds peach
- Size 7 steel crochet hook or size needed to obtain gauge
- 2 (4") squares ivory satin
- Potpourri
- Sewing needle and ivory sewing thread

Gauge: Rose = 2½" in diameter
To save time, take time to check gauge.

Pattern Note
Join rnds with a sl st unless otherwise stated.

Pattern Stitches

P: Ch 3, sl st in top of last dc made.

P shell: [3 dc, p, 2 dc] in indicated sp or st.

Double p shell (dbl p shell): [{3 dc, p} twice, 2 dc] in indicated sp or st.

Shell: [3 dc, ch 3, 3 dc] in indicated sp.

Cl: Holding back on hook last lp of each st, 5 dc in indicated st or sp, yo, draw through all 6 lps on hook.

Rose

Rnd 1: With peach, ch 8, join to form a ring, ch 1, 16 sc in ring, join in beg sc. (16 sc)

Rnd 2: Ch 5 (counts as first dc, ch-2), sk next st, [dc in next st, ch 2, sk next st] rep around, join in 3rd ch of beg ch-5. (8 ch-2 sps)

Rnd 3: Sl st in first sp, ch 1, [sc, hdc, dc, hdc, sc] in each sp around, join in beg sc. (8 petals)

Rnd 4: Working behind petals of last rnd, sl st around post of each of next 2 sts, ch 1, sc around post of same st as last sl st, ch 3, [sc around post of center dc of next petal, ch 3] rep around, join in beg sc. (8 ch-3 sps)

Rnd 5: Sl st in first sp, ch 1, [sc, hdc, 3 dc, hdc, sc] in each sp around, join in beg sc. (8 petals)

Rnd 6: Working behind petals of last rnd, sl st around post of each of next 3 sts, ch 1, sc around post of same st as last sl st, ch 5, [sc around post of center dc of next petal, ch 5] rep around, join in beg sc. (8 ch-5 sps)

Rnd 7: Sl st in first sp, ch 1, [sc, hdc, 5 dc, hdc, sc] in each sp around, join in beg sc.

Rnd 8: Working behind petals of last rnd, sl st around post of each of next 4 sts, ch 1, sc around post of same st as last sl st, ch 7, [sc around post of center dc of next petal, ch 7] rep around, join in beg sc. (8 ch-7 sps)

Rnd 9: Sl st in first sp, ch 1, [sc, hdc, 7 dc, hdc, sc] in each sp around, join in beg sc, fasten off. (8 petals)

Leaf (make 3)

Row 1: With jade green, ch 17, sc in 3rd ch from hook and in each of next 13 chs, 3 sc in last ch; working in rem lps across opposite side of foundation ch, sc in each of next 15 sts, ch 1, turn.

Row 2: Sk first st, sc in each of next 15 sts, 3 sc in next st, sc in each of next 12 sts, ch 1, turn.

Row 3: Working in back lps only this row, sk first st, sc in each of next 12 sts, 3 sc in next st, sc in each of next 13 sc, ch 1, turn.

Row 4: Sk first st, sc in each of next 13 sts, 3 sc in next st, sc in each of next 10 sts, ch 1, turn.

Row 5: Working in back lps only this row, sk first st, sc in each of next 10 sts, 3 sc in next st, sc in each of next 11 sts, ch 1, turn.

Row 6: Sk first st, sc in each of next 11 sts, 3 sc in next st, sc in each of next 8 sts, ch 1, turn.

Row 7: Working in back lps only this row, sk first st, sc in each of next 8 sts, 3 sc in next st, sc in each of next 9 sts, fasten off.

Mesh Square (make 2)

Row 1 (RS): With cream, ch 35, dc in 4th ch from hook, dc in next ch, [ch 3, sk 3 chs, dc in each of next 3 chs] rep across, turn. (18 dc, counting last 3 chs of foundation ch as first dc; 5 ch-3 sps)

Row 2: Ch 5 (counts as first dc, ch-2), 3 dc in next sp, [ch 3, 3 dc in next sp] 4 times, ch 2, dc in 3rd ch of turning ch-3, turn.

Row 3: Ch 3 (counts as first dc throughout), 2 dc in next sp, ch 3, [3 dc in next sp, ch 3] 4 times, 3 dc in last sp, turn.

Rows 4–11: Rep Rows 2 and 3 alternately; at end of Row 11, do not turn; do not fasten off.

Rnd 12: Ch 3, 2 dc in last st of last row, *ch 3, working over end sps of rows, [3 dc in next sp, ch 3] 5 times *, shell in first rem lp of foundation ch, **ch 3, [3 dc in next sp, ch 3] 5 times **, shell in last rem lp of foundation ch, rep from * to *, shell in top of first dc of last row, rep from ** to **, [3 dc, ch 3] in same st as beg ch-3, join in 3rd ch of beg ch-3, fasten off.

Sew leaves and flowers to 1 mesh square, referring to photo.

Lining

With RS tog, sew 2 pieces of ivory satin tog with a ¼" seam, leaving a 2" opening on 1 side. Trim corners and turn RS out. Press. Fill lining with potpourri and sew opening shut.

Joining Mesh Squares

With WS of mesh squares tog, working through both thicknesses at once, attach cream with a sl st in any corner sp, ch 3, [2 dc, p, 3 dc, p, 2 dc] in same sp, *sc in center dc of next 3-dc group, [p shell in next sp, sc in center dc of next 3-dc group] rep across to corner sp **, dbl p shell in corner sp, rep from * around until 3 sides have been joined, ending last rep at **, slip lining between mesh squares, continue across last side as established, join in 3rd ch of beg ch-3, fasten off. ♥

Tresses Trio

Continued from page 148

made); working in rem lps across opposite side, ch 3, sc in 2nd ch from hook, dc in next ch, sl st in rem lp of ch at base of dc on 25th point, [ch 3, sc in 2nd ch from hook, dc in next ch, sl st in rem lp of ch at base of dc on next point] rep across, fasten off.

Finishing

With sewing needle and white thread, sew 1 pearl at center of each flower. Sew 6 pearls around center pearl on each flower over ch-1 sps of Rnd 1. Glue edging around edge of barrette plate. Glue flowers evenly sp across top of barrette plate. Glue barrette back to back of barrette plate. ♥

Rose Garden Accessories

Design by Sandra Abbate

Pretty pastels nestled among her curly locks are sure to delight a young girl. Crochet the barrette and matching button covers for a lovely matching ensemble.

Let's Begin!

Experience Level: Intermediate

Finished Measurements: Barrette: 1¾" x 3¾"

Button Cover: 1½" in diameter

Materials

- Crochet cotton size 10: small amount each pink (A), lavender (B), yellow (C), blue (D) and green (E)
- Size 8 steel crochet hook or size needed to obtain gauge
- 2½"-long barrette back
- 3 (¾") covered button backs
- 6 (⅛") pearls
- Craft glue
- Tapestry needle

Gauge: Rose = 1¼" in diameter

To save time, take time to check gauge.

Pattern Note

Join rnds with a sl st unless otherwise stated.

Rose

Note: Make 2 each A, B and C.

Rnd 1: Ch 4, join to form a ring, ch 1, [sc in ring, ch 4] 5 times, join in beg sc. (5 ch-4 sps)

Rnd 2 (WS): [Sc, hdc, 3 dc, hdc, sc] in each ch-4 sp around, do not join. (5 petals)

Rnd 3: Working in front of petals of last rnd, sc around post of first unworked sc of Rnd 1, ch 5, [sc around post of next unworked sc of Rnd 1, ch 5] rep around, join in beg sc. (5 ch-5 sps)

Rnd 4: [Sc, hdc, 5 dc, hdc, sc] in each ch-5 sp around, join in beg sc, fasten off.

Leaf Cluster (make 6)

With E, ch 14, *sc in 2nd ch from hook, hdc in next ch, dc in next ch, tr in each of next 3 chs, dc in next ch, hdc in next ch, sc in next ch, sl st in next ch *, [ch 11, rep from * to *] twice, sl st in each of last 3 chs of ch-14, fasten off.

Forget-Me-Not (make 6)

Rnd 1: With D, ch 4, join to form a ring, ch 1, [sc in ring, ch 3] 6

Continued on page 165

Pineapple Rose Doily

Design by Sandra Abbate

Accent a tiny shelf or small area of a desk or table with this uniquely shaped doily. Combine the popular pineapple design with a favorite flower—the rose—to add a special decorative touch in your home.

Let's Begin!

Experience Level: Intermediate

Finished Measurements: 5½" x 8"

Materials

- Crochet cotton size 10: small amount each white (MC) and yellow (CC)
- Size 8 steel crochet hook or size needed to obtain gauge

Gauge: Rose = 1¾" in diameter
To save time, take time to check gauge.

Pattern Note

Join rnds with a sl st unless otherwise stated.

Pattern Stitches

P: Ch 3, sl st in 3rd ch from hook.

Shell: [2 dc, ch 3, 2 dc] in indicated sp or st.

Beg shell: [Ch 3, dc, ch 3, 2 dc] in indicated sp or st.

Rose (make 2)

Rnd 1: With CC, ch 4, join to form a ring, ch 1, [sc in ring, ch

5] 6 times, join in beg sc. (6 ch-5 sps)

Rnd 2: [Sc, hdc, 5 dc, hdc, sc] in each ch-5 sp around, do not join.

Rnd 3: Working behind petals, sc in first unworked sc of rnd before last, ch 7, [sc in next unworked sc of rnd before last, ch 7] rep around, join in beg sc. (6 ch-7 sps)

Rnd 4: [Sc, hdc, 7 dc, hdc, sc] in each ch-7 sp around, do not join.

Rnd 5: Rep Rnd 3, fasten off.

First Pineapple

Row 1 (RS): With MC, ch 4, 9 dc in 4th ch from hook, turn. (10 dc, counting last 3 chs of ch-4 as first dc)

Row 2: Ch 5 (counts as first tr, ch-1), tr in next dc, [ch 1, tr in next st] rep across, turn. (10 tr, 9 ch-1 sps)

Row 3: Sl st in first ch-1 sp, ch 1, sc in same sp, [ch 5, sc in next sp] 7 times, ch 2, dc in last sp to form last ch-5 sp, turn. (8 ch-5 sps)

Rows 4–8: Ch 1, sc in sp just formed, [ch 5, sc in next sp] rep across to next-to-last sp, ch 2, dc in last sp to form last ch-5 sp, turn. (3 ch-5 sps at end of Row 8)

Row 9: Ch 1, sc in sp just formed, ch 5, sc in next sp, ch 2, dc in last sp, turn. (2 ch-5 sps)

Row 10: Ch 1, sc in sp just formed, ch 2, dc in next sp, fasten off.

Second Pineapple

Row 1: With RS facing, attach MC with a sl st in rem lp of first ch of ch-4 on Row 1 of first pineapple, ch 3 (counts as first dc), 9 dc in same st, turn.

Rows 2–10: Rep Rows 2–10 of first pineapple; do not fasten off at end of Row 10; turn.

Border

Rnd 1: Beg shell in sp just formed, *[shell over end sp of next row] 6 times, 2 dc over end sp of next row, ch 1, sl st in any ch-7 sp on Rnd 5 of rose, ch 1, 2 dc in same end sp as last 2 dc made, 2 dc over end st of next row, ch 1, sl st in next ch-7 sp of rose, ch 1, 2 dc over same end st as last 2 dc made, 2 dc over end st of Row 2 on next pineapple, ch 1, sl st in same ch-7 sp on rose, ch 1, 2 dc over same end st as last 2 dc made, 2 dc over end sp of next row, ch 1, sl st in next ch-7 sp on rose, ch 1, 2 dc in same end sp as last 2 dc made, [shell over end sp of next row] 6 times *, shell in sp at tip of first pineapple, rep from * to *, joining rem rose; join in 3rd ch of beg ch-3.

Rnd 2: Sl st in next dc and in ch-3 sp, ch 3 (counts as first dc), [dc, ch 5, 2 dc] in same sp, *[shell in next shell sp] 6 times, [2 shells in next ch-7 sp on rose] 3 times, [shell in next unworked shell sp] 6 times *, [2 dc, ch 5, 2 dc] in next shell sp, rep from * to *, join in 3rd ch of beg ch-3.

Rnd 3: Sl st in next dc and in ch-5 sp, ch 1, [sc, ch 3, p, ch 3, sc] in same sp, *[ch 3, p, ch 3, sc in next shell sp] 18 times, ch 3, p, ch 3 *, [sc, ch 3, p, ch 3, sc] in next ch-5 sp, rep from * to *, join in beg sc, fasten off. ♥

Stocking Stuffer

Looking for a new way to present your holiday jams, jellies and preserves? Crochet a Christmas stocking and slip the jar of jam or jelly into the stocking. The happy recipient will enjoy the stocking long after the edible good is gone!

Joining Motifs

Some tablecloth and/or bedspread patterns are notorious for using difficult or next-to-impossible directions for joining motifs. If you want your work to lie flat, put all four corners together with a slip stitch. Use a single crochet if you want a decorative joining that will stand up.

December Birthdays

Does your little girl have a December birthday? For favors for her party, crochet tiny Christmas stockings and fill each with a crocheted 11½" fashion doll outfit, a candy cane and hair barrettes. Her little guests will be delighted.

Newlywed Ornaments

So many newlyweds don't have many Christmas ornaments at first. If you're a grandma (or grandpa), crochet all of your grandchildren some Christmas decorations each year. By the time they are married, they'll have a set of ornaments that will be nice reminders of happy memories of Christmases past.

Delightful Gifts

When sending a Christmas card to a friend, enclose a small crocheted item as a special gift. Small doilies, bookmarks, coasters and ornaments (such as a hanging candy cane) make inexpensive and delightful gifts that may be used year after year.

Chain of Daisies Chest

Design by Maggie Petsch Chasalow

Add the charm of a filigree chain adorned with sparkling daisies and soft pearls to create a special hope chest from a simple wooden box. What an appropriate place to store love letters and precious items!

Let's Begin!

Experience Level: Intermediate

Finished Measurements: 4¼" x 5¾"

Materials

- Crochet cotton size 10: small amount each yellow (A) and dark green (B)
- Crochet cotton size 20: small amount each white (C) and yellow (D)
- Kreinik Blending Filament (55 yds per spool): 1 spool each pearl #032-BF (BFA), yellow #091-BF (BFB) and green #008-BF (BFC)
- Size 9 steel crochet hook or size needed to obtain gauge
- Size 7 steel crochet hook
- ½"-wide hairpin frame
- 4¼" x 5¾" green box
- 16 (2.5mm) white pearls
- 12 (3mm) white pearls
- Sewing needle and white sewing thread
- White craft glue

Gauge: Daisy =1½" in diameter with size 20 thread and smaller hook

To save time, take time to check gauge.

Pattern Note

Join rnds with a sl st unless otherwise stated.

Daisy

Rnd 1: With D and 1 strand BFB held tog, using smaller hook, ch 2, 6 sc in 2nd ch from hook, do not join. (6 sc)

Rnd 2: 2 sc in each sc around, join in beg sc, fasten off. (12 sc)

Rnd 3: With smaller hook, join C and 1 strand BFA held tog with a sl st in front lp only of any Rnd 2 sc; working in front lps only this rnd, [ch 7, sc in 2nd ch from hook, dc in each of next 5 chs, sk next sc on Rnd 2, sl st in next sc] 6 times. (6 petals)

Rnd 4: Ch 1, sl st in back lp only of next unworked sc on Rnd 2; working in back lps only this rnd, [ch 7, sc in 2nd ch from hook, dc in each of next 5 chs, sk next sc on Rnd 2, sl st in next unworked sc] 6 times, fasten off. (6 petals)

First Leaf

Rnd 1: With B and BFC, using larger hook, ch 8, sc in 2nd ch from hook *, dc in next ch, tr in next ch, 2 tr in next ch, tr in next ch, dc in next ch *, 3 sc in last ch; working in rem lps across opposite side of foundation ch, rep from * to *, 2 sc in same ch as beg sc, do not join, do not fasten off.

Stem

Ch 9, sl st in 2nd ch from hook and in each rem ch across, sl st in beg sc on Rnd 1 of first leaf, fasten off.

Second leaf

Rnd 1: With B and BFC, using larger hook, ch 6, sc in 2nd ch from hook *, dc in next ch, 2 tr in next ch, dc in next ch *, 3 sc in last ch; working in rem lps across opposite side of foundation ch, rep from * to *, 2 sc in same ch as beg sc, do not join, do not fasten off.

Stem

Ch 4, sl st in right-hand side of first stem, approximately ⅜" from bottom of stem, sl st in each of last 4 chs, sl st in beg sc on Rnd 1 of 2nd leaf, fasten off.

Corner Flower (make 4)

Rnd 1: With A and 1 strand BFB held tog, using larger hook, ch 2, 8 sc in 2nd ch from hook, join in front lp only of beg sc. (8 sc)

Rnd 2: Working in front lps only this rnd, [ch 3, sl st in next sc] 8 times, fasten off. (8 petals)

Continued on page 166

Circles Chatelaine

Design by Shirley Patterson

Mimic crocheters from generations ago and equip yourself with this pretty and practical sewing tool. The chatelaine made from circles will give you a decorative way to keep your scissors and pins close at hand.

Let's Begin!

Experience Level: Intermediate

Finished Measurements: Approximately 2⅝" wide x 50" long not including scissors

Materials

- Crochet cotton size 10: small amounts assorted colors
- Size 5 steel crochet hook or size needed to obtain gauge
- ¼" bead
- 14" ⅜"-wide satin ribbon
- Pair of scissors
- Tapestry needle
- Polyester fiberfill

Gauge: Circle = 1¼" in diameter

To save time, take time to check gauge.

Pattern Note

Join rnds with a sl st unless otherwise stated.

Pattern Stitches

X-st: Sk next unworked st, dc in next st, dc in sk st.

P: Ch 3, sl st in 3rd ch from hook.

Strap

Circle

Note: Make 24 in assorted colors.

Rnd 1 (RS): Ch 8, join to form a ring, ch 3 (counts as first dc), 23 dc in ring, join in 3rd ch of beg ch-3. (24 dc)

Rnd 2: Ch 1, sc in same st as joining, sc in each rem dc around, join in beg sc, fasten off. (24 sc)

Joining circles

Rnd 1: Beg at pincushion end of chatelaine, with desired color, ch 7; with RS facing, sl st in each of 4 sc on any circle, [ch 10, sl st in each of 4 sc on next circle] 23 times, ch 16, sk next 8 sc on same circle on which last 4 sl sts were worked, sl st in each of next 4 sc on same circle, [ch 10, sk next 8 unworked sc on next circle, sl st in each of next 4 sc] 23 times, ch 15, join in first ch of beg ch-7; do not fasten off.

Edging

Rnd 2: Ch 1, 2 sc in same st as joining, sc in each of next 6 chs, *sc in each of next 4 sl sts, [sc in each of next 10 chs, sc in each of next 4 sl sts] 23 times *, sc in each of next 3 chs, 3 sc in next ch, sc in each of next 8 chs, 3 sc in next ch, sc in each of next 3 chs, rep from * to *, sc in each of next 6 chs, 3 sc in next ch, sc in each of next 8 chs, sc in same ch as beg sc, join in beg sc.

Rnd 3: Ch 3 (counts as first dc), 2 dc in same st as joining, *[X-st over next 2 sts] rep across to next 3-sc group **, 3 dc in center sc of 3-sc group, rep from * around, ending last rep at **, join in 3rd ch of beg ch-3, fasten off.

Rnd 4: With RS facing, attach next color with a sl st in center dc of any 3-dc group, ch 1, beg in same st, *3 sc in center dc of 3-dc group, sc in each st across to center dc of next 3-dc group, rep from * around, join in beg sc, fasten off.

Rnd 5: With RS facing, attach next color with a sl st in center sc of any 3-sc group, ch 1, 3 sc in same st, sc in next st, p, [sc in each of next 4 sts, p] rep around, working 3 sc in center sc of each 3-sc group, join in beg sc, fasten off.

Scissors Holders

Circle (make 4)

Rnds 1 & 2: Rep Rnds 1 and 2 of circles for strap.

Rnd 3: With RS facing, attach next color in any sc of Rnd 2, ch 1, sc in same st and in each rem st around, join in beg sc, fasten off.

Rnd 4: With RS facing, attach next color in any sc of Rnd 3, ch 1, sc in same st, sc in each of next 2 sts, p, [sc in each of next 3 sts, p] rep around, join in beg sc, fasten off, leaving 24" length for finishing on any 2 circles.

Joining scissors to scissors holders

Holding 2 circles, 1 with 24" length for finishing and 1 without, tog with 1 corner of scissors end of chatelaine between, sew 9 sts of last rnd of circles tog with tapestry needle, slip either handle of scissors between circles and sew opening tog. Rep for rem 2 circles and other handle of scissors.

Pincushion

Motif

Note: Do not join rnds unless otherwise stated; mark first st of each rnd with safety pin or other small marker.

Rnd 1 (RS): With any color, ch 2, 6 sc in 2nd ch from hook. (6 sc)

Rnd 2: 2 sc in each st around. (12 sc)

Rnd 3: [Sc in next st, 2 sc in next st] rep around, join in beg sc. (18 sc)

Rnd 4: *Ch 10, dc in 6th ch from hook, dc in sk ch immediately to the right of dc just made, [X-st over next 2 chs] twice, sk next 2 sc on Rnd 3, sl st in next st, rep from * around, join in rem lp of first ch of beg ch-10. (6 petals)

Rnd 5: Ch 1, sc in same st as joining, *sc in each of next 5 rem lps, 5 sc over sp at tip of petal, sc in each of next 6 dc **, sc in first rem lp at base of next petal, rep from * around, ending last rep at **, join in beg, fasten off.

Set aside.

Pincushion side (make 2)

Rnd 1 (RS): With any color, ch 4, 11 dc in 4th ch from hook, join in 4th ch of beg ch-4. (12 dc, counting last 3 chs of beg ch-4 as first dc)

Rnd 2: Ch 3 (counts as first dc throughout), dc in same st as joining, 2 dc in each rem dc around, join in 3rd ch of beg ch-3. (24 dc)

Rnd 3: Ch 3, 2 dc in next st, [dc in next st, 2 dc in next st] rep around, join in 3rd ch of beg ch-3. (36 dc)

Rnd 4: Ch 3, dc in next st, 2 dc in next st, [dc in each of next 2 sts, 2 dc in next st] rep around, join in 3rd ch of beg ch-3. (48 dc)

Rnd 5: Ch 3, dc in each of next 2 sts, 2 dc in next st, [dc in each of next 3 sts, 2 dc in next st] rep around, join in 3rd ch of beg ch-3, fasten off. (60 dc)

Assembly

Rnd 6: Holding both pieces of pincushion with WS tog and working through both thicknesses at once, attach next color with a sl st in any dc of Rnd 5, ch 1, sc in same st and in each of next 8 sts, place pincushion motif with RS up on top of pincushion, working through 3 thicknesses, 3 sc in center sc of 5-sc group at tip of any petal on motif and in next st on pincushion at the same time, [sc in each of next 9 sts of pincushion, sc in center sc of 5-sc group at tip of next petal and in next st on pincushion at the same time] rep around, stuffing pincushion with polyester fiberfill just before closing, fasten off.

Rnd 7: Attach next color with a sl st in any sc of Rnd 6, ch 1, beg in same st, [sc in each of next 4 sts, p] rep around, join in beg sc, fasten off.

With tapestry needle, tack pincushion to center and each corner of opposite end of strap from scissors, placing any petal of pincushion motif at center of strap edge.

Finishing

Sew bead to center of pincushion motif. Tie ribbon into bow. Tack on petal of pincushion motif at center of strap edge. ♥

Double-Tiered Star Scrunchies

Designs by Shirley Guess

Sport a scrunchie on your ponytail to add some fun to your accessories on casual-dress days at the office. Make several in a variety of colors using both sizes to go with a variety of outfits!

Let's Begin!

Experience Level: Intermediate

Gauge: Work evenly and consistently

Pattern Note

Join rnds with a sl st unless otherwise stated.

Mini Scrunchie

Finished Measurement

Approximately 4" in diameter

Materials

- Crochet cotton size 10: 20 yds MC and 8 yds CC
- Size 6 steel crochet hook
- Adult-size ponytail holder

Scrunchie

Rnd 1: Attach MC with a sl st to ponytail holder, ch 2 (counts as first hdc), work 83 more hdc evenly sp around ponytail holder, join in 2nd ch of beg ch-2. (84 hdc)

Rnd 2: Ch 1, sc in same st as joining, *ch 1, sk next 2 sts, [{tr, ch 2} 3 times, tr] in next st, ch 1, sk next 2 sts **, sc in next st, rep from * around, ending last rep at **, join in beg sc.

Rnd 3: Ch 1, sc in same st as joining, *ch 3, sc in next ch-2 sp, ch 3, [sc, ch 3, sc] in next ch-2 sp, ch 3, sc in next ch-2 sp, ch 3 **, sc in next sc, rep from * around, ending last rep at **, join in beg sc.

Rnd 4: Working behind last 2 rnds, *ch 6, sk next 2 tr of Rnd 2, sl st in next ch-2 sp of Rnd 2 between 2 sc of Rnd 3, ch 6, sk next 2 tr of Rnd 2 **, sl st around post of next sc of Rnd 3, rep from * around, ending last rep at **, join in joining st of last rnd, fasten off. (28 ch-6 sps)

Rnd 5: Attach CC with a sl st in any ch-6 sp, ch 5 (counts as first hdc, ch-3), [{hdc, ch 3} 3 times, hdc] in same sp, [{hdc, ch 3} 4 times, hdc] in each rem sp around, join in 2nd ch of beg ch-5, fasten off.

Continued on page 166

Gauge: Rnds 1–4 = ⅜"(¾")(1¼") in diameter
To save time, take time to check gauge

Pattern Notes

Join rnds with a sl st unless otherwise stated.

Directions are given for size small; directions for sizes medium and large follow in parentheses. When only 1 set of directions is given, it applies to all sizes.

Pattern Stitches

Shell: [3 dc, ch 2, 3 dc] in indicated sp or st.
Beg shell: [Ch 3, 2 dc, ch 2, 3 dc] in indicated sp or st.

Crib Afghan

Rnd 1: With A, ch 4, join to form a ring, ch 6 (counts as first dc, ch-3), [dc in ring, ch 3] 3 times, join in 3rd ch of beg ch-6. (4 ch-3 sps)
Rnd 2: [Sc, 3 dc, sc] in each ch-3 sp around, do not join. (4 petals)
Rnd 3: Working behind petals of last rnd, sc in 3rd ch of beg ch-6 on Rnd 1, ch 3, sc at base of center dc of first petal, ch 3, [sc in next unworked dc of Rnd 1, ch 3, sc at base of center dc of next petal, ch 3] rep around, join in beg sc, fasten off. (8 ch-3 sps)
Rnd 4: Attach MC(B)(MC) with a sl st in any ch-3 sp, ch 1, beg in same sp, [sc, 4 dc, sc] in each sp around, do not join. (8 petals)
Rnd 5: Working behind petals of last rnd, sc in first unworked sc of Rnd 3, ch 4, [sc in next unworked sc of Rnd 3, ch 4] rep around, join in beg sc, fasten off. (8 ch-4 sps)
Rnd 6: Attach B(C)(B) with a sl st in any ch-4 sp, ch 1, sc in same sp, *ch 3, shell in next sp, ch 3 **, sc in next sp, rep from * around, ending last rep at **, join in beg sc, fasten off.
Rnd 7: Attach C(D)(C) with a sl st in any ch-2 shell sp, ch 1, beg in same sp, [sc in shell sp, ch 3, shell in next sc, ch 3] rep around, join in beg sc, fasten off.
Rnd 8: Attach MC with a sl st in any shell sp, ch 1, beg in same sp, *[sc, ch 3, sc] in shell sp, ch 3, sc between 2nd and 3rd dc of same shell, [3 dc, sc] in next sp, 3 dc in next sc, [sc, 3 dc] in next sp, sc between first and 2nd dc of next shell, ch 3, rep from * around, join in beg sc.
Rnd 9: Sl st in first ch-3 sp, beg shell in same sp, *ch 3, sc in next ch-3 sp, 3 dc in next sc, [sc in center dc of next 3-dc group, 3 dc in next sc] 3 times, sc in next ch-3 sp, ch 3 **, shell in corner ch-3 sp, rep from *around, ending last rep at **, join in 3rd ch of beg ch-3.
Rnd 10: Sl st in each of next 2 dc and in corner sp, beg shell in same sp, *ch 3, sc between 2nd and 3rd dc of same shell, 3 dc in next sc, [sc in center dc of next 3-dc group, 3 dc in next sc] 4 times, sc between first and 2nd dc of next shell, ch 3 **, shell in corner sp, rep from * around, ending last rep at **, join in 3rd ch of beg ch-3, do not fasten off.

First End

Row 1: Sl st in each of next 2 dc and in corner sp, *ch 3 (counts as first dc throughout), 3 dc in same sp, 3 dc in next ch-3 sp, [3 dc in center dc of next 3-dc group] 5 times, 3 dc in next ch-3 sp, 4 dc in corner sp, turn. (29 dc)
Row 2: Ch 6 (counts as first dc, ch-3 throughout), 3 dc between first 4-dc group and next 3-dc group, [3 dc between next 2 3-dc groups] 6 times, 3 dc between next 3-dc group and last 4-dc group, ch 3, dc in 3rd ch of turning ch-3, turn.
Row 3: Sl st in ch-3 sp, ch 3, 3 dc in same sp, [3 dc between next 2 3-dc groups] 7 times, 4 dc in turning ch-6 sp, turn. (29 dc)
Row 4: Rep Row 2, do not turn; fasten off.

Second End

Row 1: With RS facing, attach MC with a sl st in corner sp of Rnd 10 at right-hand corner on opposite end, beg at *, rep Row 1 of first end.
Rows 2 & 3: Rep Rows 2 and 3 of first end.
Row 4: Ch 6, 3 dc between first 4-dc group and next 3-dc group, [3 dc between next 2 3-dc groups] 6 times, 3 dc between next 3-dc group and last 4-dc group, ch 6, sl st in 3rd ch of turning ch 3, turn.
Rnd 11: Sl st in ch-6 sp, beg shell in same sp, *ch 3, [sc in first dc of next 3-dc group, 3 dc in next dc of same group] 8 times, [sc, ch 3, shell] in corner sp, ch 3; working across long edge, [sc, 3 dc] over end st of Row 2, [sc, 3 dc] over end st of Row 1, sc in next dc of corner shell on Rnd 10, 3 dc in next dc of same shell, sc in next ch-3 sp, [3 dc in next sc, sc in center dc of next 3-dc group] 5 times, 3 dc in next sc, sc in next sp, 3 dc in 2nd dc of next shell, sc in next dc of same shell, [{3 dc, sc} over end st of next row] twice, ch 3 **, shell in corner sp of Row 4, rep from * around, ending last rep at **, join in 3rd ch of beg ch-3.
Rnd 12: Sl st in each of next 2 dc and in corner sp, ch 1, beg in same sp, *[sc, ch 3, sc] in corner sp, ch 3, sc between 2nd and 3rd dc of same shell, [3 dc in next sc, sc in center dc of next 3-dc group] rep across to last 3-dc group before corner shell, 3 dc in next sc, sc between first and 2nd dc of corner shell, ch 3, rep from * around, join in beg sc. (9 3-dc groups between shells on short edges; 13 3-dc groups between shells on long edges)
Rnd 13: Sl st in corner ch-3 sp, beg shell in same sp, *ch 3, sc in next ch-3 sp, [3 dc in next sc, sc in center dc of next 3-dc group] rep across to last 3-dc group before corner shell, 3 dc in next sc, sc in next ch-3 sp, ch 3 **, shell in corner sp, rep from * around, ending last rep at **, join

in 3rd ch of beg ch-3. (10 3-dc groups between shells on short edges; 14 3-dc groups between shells on long edges)

Rnd 14: Rep Rnd 12. (11 3-dc groups between shells on short edges; 15 3-dc groups between shells on long edges)

Rnd 15: Sl st in corner sp, ch 5 (counts as first tr, ch-1), [{tr, ch 1} twice, tr] in same sp, *ch 1, tr in next ch-3 sp, ch 1, tr in next sc, [ch 1, tr in center dc of next 3-dc group, ch 1, tr in next sc] rep across to next corner, ch 1, tr in first of 3 corner ch-3 sps, ch 1 **, [{tr, ch 1} 3 times, tr] in next corner sp, rep from * around, ending last rep at **, join in 4th ch of beg ch-5.

Rnd 16: Sl st in next sp, ch 1, sc in same sp, *ch 3, shell in center sp, ch 3, sc in next sp, sk next sp, [{dc, ch 1} 4 times, dc] in next sp, *sk next sp, sc in next sp, sk next sp, [{dc, ch 1} 4 times, dc] in next sp, rep from * 5 times, sc in next sp, ch 3, shell in corner sp, ch 3, sc in next sp, sk next sp, [{dc, ch 1} 4 times, dc] in next sp, **sk next sp, sc in next sp, sk next sp, [{dc, ch 1] 4 times, dc] in next sp, rep from ** 7 times †, sc in next sp, rep from * around, ending last rep at †, join in beg sc.

Rnd 17: Sl st in each of next 3 chs, in each of next 3 dc and in corner sp, [sc, ch 3, sc] in same sp, *ch 3, sc between 2nd and 3rd dc of same shell, ch 3, sc in next ch-3 sp, [ch 3, sc in next ch-1 sp] rep across to next corner, ch 3, sc in ch-3 sp, ch 3, sc between first and 2nd dc of corner shell, ch 3 **, [sc, ch 3, sc] in shell sp, rep from * around, ending last rep at **, join in beg sc.

Rnd 18: Sl st in ch-3 sp, beg shell in same sp, *ch 3, sc in next sp, [sk next sp, {dc, ch 1} 5 times in next sp, sk next sp, sc in next sp] rep across to next corner, ch 3 **, shell in corner ch-3 sp, rep from * around, ending last rep at **, join in 3rd ch of beg ch-3.

Rnd 19: Sl st between same st in which joining st was made and next dc, ch 1, sc in same sp, *ch 3, [sc, ch 3, sc] in corner sp, ch 3, sc between 2nd and 3rd dc of same shell, ch 3, sc in next sp, ch 3, [{sc in next ch-1 sp, ch 3} 4 times, sk next ch-1 sp] rep across to next corner, sc in next ch-3 sp, ch 3 **, sc between first and 2nd dc of corner shell, rep from * around, ending last rep at **, join in beg sc, fasten off.

Finishing

Weave lengths of green satin ribbon through ch-1 sps of Rnd 15 on each side of crib afghan. Tie ends in bow at corners. Cut 1 (1½)" length of light pink ribbon for each corner, gather each length into 3 lps and sew 1 at each corner for roses. Cut a 1" length of dark pink ribbon for each corner; tack next to rose at each corner for rosebuds.

Pillow

Rnds 1–7: Rep Rnds 1–7 of Crib Afghan.

Rnd 8: With RS facing, attach MC with a sl st in any shell sp, ch 1, beg in same sp, *[sc, ch 3, sc] in shell sp, *ch 3, sc between 2nd and 3rd dc of same shell, [3 dc, sc, 3 dc] in next sp, sc in next sc, [3 dc, sc, 3 dc] in next sp, sc between first and 2nd dc of next shell, ch 3, [sc, ch 3, sc] in corner sp, ch 3, sc between 2nd and 3rd dc of same shell, [3 dc, sc] in next sp, 3 dc in next sc, [sc, 3 dc] in next sp, sc between first and 2nd dc of next shell, ch 3, rep from * around, join in beg sc.

Rnd 9: Sl st in corner ch-3 sp, beg shell in same sp, *ch 3, sc in next ch-3 sp, 3 dc in next sc, [sc in center dc of next 3-dc group, 3 dc in next sc] rep across to next corner, sc in next ch-3 sp, ch 3 **, shell in corner ch-3 sp, rep from * around, ending last rep at **, join in 3rd ch of beg ch-3. (5 3-dc groups across 2 sides; 4 3-dc groups across 2 opposite sides)

Rnd 10: Sl st in next dc, ch 5 (counts as first tr, ch-1), *[tr, ch 1] 4 times in corner sp, sk next dc, [tr, ch 1] in next dc, [tr, ch 1] in next ch-3 sp, [tr, ch 1] in next sc, [{tr, ch 1} in center dc of next 3-dc group, {tr, ch 1} in next sc] rep across to next corner, [tr, ch 1] in next ch-3 sp, sk next dc **, [tr, ch 1] in next dc, rep from * around, ending last rep at **, join in 4th ch of beg ch-5. (4 tr in each corner sp; 15 tr on each of 2 sides; 13 tr on each of opposite 2 sides)

Rnd 11: Sl st in first ch-1 sp, [sc, ch 3] twice in same sp, *[sc, ch 3] 3 times in next sp, [sc, ch 3] 4 times in corner sp, [sc, ch 3] 3 times in next sp, [sk next sp, {sc, ch 3} twice in next sp, sk next sp, {sc, ch 3} 3 times in next sp] 4 times, [sc, ch 3] 3 times in next sp, [sc, ch 3] 4 times in corner sp, [sc, ch 3] 3 times in next sp, [sk next sp, {sc, ch 3} twice in next sp, sk next sp, {sc, ch 3} 3 times in next sp] 3 times, sk next sp **, [sc, ch 3] twice in next sp, rep from * around, ending last rep at **, join in beg sc.

Rnds 12 & 13: Sl st in next ch-3 sp, ch 1, beg in same sp, [sc, ch 3] in each sp around, join in beg sc; at end of Rnd 13, fasten off.

Finishing

Rep finishing instructions for Crib Afghan, weaving satin ribbon through ch-1 sps of Rnd 10. Make pillow form with satin fabric and stuff with polyester fiberfill. Sew pillow top to pillow form.

Pansy Garden Doily

Design by Sandra Abbate

Add a splash of color to the base of a favorite bud vase with this enchanting doily. Not only will the flowers in the vase bring special oohs and aahs, but this creative, colorful doily will as well.

Let's Begin!

Experience Level: Intermediate

Finished Measurement: 5¾" in diameter

Materials

- Crochet cotton size 10: small amount each dark green (MC), yellow (A), dark blue (B), lavender (C), burgundy (D), turquoise (E), light blue (F), purple (G) and pink (H)
- Size 8 steel crochet hook or size needed to obtain gauge

Gauge: Rnds 1–3 of center = 1½" in diameter

To save time, take time to check gauge.

Pattern Note

Join rnds with a sl st unless otherwise stated.

Pattern Stitches

P: Ch 3, sl st in 3rd ch from hook.

Cl: Holding back on hook last lp of each st, 3 dc in indicated st or sp, yo, draw through all 4 lps on hook.

Beg cl: Ch 2; holding back on hook last lp of each st, 2 dc in same sp or st, yo, draw through all 3 lps on hook.

Pansies

Note: Make 1 each of A–H in alphabetical order.

First pansy

Rnd 1 (RS): Ch 4, join to form a ring, ch 1, [sc in ring, ch 7] twice, [sc in ring, ch 5] 3 times, join in beg sc.

Rnd 2: [Sc, hdc, dc, 7 tr, dc, hdc, sc] in each of first 2 ch-7 sps, [sc, hdc, 5 dc, hdc, sc] in each of next 3 ch-5 sps, join in beg sc. (2 large petals and 3 small petals)

Row 3: Ch 1, [sc in next st, {ch 3, sc in next st} 11 times] twice, sl st in next st, fasten off.

Second pansy

Rnds 1 & 2: Rep Rnds 1 and 2 of first pansy.

Row 3: *Ch 1, sc in next st, [ch 3, sc in next st] twice, ch 1, sl st in corresponding ch-3 sp on Rnd 3 of previous pansy, ch 1, sc in next st on working pansy *, continue across as for first pansy, fasten off.

Next 5 pansies

Rnds 1 & 2: Rep Rnds 1 and 2 of first pansy.

Row 3: Rep Row 3 of 2nd pansy.

Last pansy

Rnds 1 & 2: Rep Rnds 1 and 2 of first pansy.

Row 3: Rep Row 3 of 2nd pansy from * to *, [ch 3, sc in next st on working pansy] 8 times, sc in next st, [ch 3, sc in next st] 8 times, ch 1, sl st in corresponding ch-3 sp on first pansy, ch 1, sc in next st on working pansy, [ch 3, sc in next st on working pansy] twice, sl st in next st, fasten off.

Center

Rnd 1: With MC, ch 4, join to form a ring, [beg cl, ch 3, {cl, ch 3} 3 times] in ring, join in top of beg cl. (4 ch-3 sps)

Rnds 2 & 3: Sl st in first ch-3 sp, [beg cl, ch 3, cl, ch 3] in same sp, [cl, ch 3] twice in each sp around, join in top of beg cl. (16 ch-3 sps at end of Rnd 3)

Rnd 4: Sl st in first ch-3 sp, [beg cl, ch 3, cl, ch 3] in same sp, *sc in next ch-3 sp, ch 3**, [cl, ch 3] twice in next sp, rep from * around, ending last rep at **, join in top of beg cl.

Rnd 5: Sl st in first ch-3 sp, [beg cl, ch 3, cl, ch 3] in same sp, *[sc in next sp, ch 3] twice **, [cl, ch 3] twice in next sp, rep from * around, ending last rep at **, join in top of beg cl.

Rnd 6: Sl st in first ch-3 sp, [beg cl, ch 3, cl, ch 3] in same sp, *sk next sp, sc in next sp, ch 3, sk next sp **, [cl, ch 3] twice in next sp, rep from * around, ending last rep at **, join in top of beg cl.

Rnd 7: Rep Rnd 5.

Rnd 8: Sl st in first ch-3 sp, [beg cl, p, cl] in same sp, sl st in center dc of first small petal to the right on any pansy, *[ch 3, sc in next sp on center] twice, ch 1, sl st in center dc of next small petal on same pansy, ch 1, sc in same sp on center as last sc, ch 3, sc in next sp on center, ch 3, sl st in center dc of next small petal on same pansy **, [cl, p, cl] in next

sp on center, sl st in center dc of next small petal on next pansy, rep from * around, ending last rep at **, join in top of beg cl, fasten off. ❤

Rose Garden Accessories

Continued from page 151

times, join in beg sc, fasten off. With tapestry needle and C, work a French knot in the center of each forget-me-not.

Finishing

Glue 1 leaf cluster at each end of barrette and 1 in the center on either edge. Glue yellow rose at center of barrette and 1 pink rose and 1 lavender rose on opposite sides. Glue 1 forget-me-not on center leaf of each leaf cluster. Glue 1 pearl to center of each rose. Glue 1 leaf cluster to edge of each covered button back and 1 rose over center of each covered button back. Glue 1 forget-me-not to center leaf of each leaf cluster and 1 pearl to center of each rose. ❤

Gingerbread Swag

Design by Sandra Abbate

Hang this charming swag on your fireplace mantel or over a doorway to bring holiday cheer to your family and friends.

Let's Begin!

Experience Level
Intermediate

Finished Measurements
Approximately 31" long x 8" high

Materials
- Red Heart Super Saver worsted weight yarn (3 oz per skein): 1 skein each white #311, warm brown #336 and hot red #390
- Red Heart sport weight yarn (2½ oz per skein): small amount each white #1 and jockey red #904
- Size G/6 crochet hook or size needed to obtain gauge
- Size D/3 crochet hook
- 4 (7/16") black shank buttons
- 5 (7/16") white buttons
- 4 (½") red satin ribbon roses with leaves
- 2⅔ yds ⅜"-wide red satin ribbon
- 2 yds ⅜"-wide green satin ribbon
- Tapestry needle
- Craft glue or glue gun
- Polyester fiberfill
- ½" jingle bell
- Safety pin or other small marker

Gauge: 4 sts and 4 rows = 1" in sc with larger hook and worsted weight yarn

To save time, take time to check gauge.

Pattern Note
Join rnds with a sl st unless otherwise stated.

Pattern Stitches
V-st: [Dc, ch 2, dc] in indicated st or sp.
Beg V-st: [Ch 5, dc] in indicated st or sp.

Gingerbread Boy & Girl

Front & Back

Note: Make 1 front and 1 back each for gingerbread boy and gingerbread girl.

Head
Note: Do not join rnds unless otherwise stated; mark first st of each rnd with safety pin or other small marker.
Rnd 1: With larger hook and warm brown, ch 2, 6 sc in 2nd ch from hook. (6 sc)
Rnd 2: 2 sc in each st around. (12 sc)
Rnd 3: [Sc in next st, 2 sc in next st] rep around. (18 sc)
Rnd 4: [Sc in each of next 2 sts, 2 sc in next st] rep around. (24 sc)
Rnd 5: [Sc in each of next 3 sts, 2 sc in next st] rep around. (30 sc)

Neck
Row 6 (RS): Sc in each of next 5 sts, ch 1, turn. (5 sc)
Row 7: 2 sc in first st, sc in each of next 3 sts, 2 sc in last st, ch 7, turn. (7 sc)

Arms & torso
Row 8: Sc in 2nd ch from hook and in each of next 5 chs, sc in each of next 7 sc, ch 7, turn.
Row 9: Sc in 2nd ch from hook and in each of next 5 chs, sc in each rem sc across, ch 1, turn. (19 sc)
Row 10: Sc in each sc across, ch 1, turn. (19 sc)
Row 11: Sc in each of first 14 sc, leave rem sts unworked, ch 1, turn. (14 sc)
Row 12: Sc in each of first 9 sc, leave rem sts unworked, ch 1, turn. (9 sc)
Row 13: Rep Row 10. (9 sc)
Row 14: 2 sc in first st, sc in each of next 7 sts, 2 sc in last st, ch 1, turn. (11 sc)
Row 15: Rep Row 10. (11 sc)

First leg
Row 16: Sc in each of first 4 sts, ch 1, turn.
Rows 17–19: Rep Row 10. (4 sc)
Row 20: 2 sc in first st, sc in each of next 3 sts, ch 1, turn. (5 sc)
Row 21: Sc in each of first 4 sts, 2 sc in last st, ch 1, turn. (6 sc)
Row 22: Sc in each sc across, fasten off.

Second leg
Row 16: With RS facing, sk next 3 sts on Row 15, attach warm brown with a sl st in next st, ch 1, sc in same st, sc in each of next 3 sts, ch 1, turn.

Gold Glitter Stockings

Design by Colleen Sullivan

Crochet each member of the family his or her own mini stocking to be hung on the tree on Christmas Eve. Fill each with small gifts and goodies to be enjoyed on Christmas morning!

Let's Begin!

Experience Level: Intermediate

Finished Measurement: Approximately 6" long

Materials

- Caron Victorian Christmas Gold yarn (1¾ oz per skein): 1 skein lace #1902 (MC) and small amount balsam #1901 or cranberry #1900 (CC)
- Size H/8 crochet hook or size needed to obtain gauge
- 8" ¼"-wide gold metallic ribbon
- Tapestry needle

Gauge: 10 sts and 9 rows = 3" in sc

To save time, take time to check gauge.

Pattern Note

Join rnds with a sl st unless otherwise stated.

Pattern Stitches

Pattern St 1 (Worked on an even number of sts)

Rnd 1: [Sc in back lp of next st, sc in front lp of next st] rep around.

Rep Rnd 1 for pattern.

Pattern St 2 (Worked on an even number of sts)

Rnd 1: [Sc in back lp of next st, sc in front lp of next st] rep around.

Rnd 2: [Sc in front lp of next st, sc in back lp of next st] rep around.

Rep Rnds 1 and 2 alternately for pattern.

Stocking

Note: Do not join rnds unless otherwise indicated. Mark first st of each rnd with safety pin or other small marker.

Foundation row: Beg at top of stocking, with MC ch 20, taking care not to twist ch, join to form a ring, ch 1, sc in each ch around. (20 sc)

Rnds 1–9: Work in pattern st 1 or pattern st 2 as desired, ending with Rnd 1 for pattern st 2; at end of Rnd 9, join in beg sc, fasten off.

Heel Shaping

Row 1 (RS): Attach CC with a sl st in joining st of Rnd 9, ch 1, sc in same st and in each of next 9 sc, ch 1, turn. (10 sc)

Rows 2–5: Sk first sc, sc in each rem sc across to last 2 sc, sk next sc, sc in last sc, ch 1, turn. (2 sc at end of Row 5)

Row 6: 2 sc in each sc across, ch 1, turn. (4 sc)

Rows 7–9: 2 sc in first sc, sc in each sc across to last sc, 2 sc in last sc, ch 1, turn; at end of Row 9, do not ch 1; fasten off. (10 sc at end of Row 9)

Foot

Note: Do not join rnds unless otherwise indicated. Mark first st of each rnd with safety pin or other small marker.

Rnd 1: Attach MC with a sl st in first sc at right-hand edge of Row 9 of heel, ch 1, sc in same st and in each of next 9 heel sts, continue in pattern st 1 or pattern st 2 across next 10 unworked sts of Rnd 9 of stocking. (20 sc)

Rnds 2–5: Continue in pattern st 1 or pattern st 2 on 20 sts around; at end of Rnd 5, join in beg sc, fasten off.

Toe Shaping

Rnd 1: Attach CC with a sl st in joining st of Rnd 5 of foot, ch 1, sc in same st and in each of next 2 sts, sc dec, [sc in each of next 3 sts, sc dec] rep around, join in beg sc. (16 sts)

Rnd 2: Ch 1, sc in same st as joining and in next st, sc dec, [sc in each of next 2 sts, sc dec] rep around, join in beg sc. (12 sts)

Rnd 3: Ch 1, sc in same st as joining, sc dec, [sc in next st, sc dec] rep around, join in beg sc, fasten off, leaving long end for sewing. (8 sts)

Continued on page 188

Country Christmas Booties

Designs by Sharon Volkman

Capture old-fashioned country charm in this pair of little stockings. Those tiny bits of yarn you couldn't bear to toss can now be used as patches or stripes in these darling folk ornaments.

Let's Begin!

Experience Level: Intermediate

Finished Measurements: 4¼" wide x 4½" long

Materials

Striped Stocking

- Sport weight yarn: small amount each red, green and white
- 16" ¼"-wide green ribbon

Patchwork Stocking

- Sport weight yarn: small amount each red, green, white, blue and yellow
- ½" buttons: 2 white and 1 each yellow, blue, red and green
- Sewing needle and sewing thread

Both Projects

- Size G/6 crochet hook or size needed to obtain gauge
- Bobbins (optional)

Gauge: 9 sts and 10 rows = 2" in sc
To save time, take time to check gauge.

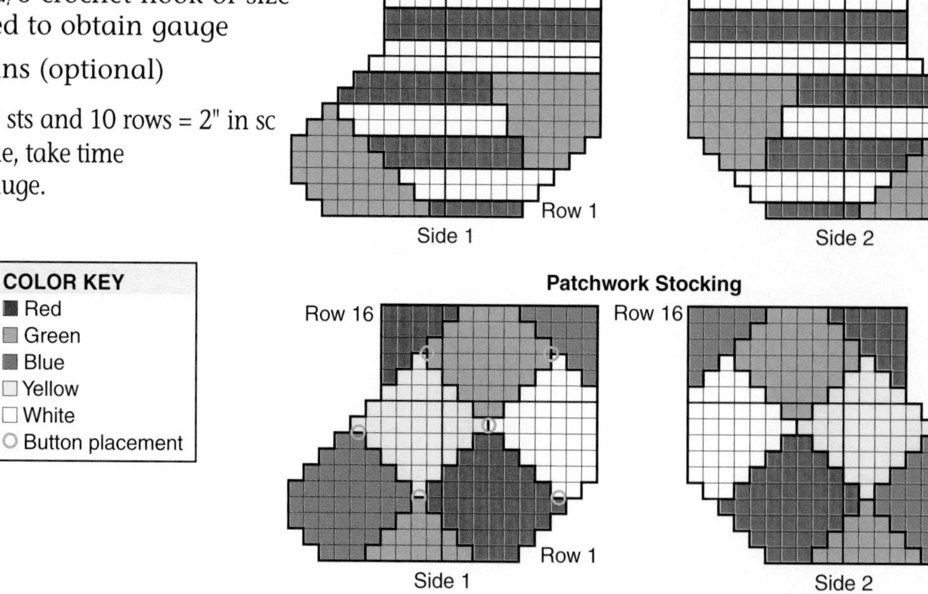

Pattern Notes

Join rnds with a sl st unless otherwise stated.

To change color in sc, work last st before color change as follows: Insert hook in next st, yo with working color, draw up a lp, drop working color to WS, yo with next color, complete sc.

When working from chart, read all odd-numbered (RS) rows from right to left, all even-numbered (WS) rows from left to right.

Do not carry color not in use across WS of work. Use bobbins or wind small balls of yarn for each separate color section.

Striped Stocking

First Side

Row 1 (RS): With green, ch 5, drop green to WS, yo with red, draw through lp on hook, ch 6 with red, 2 sc in 2nd ch from hook, sc in each of next 4 chs, changing to green in last sc; sc in each of next 5 chs with green, 2 sc in last ch, ch 1, turn. (6 red sc; 7 green sc)

Rows 2–16: Follow Striped Stocking chart for first side, changing colors and working sc incs and sc decs at begs and ends of rows as indicated; ch 1, turn at end of each row; at end of Row 16, do not fasten off; ch 1, turn.

Edging

2 sc in first st, sc in each st across to last st, 3 sc in last st; working in red over red-and-white striped sections and in green over green sections, sc over end st of each row and in each rem lp of foundation ch around, join in beg sc, fasten off.

Second Side

Row 1 (RS): With red, ch 4, drop red to WS, yo with green, draw through lp on hook, ch 7 with green, 2 sc in 2nd ch from hook, sc in each of next 5 chs, changing to red in last st; sc in each of next 4 chs with red, 2 sc in last st, ch 1, turn. (7 green sc; 6 red sc)

Rows 2–16: Follow Striped Stocking chart for 2nd side, changing colors and working sc incs and sc decs at begs and ends of rows as indicated; ch 1, turn at end of each row; at end of Row 16, do not fasten off; ch 1, turn.

Edging

Rep instructions for edging for first side.

With RS tog, using tapestry needle and matching yarn to sections being joined, sew first and 2nd sides tog. Turn stocking RS out.

Cuff

Rnd 1: With RS facing, attach white with a sl st at top back seam, ch 1, beg in same st, work 32 sc evenly sp around, join in beg sc.

Rnd 2: Ch 1, sc in same st as joining and in each rem st around, join in beg sc. (32 sc)

Rnd 3: Ch 3 (counts as first dc), dc in each rem st around, join in 3rd ch of beg ch-3. (32 dc)

Rnd 4: Ch 1, sc in same st as joining, *sk next st, 3 dc in next st, sk next st **, sc in next st, rep from * around, ending last rep at **, join in beg sc, ch 12 for hanging lp, sl st in joining st, fasten off.

Finishing

Beg at center on first side, weave ribbon through dcs of Rnd 3. Tie ends in bow.

Patchwork Stocking

First Side

Row 1: With red, ch 12, 2 sc in 2nd ch from hook, sc in next ch, changing to green; sc in each of next 7 chs, changing to blue in last sc; sc in next ch with blue, 2 sc in last ch, ch 1, turn. (13 sc)

Rows 2–16: Follow Patchwork Stocking chart for first side,

Continued on page 188

Potpourri Pillows

Designs by Sandra Abbate

Tuck a potpourri-filled pillow in a corner to give your home a pleasant scent throughout the holidays. The scent of cinnamon, cranberry or pine potpourri is sure to become your family's favorite!

Let's Begin!

Experience Level: Beginner

Finished Measurements
Star: Approximately 9" across widest point
Bell: Approximately 9¾" high x 8" wide
Tree: Approximately 8" high x 6" wide

Materials

- Red Heart Super Saver worsted weight yarn (8 oz per skein): 1 skein each cherry red #319 and jade #369 and small amount white #311
- Size F/5 crochet hook or size needed to obtain gauge
- ½ yd ¼"-wide white satin ribbon
- 1¾ yds ¼"-wide red satin ribbon
- Tapestry needle
- Polyester fiberfill
- Potpourri
- Craft glue

Gauge: 8 sts and 8 rows = 2" in sc
To save time, take time to check gauge.

Pattern Note
Join rnds with a sl st unless otherwise stated.

Star

Diamond Motif
Note: Make 6 cherry red and 6 jade.

First half
Row 1 (RS): Ch 9, sc in 2nd ch from hook and in each rem ch across, ch 1, turn. (8 sc)
Row 2: Sc dec, sc in each st across to last 2 sts, sc dec, ch 1, turn. (6 sts)
Row 3: Sc in each st across, ch 1, turn. (6 sc)
Rows 4 & 5: Rep Rows 2 and 3. (4 sc)
Row 6: [Sc dec] twice, ch 1, turn. (2 sts)
Row 7: Rep Row 3. (2 sc)
Row 8: Sc dec, ch 1, turn. (1 st)
Row 9: Sc in sc, fasten off. (1 sc)

Second half
Row 1: With RS facing, attach yarn with a sl st in first rem lp of foundation ch, ch 1, sc in same st and in each rem lp across, ch 1, turn. (8 sc)
Rows 2–9: Rep Rows 2–9 of first half, do not fasten off at end of Row 9, ch 1.

Border
Working over row ends, work 9 sc evenly sp to first point, 3 sc at

point, [work 9 sc evenly sp to next point, 3 sc at point] 3 times, join in beg sc, fasten off.

Finishing

First side

With tapestry needle, using photo as a guide and alternating 1 cherry red and 1 jade diamond, sew 6 diamonds tog to form a star.

Second side

Rep as for first side.

With RS tog, pairing cherry red points on 1 side with jade points on other side, sew first and 2nd sides tog, leaving opening for stuffing. Turn star RS out; fill points with polyester fiberfill and center with potpourri. Sew opening closed. Cut white ribbon in half and make 2 bows. Sew 1 bow to center of each side.

Bell

Side (make 2)

Row 1: Beg at bottom with cherry red, ch 22, 2 sc in 2nd ch from hook, sc in each rem ch across to last ch, 2 sc in last ch, ch 1, turn. (23 sc)

Row 2 (RS): 2 sc in first st, sc in each rem st across to last st, 2 sc in last st, ch 1, turn. (25 sc)

Rows 3–6: Rep Row 2. (33 sc at end of Row 6)

Row 7: Sc dec, sc in each rem st across to last 2 sts, sc dec, ch 1, turn. (31 sts)

Rows 8–10: Rep Row 7, fasten off at end of Row 10. (25 sts at end of Row 10)

Row 11: With WS facing, attach jade in first st, ch 1, sc in same st and in each rem st across, turn. (25 sc)

Row 12: Ch 4 (counts as first dc, ch-1), sk next sc, dc in next sc, [ch 1, sk next sc, dc in next sc] rep across, ch 1, turn. (12 ch-1 sps)

Row 13: Sc in each dc and in each ch-1 sp across with last sc in 3rd ch of beg ch-4, fasten off. (25 sc)

Row 14: With RS facing, attach cherry red with a sl st in first sc, ch 1, sc in same st and in each rem sc across, ch 1, turn. (25 sc)

Rows 15–24: Sc in each sc across, ch 1, turn.

Row 25: Rep Row 7. (23 sts)

Row 26: Sc in each sc across, ch 1, turn.

Rows 27–32: Rep Rows 25 and 26 alternately.

Rows 33–35: Rep Row 25. (11 sts at end of Row 35)

Row 36: Sc in each of first 2 sts, hdc in each of next 2 sts, dc in each of next 3 sts, hdc in each of next 2 sts, sc in each of last 2 sts, fasten off.

Clapper

Row 1: Working in rem lps of foundation ch, sk first 9 chs, attach jade with a sl st in next ch, ch 1, sc in same st, sc in each of next 4 sts, ch 1, turn. (5 sc)

Row 2: Sc dec, sc in next st, sc dec, ch 1, turn. (3 sts)

Row 3: Pick up lp in each of 3 sts, yo and through all 4 lps on hook, fasten off.

Finishing

With WS tog, sew pieces of bell tog, leaving opening at bottom for stuffing. Weave 24" length red ribbon through ch-1 sps on Row 12 of bell; tie in bow at front. Trim ends. Stuff with polyester fiberfill around edges and potpourri at center. Sew opening closed.

Tree

Side (make 2)

Note: Work all sts in back lps only unless otherwise stated.

Row 1: Beg at bottom with jade, ch 38, sc in 2nd ch from hook and in each rem ch across, ch 1, turn. (37 sc)

Row 2 (RS): Sk first st, sc in each of next 17 sts, 3 sc in next st, sc in each of next 17 sts, leave last st unworked, fasten off, turn. (37 sc)

Row 3: With WS facing, attach white with a sl st in 2nd st from right edge, ch 1, sc in same st and in each st across to center sc, 3 sc in center sc, sc in each rem st across to last sc, leave last sc unworked, ch 1, turn. (37 sc)

Row 4: Sk first st, sc in each st across to center sc, 3 sc in center sc, sc in each rem st across to last sc, leave last sc unworked, fasten off, turn. (37 sc)

Row 5: With WS facing, attach jade with a sl st in 4th st from right edge, ch 1, sc in each st across to center sc, 3 sc in center sc, sc in each rem st across to last 3 sc, leave last 3 sc unworked, ch 1, turn. (33 sc)

Row 6: Rep Row 4. (33 sc)

Rows 7 & 8: Rep Rows 3 and 4. (33 sc)

Rows 9–20: Rep Rows 5–8, fasten off at end of Row 20. (21 sts on each of last 4 rows)

Base

Note: Work all sts in both lps unless otherwise stated.

Row 1: Working in rem lps on opposite side of foundation ch, with RS facing, sk first 12 sts, attach cherry red with a sl st in next st, ch 1, sc in same st and in each of next 3 sts, hdc in next st, dc in each of next 3 sts, hdc in next st, sc in each of next 4 sts, leave rem sts unworked, ch 1, turn. (13 sts)

Row 2: Sc in each st across, ch 1, turn.

Row 3: Sc dec, sc in each st across to last 2 sts, sc dec, ch 1, turn. (11 sts)

Rows 4–7: Rep Rows 2 and 3 alternately. (7 sts at end of Row 7)

Rows 8 & 9: Rep Row 2, do not ch 1 at end of Row 9; fasten off.

Finishing

Holding WS tog, sew 2 pieces of tree tog with tapestry needle, leaving opening at bottom for stuffing. Stuff edges with polyester fiberfill; stuff center with potpourri. Sew opening closed.

Cut 2 (6") lengths of red ribbon. Knot 1 at top center of tree base and 1 at center of tree; trim ends.

Tie 24" length of ribbon into bow through st at top center of tree. Using photo as a guide, glue streamers over ends of every other row down each side of tree, leaving slack between joinings. ❤

Tiny Tannenbaum

Design by Isabelle Wolters

Suspend this tiny tree from your larger Christmas tree among many other bright ornaments. Or hang it by itself from a peg, light switch, suction cup on a window or any other spot that needs a touch of tannenbaum.

Let's Begin!

Experience Level: Intermediate

Finished Measurements: 2¾" x 5"

Materials

- Worsted weight yarn: small amount each green, red, yellow and white
- Size G/6 crochet hook or size needed to obtain gauge
- Tapestry needle
- Sewing needle and white sewing thread
- 7" length gold metallic cord

Gauge: 4 sts and 2 rows = 1" in dc

To save time, take time to check gauge.

Tree

Row 1 (RS): With green, ch 4, dc in 4th ch from hook, turn. (2 dc, counting last 3 chs of ch-4 as first dc)

Row 2: Ch 3 (counts as first dc throughout), dc in first st, 2 dc in next st, turn. (4 dc)

Row 3: Ch 3, 2 dc in first st, dc in each st across to last st, 3 dc in last st, turn. (8 dc)

Row 4: Sl st in each of first 2 dc, ch 3, dc in each of next 5 dc, turn. (6 dc)

Row 5: Rep Row 3. (10 dc)

Row 6: Sl st in each of first 3 dc, ch 3, dc in each of next 5 dc, turn. (6 dc)

Row 7: Rep Row 3, fasten off. (10 dc)

Tree Stand

Row 1: With RS facing, attach red with a sl st in 4th st of Row 7, ch 1, sc in same st, sc in each of next 3 sts, ch 1, turn. (4 sc)

Row 2: Sc in each sc across, fasten off. (4 sc)

Star

With yellow, ch 2, sl st in 2nd ch from hook (center of star), [ch 2, sl st in 2nd ch from hook, sl st in center of star] 5 times, fasten off, leaving short length for sewing.

Garland

With RS facing, attach white with a sl st over post of end dc of Row 2, work a ch 16" long; do not fasten off. Drape ch around front and back of tree from top to bottom to resemble garland. Add or remove chs at end, as necessary. Fasten off. With sewing needle and white thread, tack garland to tree.

Finishing

With tapestry needle, sew star to top of tree. Using photo as a guide, with red and tapestry needle, embroider French knots on tree as ornaments. Rep with yellow yarn. Attach gold cord to top of tree for hanging lp. ❤

Petite Christmas Coaster

Design by Linda Driscoll for DMC

Accent a small Christmas decoration by placing it on this petite coaster. The dainty red-and-green edging will create just the proper setting for making a holiday ornament even more festive.

Let's Begin!

Experience Level: Intermediate

Finished Measurement: 5" in diameter

Materials

- DMC Baroque crochet cotton size 10 (400 yds per skein): small amount each white #1 (MC), Christmas red #666 (A) and Christmas green #699 (B)
- Size 5 steel crochet hook or size needed to obtain gauge

Gauge: Rnds 1–4 = 2" in diameter
To save time, take time to check gauge.

Pattern Note

Join rnds with a sl st unless otherwise stated.

Pattern Stitches

Shell: [2 dc, ch 3, 2 dc] in indicated sp or st.

Popcorn (pc): Work 3 dc in indicated sp or st, remove hook from lp, insert hook from RS to WS in first of last 3 dc made, pick up dropped lp, draw through st on hook.

Coaster

Rnd 1 (RS): With MC, ch 3, join to form a ring, ch 4 (counts as first dc, ch-1), [dc, ch 1] 5 times in ring, join in 3rd ch of beg ch-4. (6 ch-1 sps)

Rnd 2: Sl st into first ch-1 sp, ch 4 (counts as first dc, ch-1), dc in same sp, ch 2, [{dc, ch 1, dc} in next sp, ch 2] rep around, join in 3rd ch of beg ch-4.

Rnd 3: Sl st in ch-1 sp, ch 1, [sc, ch 3, sc] in same sp, *ch 4, 3 tr in next ch-2 sp, ch 4 **, [sc, ch 3, sc] in next ch-1 sp, rep from * around, ending last rep at **, join in beg sc.

Rnd 4: Sl st in next ch-3 sp, ch 3 (counts as first dc), 2 dc in same sp, *ch 1, sc in next ch-4 sp, ch 3, sk next 3 tr, sc in next ch-4 sp, ch 1 **, 3 dc in next ch-3 sp, rep from * around, ending last rep at **, join in 3rd ch of beg ch-3.

Rnd 5: Sl st between first and 2nd dc of first 3-dc group, ch 1, sc in same sp, *ch 3, sc between next 2 dc, ch 3, shell in next ch-3 sp, ch 3 **, sc between first and 2nd dc of next 3-dc group, rep from * around, ending last rep at **, join in beg sc.

Rnd 6: Sl st in first ch-3 sp, ch 6 (counts as first dc, ch-3), *[{pc, ch 2} twice, pc] in next shell sp, ch 3, sk next ch-3 sp **, dc in next ch-3 sp, ch 3, rep from * around, ending last rep at **, join in 3rd ch of beg ch-6.

Continued on page 189

Decorative Candy Dish

Design by Beverly Mewhorter

Individually wrapped candy canes, chocolates and other confectionery delights will be pleasing to the eye as well as the palate on this festive holiday project.

Let's Begin!

Experience Level: Beginner

Finished Measurement: Fits 9½"-diameter wicker plate

Materials

- Caron Christmas Glitter worsted weight yarn (1.75 oz per skein): 1 skein each red #7202 and green #7203
- Size G/6 crochet hook or size needed to obtain gauge
- 1⅓ yds ¼"-wide white ribbon
- 9½"-diameter wicker plate

Gauge: Rnds 1–3 = 4" in diameter

To save time, take time to check gauge.

Pattern Note

Join rnds with a sl st unless otherwise stated.

Candy Dish Cover

Rnd 1 (RS): With green, ch 4, 11 dc in 4th ch from hook, join in 4th ch of beg ch-4. (12 dc, counting last 3 chs of ch-4 as first dc)

Rnd 2: Ch 3 (counts as first dc throughout), dc in same st as joining, 2 dc in each rem dc around, join in 3rd ch of beg ch-3. (24 dc)

Rnd 3: Ch 3, dc in same st as joining, dc in next st, [2 dc in next st, dc in next st] rep around, join in 3rd ch of beg ch-3, fasten off. (36 dc)

Rnd 4: With RS facing, attach red with a sl st in same st as joining, ch 3, dc in same st, dc in each of next 2 sts, [2 dc in next st, dc in each of next 2 sts] rep around, join in 3rd ch of beg ch-3, fasten off. (48 dc)

Rnd 5: With RS facing, attach green with a sl st in same st as joining, ch 3, dc in same st, dc in each of next 3 sts, [2 dc in next st, dc in each of next 3 sts] rep around, join in 3rd ch of beg ch-3. (60 dc)

Rnd 6: Ch 3, dc in same st as joining, dc in each of next 4 sts, [2 dc in next st, dc in each of next 4 sts] rep around, join in 3rd ch of beg ch-3. (72 dc)

Rnd 7: Ch 3, dc in same st as joining, dc in each of next 5 sts, [2 dc in next st, dc in each of next 5 sts] rep around, join in 3rd ch of beg ch-3. (84 dc)

Rnd 8: Ch 3, dc in same st as joining, dc in each of next 6 sts, [2 dc in next st, dc in each of next 6 sts] rep around, join in 3rd ch of beg ch-3, fasten off. (96 dc)

Rnd 9: With RS facing, attach red with a sl st in same st as joining, ch 1, 2 sc in same st, sc in each of next 7 sts, [2 sc in next st, sc in each of next 7 sts] rep around, join in front lp only of beg sc. (108 sc)

Rnd 10: Working in front lps only this rnd, ch 3, 4 dc in same st as joining, 5 dc in each rem st around, join in 3rd ch of beg ch-3, fasten off.

Continued on page 189

Christmas Cuties

Designs by Vicky Tignanelli

Santa and Mrs. Claus will feel welcome in your home when they see you have "extras" for them in case they get wet and cold. Crochet these cute little essentials for Santa's wardrobe to add Christmas cheer to this festive season.

Let's Begin!

Experience Level: Intermediate

Finished Measurements: Stocking: 3" long
Coat: 2¼" x 3¾"
Hat: 2" x 2½"

Materials

- Sport weight yarn: small amount each red, green and white
- Size F/5 crochet hook or size needed to obtain gauge
- Small amount gold metallic cord for hanger
- ¼" white pompom for hat
- ⅝" circle magnet for refrigerator magnet
- Hot-glue gun
- Tapestry needle
- Sewing needle and red sewing thread
- 2 size 4/0 snaps for coat

Gauge: 5 sts and 6 rnds = 1" in sc
To save time, take time to check gauge.

Pattern Note

Join rnds with a sl st unless otherwise stated.

Stocking

Note: Do not join rnds unless otherwise stated; mark first st of each rnd with safety pin or other small marker.

Rnd 1 (RS): Beg at toe, with red or green, ch 6, 2 sc in 2nd ch from hook, sc in next ch, hdc in each of next 2 chs, 6 dc in last ch; working in rem lps across opposite side of foundation ch, hdc in each of next 2 chs, sc in next ch, 2 sc in last ch. (16 sts)

Rnd 2: Sc in each sc around. (16 sc)

Shape Toe

Row 3: Fold work in half with WS tog; working through both thicknesses, sc first 3 sts tog.

Upper Stocking

Rnd 4: Working through 1 thickness only, [sc in each of next 3 sc, 2 sc in next sc] twice, sc in each of next 2 sc. (12 sc)

Rnds 5–17: Sc in each sc around; at end of Rnd 17, join in beg sc, fasten off. (12 sc)

Cuff

Rnd 18: With RS facing, attach white with a sl st in beg sc, ch 1, sc in same st and in each rem sc around, join in beg sc, turn. (12 sc)

Rnd 19: Ch 3 (counts as first dc), dc in each rem sc around, join in 3rd ch of beg ch-3. (12 dc)

Rnd 20: Ch 1, sc in same st as joining, ch 2, [sc in next dc, ch 2] rep around, join in beg sc, fasten off.

Finishing

Turn cuff down. With tapestry needle and green, embroider 3 leaves on Rnd 19 at front of stocking cuff using lazy-daisy st. With red, embroider 3 berries on top of leaves with French knots.

For ornament: Cut 12" length of metallic cord. With tapestry needle, thread cord through top back of cuff and tie ends tog.

For refrigerator magnet: Glue magnet to back of stocking.

Coat

Row 1 (WS): With red, ch 11, sc in 2nd ch from hook and in each rem ch across, ch 1, turn. (10 sc)

Row 2: 2 sc in each sc across, ch 1, turn. (20 sc)

Row 3: Sc in each of first 4 sc, *ch 2, sk next 3 sc for armhole *, sc in each of next 6 sc, rep from * to *, sc in each of last 4 sc, ch 1, turn.

Row 4: Sc in each sc and each ch across, turn. (18 sc)

Row 5: Ch 3 (counts as first dc throughout), 2 dc in first st, 3 dc in each rem st across, turn. (54 dc)

Row 6: Ch 3, dc in each rem dc across, fasten off. (54 dc)

Sleeve

Note: Do not join rnds unless otherwise stated; mark first st of each rnd with safety pin or other small marker.

Rnd 1: With RS facing, attach red with a sl st in rem lp of first ch at either underarm, ch 1, sc in same st, sc in next ch, sc over side of end st of next row, sc in each of next 3 unworked sc of Row 2, sc over side of end st of next row. (7 sc)

Rnds 2–4: Sc in each sc around; at end of Rnd 4, join in beg sc, fasten off. (7 sc)

Rnd 5: With RS facing, attach white with a sl st in beg sc, ch 1, beg in same st, [sc, ch 1] in each st around, join in beg sc, fasten off.

Rep on rem underarm.

Edging

With RS facing, attach white with a sl st at bottom corner of left front coat opening, ch 1, [sc, ch 1] in each st across bottom of coat to next corner, [sc, ch 1] evenly sp over row ends up front opening of coat to neck, [sc, ch 1] in rem lp of each ch of foundation ch across neck, [sc, ch 1] evenly sp over row ends down rem front opening of coat, join in beg sc, fasten off.

Finishing

With tapestry needle and green, embroider 3 leaves with lazy-daisy st over edging at left front neck. Embroider 3 berries in red with French knots over leaves. Sew 1 snap at top and 1 at bottom of front opening.

For ornament: Cut 12" length of metallic cord. With tapestry needle, thread cord through center back neck opening and tie ends in knot.

For refrigerator magnet: Glue magnet to center back of coat.

Hat

Note: Do not join rnds unless otherwise stated; mark first st of each rnd with safety pin or other small marker.

Rnd 1 (RS): With red, ch 2, 4 sc in 2nd ch from hook. (4 sc)

Rnds 2 & 3: [Sc in next st, 2 sc in next st] rep around. (9 sc at end of Rnd 3)

Rnd 4: Sc in each sc around. (9 sc)

Rnd 5: [Sc in each of next 2 sc, 2 sc in next sc] rep around. (12 sc)

Rnd 6: [Sc in each of next 3 sc, 2 sc in next sc] rep around. (15 sc)

Rnd 7: Rep Rnd 4. (15 sc)

Rnd 8: [Sc in each of next 4 sc, 2 sc in next sc] rep around. (18 sc)

Rnd 9: Rep Rnd 4. (18 sc)

Rnd 10: [Sc in each of next 5 sc, 2 sc in next sc] rep around. (21 sc)

Rnd 11: Rep Rnd 4. (21 sc)

Rnd 12: [Sc in each of next 6 sc, 2 sc in next sc] rep around. (24 sc)

Rnds 13–17: Rep Rnd 4; at end of Rnd 17, join in beg sc, fasten off. (24 sc)

Brim

Rnd 18: With RS facing, attach white with a sl st in beg sc, ch 1, sc in same st and in each rem st around. (24 sc)

Rnds 19–21: Rep Rnd 4; at end of Rnd 21, join in beg sc, fasten off. (24 sc)

Finishing

Fold brim of hat to RS. With tapestry needle and green, working through both thicknesses of brim, embroider 3 leaves with lazy-daisy st at left front corner. With red, using French knots, embroider 3 berries over leaves. Fold tip of hat down to back of hat and glue to hat approximately ½" from top of brim. Glue pompom to tip of hat.

For ornament: Cut 12" length of metallic cord. With tapestry needle, thread cord through folded top of hat and tie ends in knot.

For refrigerator magnet: Glue magnet to back of flattened hat. ❤

Jolly Holiday Cushion

Pattern begins on page 186

Ho-Ho-Ho Wall Hanging

Design by Barbara Roy

Add a colorful decoration to your front door with this cheery wall hanging. Your kids will love it!

Let's Begin!

Experience Level: Beginner

Finished Measurements: Approximately 17" long x 12" high

Materials

- Worsted weight yarn: 2 oz each red, green and white
- Size F/5 crochet hook or size needed to obtain gauge
- Polyester fiberfill
- Tapestry needle

Gauge: 4 sc = 1"

To save time, take time to check gauge.

Letter H

Note: Make 2 each red, green and white.

Row 1 (RS): Ch 25, sc in 2nd ch from hook and in each rem ch across, ch 1, turn. (24 sc)

Rows 2–5: Sc in each sc across, ch 1, turn; at end of Row 5, do not ch 1; fasten off, turn. (24 sc)

Row 6: With WS facing, attach yarn with a sl st in 10th sc from right edge, ch 1, sc in same st and in each of next 4 sc, ch 1, turn. (5 sc)

Rows 7–10: Sc in each sc across, ch 1, turn; at end of Row 10, do not ch 1; fasten off, turn. (24 sc)

Row 11: Ch 10, with RS facing, sl st in each of 5 sc across last row, ch 10, turn.

Row 12: Sc in 2nd ch from hook and in each of next 8 chs, sc in each of next 5 sl sts, sc in each of next 10 chs, ch 1, turn. (24 sc)

Rows 13–16: Sc in each sc across, ch 1, turn; do not ch 1 at end of Row 16; fasten off.

With tapestry needle and matching colors, sew 2 green letters H tog, 2 red letters H tog, and 2 white letters H tog, stuffing as you sew.

Letter O

Note: Make 2 each red, green and white.

Row 1 (RS): Ch 17, sc in 2nd ch from hook and in each rem ch across, ch 1, turn. (16 sc)

Rows 2–5: 2 sc in first sc, sc in each sc across to last sc, 2 sc in last sc, ch 1, turn. (24 sc at end of Row 5)

First side

Row 6: Sc in each of first 5 sc, ch 1, turn. (5 sc)

Rows 7–10: Sc in each sc across, ch 1, turn; at end of Row 10, do not ch 1; fasten off. (5 sc)

Second side

Row 6: With WS facing, sk next 14 unworked sc of Row 5, attach yarn with a sl st in next sc, ch 1, sc in same st and in each of next 4 sc, ch 1, turn. (5 sc)

Rows 7–10: Sc in each sc across, ch 1, turn. (5 sc)

Row 11: Sl st in each of first 5 sc, ch 14, sl st in each of next 5 sc of first side, ch 1, turn.

Row 12: Sc in each of first 5 sl sts, sc in each of next 14 chs, sc in each of next 5 sl sts, ch 1, turn. (24 sc)

Rows 13–16: Sc dec, sc in each st across to last 2 sts, sc dec, ch 1, turn; at end of Row 16, do not ch 1; fasten off. (16 sts at end of Row 16)

With tapestry needle and matching colors, sew 2 green letters O tog, 2 red letters O tog, and 2 white letters O tog, stuffing as you go.

Assembly

With tapestry needle, matching colors, sew green H and O tog, sew red H and O tog, and sew white H and O tog.

Using photo as a guide, sew red HO to green HO; sew white HO at center below.

Hanging Lps

Attach green with a sl st approximately 1½" down from top at outside right edge on back of green letter H, ch 5, sk 1 row, sl st over next st of next row, fasten off. Rep with green on first part of green letter O. Rep with red on first part of red letter H and on outside left edge of red letter O. ❤

Jolly Holiday Cushion

Design by Laura Gebhardt

Use your bright red and green yarn to give this pillow a jolly look that will appeal even to Santa. What a great place to lay your head for a brief nap from wrapping presents, decorating the tree or delivering a sleighful of toys.

Let's Begin!

Experience Level: Intermediate

Finished Measurements: 7¼" in diameter x 14" long

Materials

- Worsted weight yarn: 6 oz white (MC) and 1¾ oz each red (A) and green (B)
- Afghan hook size I/9 or size needed to obtain gauge
- Size G/6 crochet hook
- 6"-wide x 14"-long bolster form
- 4" square piece of cardboard

Gauge: 16 sts and 14 rows = 4" in afghan st stripe pattern with afghan hook
To save time, take time to check gauge.

Pattern Note

Join rnds with a sl st unless otherwise stated.

Pattern Stitch

Afghan St Stripe Pattern

Row 1: With MC, retaining all lps on hook, draw up a lp in 2nd ch from hook and in each rem ch across (first half of row); *yo, draw through 1 lp on hook, [yo, draw through 2 lps on hook] rep across until 1 lp rems (2nd half of row; lp that rems counts as first st of next row) *.

Row 2: Retaining all lps on hook, sk first vertical bar, [insert hook under next vertical bar, yo, draw up a lp] rep across, ending with insert hook under last vertical bar and 1 strand directly behind it, yo, draw up a lp for last st (first half of row), drop MC; with A, rep Row 1 from * to * for 2nd half of row.

Row 3: With A, rep first half of Row 2, drop A; with MC, rep Row 1 from * to * for 2nd half of row.

Row 4: With MC, rep first half of Row 2; with MC, rep Row 1 from * to * for 2nd half of row.

Row 5: With MC, rep first half of Row 2, drop MC; with B, rep Row 1 from * to * for 2nd half of row.

Row 6: With B, rep first half of Row 2, drop B; with MC, rep Row 1 from * to * for 2nd half of row.

Row 7: Rep Row 4.

Rep Rows 2–7 for afghan st stripe pattern.

Center Panel

With afghan hook and MC, ch 50.

Rows 1–72: Work in afghan st stripe pattern on 50 sts, ending with a Row 6; at end of Row 72, do not fasten off.

Row 73: Beg under 2nd vertical bar, sl st under each vertical bar across, fasten off.

Edging

Working over row ends, using crochet hook, attach MC with a sl st over end st at right-hand edge on either long edge, ch 1, beg in same st, work 72 sc evenly sp over row ends across, fasten off.

Rep across opposite long edge.

End Piece (make 2)

Rnd 1: With crochet hook and MC, ch 6, join to form a ring, ch 3 (counts as first dc throughout), 11 dc in ring, join in 3rd ch of beg ch-3. (12 dc)

Rnd 2: Ch 3, dc in same st as joining, 2 dc in each rem st around, join in 3rd ch of beg ch-3. (24 dc)

Rnd 3: Ch 3, 2 dc in next st, [dc in next st, 2 dc in next st] rep around, join in 3rd ch of beg ch-3. (36 dc)

Rnd 4: Ch 3, dc in next st, 2 dc in next st, [dc in each of next 2 sts, 2 dc in next st] rep around, join in 3rd ch of beg ch-3. (48 dc)

Rnd 5: Ch 3, dc in each of next 2 sts, 2 dc in next st, [dc in each of next 3 sts, 2 dc in next st] rep around, join in 3rd ch of beg ch-3. (60 dc)

Rnd 6: Ch 3, dc in each of next 3 sts, 2 dc in next st, [dc in each of next 4 sts, 2 dc in next st] rep around, join in 3rd ch of beg ch-3. (72 dc)

Rnd 7: Ch 1, sc in same st as joining, sc in each rem st around, join in beg sc, fasten off. (72 sc)

Continued on page 189

Christmas Treasures

Design by Katherine Eng

Add sparkle to your tree with the metallic thread used in these ornaments made from traditional Christmas colors. Little bows and braided trims make each of these orbs a unique treasure.

Let's Begin!

Experience Level: Beginner

Finished Measurements: 1½" in diameter

Materials

Each Ornament

- Metallic crochet cotton size 10: 20 yds
- Size 7 steel crochet hook or size needed to obtain gauge
- 12" ¼"-wide ribbon in coordinating color
- 10" ¼"-wide trim in coordinating color (optional)
- 1½" in Styrofoam plastic-foam ball
- Craft glue (optional)
- Tapestry needle

Gauge: Rnds 1–4 = 1" in diameter

To save time, take time to check gauge.

Pattern Note

Join rnds with a sl st unless otherwise stated.

Ornament Cover

First half

Rnd 1: Ch 4, join to form a ring, ch 1, 8 sc in ring, join in beg sc. (8 sc)

Rnd 2: Ch 1, 2 sc in same st as joining, 2 sc in each rem sc around, join in beg sc. (16 sc)

Rnd 3: Ch 1, sc in same st as joining, 2 sc in next sc, [sc in next sc, 2 sc in next sc] rep around, join in beg sc. (24 sc)

Rnd 4: Ch 1, sc in same st as joining, sc in each rem sc around, join in beg sc. (24 sc)

Rnd 5: Ch 1, sc in same st as joining, 3 dc in next sc, [sc in next st, 3 dc in next st] rep around, join in beg sc.

Rnd 6: Ch 3 (counts as first dc), *hdc in next dc, sc in next dc, hdc in next dc **, dc in next sc, rep from * around, ending last rep at **, join in 3rd ch of beg ch-3, fasten off.

Second half

Rnds 1–6: Rep Rnds 1–6 of first half; at end of Rnd 6, fasten off, leaving length for sewing.

Finishing, Without Trim

Hanging lp

Attach thread with a sl st in any st of Rnd 1 on either half, ch 40, fasten off, leaving short length for finishing. Pull end through another st of Rnd 1, fasten off on WS.

Place both halves over plastic-foam ball. With tapestry needle and rem length on 2nd half, sew last rnd of each half tog.

Tie ribbon into bow at base of hanging lp.

Finishing, With Trim

Place both halves over plastic-foam ball. With tapestry needle and rem length on 2nd half, sew last rnd of each half tog.

Hanging lp

Glue trim over seam, folding rem length of trim down to form hanging lp. Tack end in place. Tie ribbon into bow at base of hanging lp. ❤

Gold Glitter Stockings

Continued from page 172

Assembly

Turn stocking WS out. With tapestry needle, weave long end at tip of toe through sts of last rnd, pull to tighten, secure with several small sts, fasten off. Do not turn stocking RS out.

Sew heel seams.

Cuff

Rnd 1: With WS facing, attach CC with a sl st in rem lp of foundation ch at center back top of stocking, ch 1, sc in same st and in each rem st around, join in back lp only of beg sc. (20 sc)

Rnd 2: Ch 1, working in back lps only this rnd, sc in same st as joining and in each rem sc around, join in beg sc.

Rnd 3: Ch 3 (counts as first dc), dc in each rem sc around, join in 3rd ch of beg ch-3. (20 dc)

Rnd 4: Ch 3, [sk next dc, sl st in next dc, ch 3] rep around, ending with ch 3, sk last dc, join in st at base of beg ch-3.

Rnd 5: Sl st in first ch-3 lp, ch 3, [sl st in next ch-3 lp, ch 3] rep around, join in beg sl st, fasten off.

Turn stocking RS out; turn cuff down.

Hanger

Attach MC with a sl st at top center back of cuff, ch 12, sl st in same st as last sl st, fasten off.

Finishing

Tie gold metallic ribbon into bow at center of cuff. ❤

Country Christmas Booties

Continued from page 175

changing colors and working sc incs and sc decs at begs and ends of rows as indicated; ch 1, turn at end of each row; at end of Row 16, do not fasten off; ch 1, turn.

Edging

Matching color to section being worked, 2 sc in first st, sc across to last st, 3 sc in last st; with red, sc over end st of each row and in each rem lp of foundation ch around, join in beg sc, fasten off.

With sewing needle and sewing thread, using photo as a guide, sew buttons to RS at points indicated on Patchwork Stocking graph.

Second Side

Row 1: Rep Row 1 of first side.

Rows 2–16: Follow Patchwork Stocking chart for 2nd side, changing colors and working sc incs and sc decs at begs and ends of rows as indicated; ch 1, turn at end of each row; at end of Row 16, do not fasten off; ch 1, turn.

Edging

With red, rep instructions for edging for first side.

With RS tog, using tapestry needle and red, sew first and 2nd sides tog. Turn stocking RS out.

Cuff

Rnds 1 & 2: Rep Rnds 1 and 2 of cuff for Striped Stocking.

Rnd 3: Ch 3 (counts as first dc), 2 dc in same st as joining, *sk next st, sc in next st, sk next st **, 3 dc in next st, rep from * around, ending last rep at **, join in 3rd ch of beg ch-3.

Rnd 4: Sl st in next dc, ch 1, sc in same st, *[dc, ch 2, dc] in next sc **, sc in center dc of next 3-dc group, rep from * around, ending last rep at **, join in beg sc, ch 12 for hanging lp, sl st in joining st, fasten off. ❤

Petite Christmas Coaster

Continued from page 180

Rnd 7: Sl st in next ch-3 sp, ch 1, sc in same sp, *[ch 3, sc in next ch-2 sp] twice, ch 3, sc in next ch-3 sp, ch 4, [{pc, ch 2} twice, pc] in next dc, ch 4 **, sc in next ch-3 sp, rep from * around, ending last rep at **, join in beg sc.

Rnd 8: Sl st in first ch-3 sp, ch 1, sc in same sp, *ch 3, [sc, ch 3, sc] in next sp **, [ch 3, sc in next sp] 6 times, rep from * around, ending last rep at **, [ch 3, sc in next sp] 5 times, ch 3, join in beg sc, fasten off.

Rnd 9: With RS facing, attach A with a sl st in first ch-3 sp after joining st, ch 1, sc in same sp, *ch 2, [{pc, ch 2} twice, pc] in next sp, ch 2, sc in next sp, ch 3, sk next sp **, sc in next sp, rep from * around, ending last rep at **, join in beg sc, fasten off.

Rnd 10: With RS facing, attach B with a sl st in any ch-3 sp, ch 3 (counts as first dc), [2 dc, ch 1, 3 dc] in same sp, *sk next ch-2 sp, sc in next ch-2 sp, ch 3, sc in next ch-2 sp, sk next ch-2 sp **, [3 dc, ch 1, 3 dc] in next ch-3 sp, rep from * around, ending last rep at **, join in 3rd ch of beg ch-3.

Rnd 11: Ch 1, sc in same st as joining, sc in each dc and in each ch-1 sp and 3 sc in each ch-3 sp around, join in beg sc, fasten off. ❤

Decorative Candy Dish

Continued from page 181

Rnd 11: With RS facing, attach red with a sl st in any rem lp of Rnd 9, ch 1, sc in same st and in each rem st around, join in beg sc. (108 sc)

Rnd 12: Ch 1, sc in same st, sc in next st, sk next st, [sc in each of next 2 sts, sk next st] rep around, join in beg sc, fasten off.

Rnd 13: With RS facing, attach green with a sl st in same st as joining, ch 3, dc in each rem st around, join in 3rd ch of beg ch-3.

Rnd 14: Ch 3, dc in each rem st around, join in 3rd ch of beg ch-3, fasten off.

Trim

With RS facing, attach green with a sl st in any dc of Rnd 10, sl st in each rem st around, join in beg sl st, fasten off.

Finishing

Slip candy dish cover over wicker plate. Cut ribbon into 4 (12") lengths. Spacing bows evenly around, tie lengths into bows in tops of dc sts on Rnd 10. ❤

Jolly Holiday Cushion

Continued from page 186

Tassel (make 1 each A & B)

Wrap yarn 30 times around cardboard. Slip 10" length of yarn under strands across 1 edge. Knot tightly. Cut open ends at opposite edge. Cut 2nd 10" length of yarn. Tie tightly around tassel 1" from top. Sew 1 tassel to center of each end piece.

Assembly

Wrap center panel around bolster. With MC and crochet hook, sl st rem lps of foundation ch and last row of center panel tog. With crochet hook and A, sc end piece with tassel made of A to edging sts on either end of center panel; do not fasten off. Work 1 rnd reverse sc; fasten off.

With crochet hook and B, rep for end piece with tassel made of B on opposite end of center panel. ❤

General Instructions

Please review the following information before working the projects in this book. Important details about the abbreviations and symbols used are included.

Hooks

Crochet hooks are sized for different weights of yarn and thread. For thread crochet, you will usually use a steel crochet hook. Steel crochet hook sizes range from size 00 to 14. The higher the number of hook, the smaller your stitches will be. For example, a size 1 steel crochet hook will give you much larger stitches than a size 9 steel crochet hook. Keep in mind that the sizes given with the pattern instructions were obtained by working with the size thread or yarn and hook given in the materials list. If you work with a smaller hook, depending on your gauge, your project size will be smaller; if you work with a larger hook, your finished project's size will be larger.

Gauge

Gauge is determined by the tightness or looseness of your stitches, and affects the finished size of your project. If you are concerned about the finished size of the project matching the size given, take time to crochet a small section of the pattern and then check your gauge. For example, if the gauge called for is 10 dc = 1 inch, and your gauge is 12 dc to the inch, you should switch to a larger hook. On the other hand, if your gauge is only 8 dc to the inch, you should switch to a smaller hook.

If the gauge given in the pattern is for an entire motif, work one motif and then check your gauge.

Understanding Symbols

As you work through a pattern, you'll quickly notice several symbols in the instructions. These symbols are used to clarify the pattern for you: Brackets [], curlicue brackets {}, asterisks *. Brackets [] are used to set off a group of instructions worked a number of times. For example, "[ch 3, sc in ch-3 sp] 7 times" means to work the instructions inside the [] seven times. Brackets [] also set off a group of stitches to be worked in one stitch, space or loop. For example, the brackets [] in this set of instructions, "Sk 3 sc, [3 dc, ch 1, 3 dc] in next st" indicate that after skipping 3 sc, you will work 3 dc, ch 1 and 3 more dc all in the next stitch. Occasionally, a set of instructions inside a set of brackets needs to be repeated too. In this case, the text within the brackets to be repeated will be set off with curlicue brackets {}. For example, "[Ch 9, yo twice, insert hook in 7th ch from hook and pull up a loop, sk next dc, yo, insert hook in next dc and pull up a loop, {yo and draw through 2 lps on hook} 5 times, ch 3] 8 times." In this case, in each of the eight times you work the instructions included in brackets, you will work the section included in curlicue brackets five times.

Asterisks * are also used when a group of instructions is repeated. They may either be used alone or with brackets. For example, "*Sc in each of the next 5 sc, 2 sc in next sc, rep from * around, join with a sl st in beg sc" simply means you will work the instructions from the first * around the entire round.

"*Sk 3 sc, [3 dc, ch 1, 3 dc] in next st, rep from * around" is an example of asterisks working with brackets. In this set of instructions, you will repeat the instructions from the asterisk around, working the instructions inside the brackets together. ❤

Buyer's Guide

When looking for a specific material, first check your local craft stores and yarn shops. If you are unable to locate a product, contact the manufacturers listed below for the closest retail source in your area.

- **Caron International**
  200 Gurler Rd.,
  DeKalb, IL 60115,
  (815) 758-0173
- **Coats & Clark**
  Consumer Service,
  P.O. Box 12229,
  Greenville, SC
  26912-0229,
  (800) 648-1479
- **DMC Corp.**
  10 Port Kearny,
  South Kearny, NJ
  02032, (800) 275-4117
- **JHB International**
  1955 S. Quince St.,
  Denver, CO 80231,
  (303) 751-8100
- **Kreinik Manufacturing**
  3106 Timanus Ln.,
  Suite 101, Baltimore,
  MD 21244,
  (800) 537-2166
- **Lion Brand**
  34 W. 15th St., New
  York, NY 10011,
  (212) 243-8995
- **Patons**
  1001 Roselawn Ave.,
  Toronto, Ontario
  M6B 1B8, Canada,
  (800) 275-4117
- **Spinrite Yarns & Dyers, Ltd.**
  320 Livingstone Ave.,
  Listowel, Ontario
  N4W 3H3, Canada,
  (519) 291-3780
- **Wimpole Street Creations**
  419 W 500 S
  Bountiful, UT 84010,
  (801) 298-0504

Stitch Guide

Special Stitches

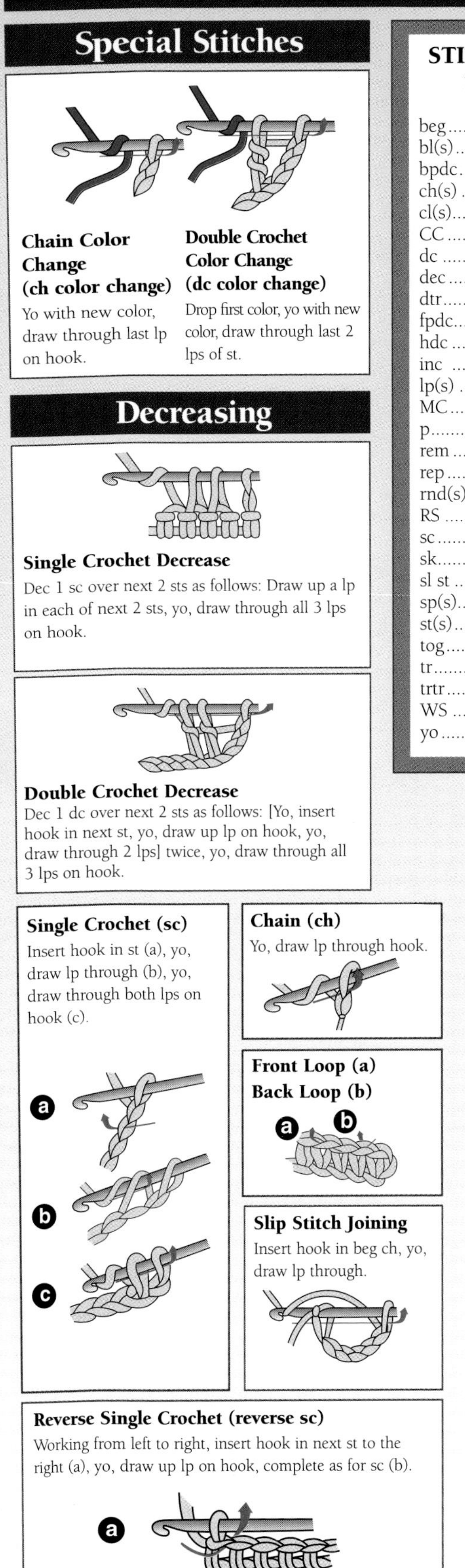

Chain Color Change (ch color change)
Yo with new color, draw through last lp on hook.

Double Crochet Color Change (dc color change)
Drop first color, yo with new color, draw through last 2 lps of st.

Decreasing

Single Crochet Decrease
Dec 1 sc over next 2 sts as follows: Draw up a lp in each of next 2 sts, yo, draw through all 3 lps on hook.

Double Crochet Decrease
Dec 1 dc over next 2 sts as follows: [Yo, insert hook in next st, yo, draw up lp on hook, yo, draw through 2 lps] twice, yo, draw through all 3 lps on hook.

Single Crochet (sc)
Insert hook in st (a), yo, draw lp through (b), yo, draw through both lps on hook (c).

Chain (ch)
Yo, draw lp through hook.

Front Loop (a)
Back Loop (b)

Slip Stitch Joining
Insert hook in beg ch, yo, draw lp through.

Reverse Single Crochet (reverse sc)
Working from left to right, insert hook in next st to the right (a), yo, draw up lp on hook, complete as for sc (b).

STITCH ABBREVIATIONS

The following stitch abbreviations are used throughout this book.

beg	begin(ning)
bl(s)	block(s)
bpdc	back post dc
ch(s)	chain(s)
cl(s)	cluster(s)
CC	contrasting color
dc	double crochet
dec	decrease
dtr	double treble crochet
fpdc	front post dc
hdc	half-double crochet
inc	increase
lp(s)	loop(s)
MC	main color
p	picot
rem	remain(ing)
rep	repeat
rnd(s)	round(s)
RS	right side facing you
sc	single crochet
sk	skip
sl st	slip stitch
sp(s)	space(s)
st(s)	stitch(es)
tog	together
tr	treble crochet
trtr	triple treble crochet
WS	wrong side facing you
yo	yarn over

CROCHET HOOKS

Metric	US
.60mm	14 steel
.75mm	12 steel
1.00mm	10 steel
1.25mm	8 steel
1.50mm	7 steel
1.75mm	5 steel
2.00mm	B/1
2.50mm	C/2
3.00mm	D/3
3.50mm	E/4
4.00mm	F/5
4.50mm	G/6
5.00mm	H/8
5.50mm	I/9
6.00mm	J/10

YARN CONVERSION

Ounces to Grams

1	28.4
2	56.7
3	85.0
4	113.4

Grams to Ounces

25	⅞
40	1⅔
50	1¾
100	3½

Crochet Abbreviations

US	UK
sc—single crochet	dc—double crochet
dc—double crochet	tr—treble crochet
hdc—half double crochet	htr—half treble crochet
tr—triple crochet	dtr—double treble crochet
dtr—double treble crochet	trip—triple treble crochet
sk—skip	miss

Yarns

Bedspread weight	No. 10 cotton or Virtuoso
Sport weight	4-ply or thin DK
Worsted weight	Thick DK or Aran

Check tension or gauge to save time.

Treble Crochet (tr)
Yo hook twice, insert hook in st (a), yo, draw lp through (b), [yo, draw through 2 lps on hook] 3 times (c, d, e).

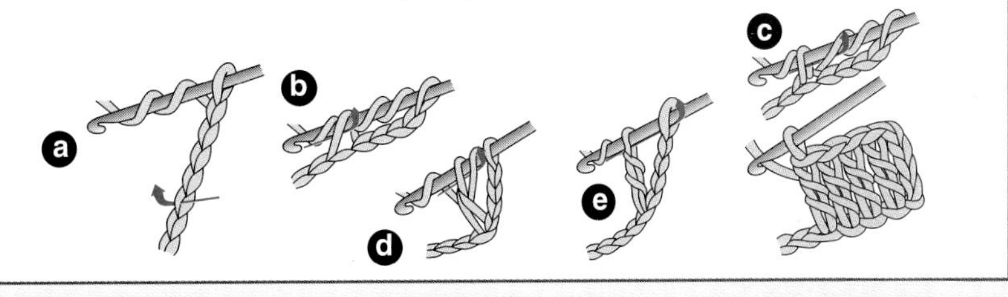

Double Crochet (dc)
Yo, insert hook in st (a), yo, draw lp through (b), [yo, draw through 2 lps] twice (c, d).

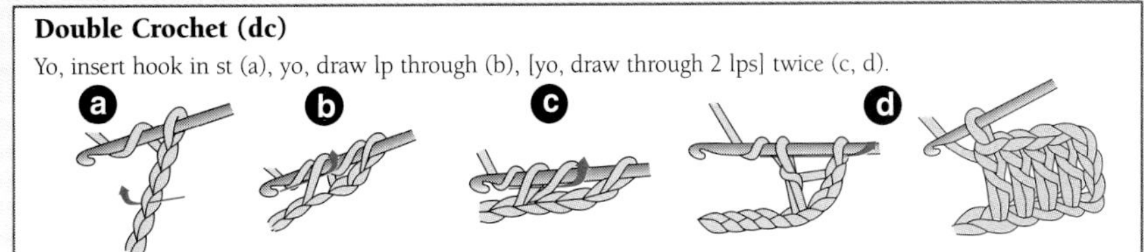

Half-Double Crochet (hdc)
Yo, insert hook in st (a), yo, draw lp through (b), yo, draw through all 3 lps on hook (c).

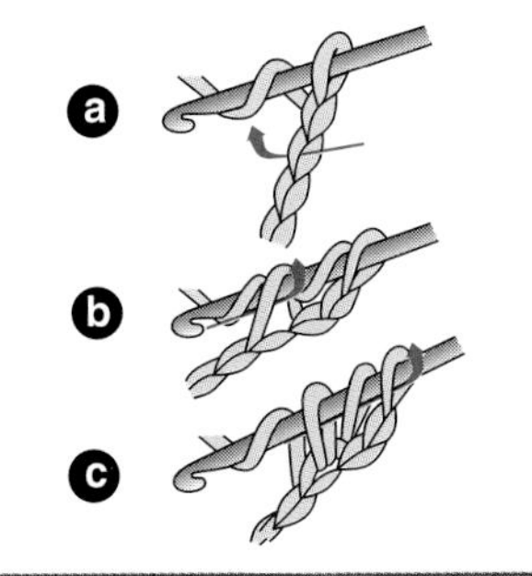

Front Post/Back Post Dc
Fpdc (a): Yo, insert hook from front to back and to front again around the vertical post (upright part) of next st, yo and draw yarn through, yo and complete dc.
Bpdc (b): Yo, reaching over top of piece and working on opposite side (right side) of work, insert hook from right to left around vertical post of next st, yo and draw yarn through, yo and complete dc.

Special Thanks

We would like to thank the following freelance designers whose original work has been published in this collection. We appreciate their creativity and dedication to crochet.

Sandra Abbate
Country Warmth Set, Daisy in the Sun Doily, Gingerbread Swag, Itzy-Bitzy Bear, Pansy Garden Doily, Pineapple Rose Doily, Potpourri Pillows, Rose Garden Accessories, Sitting Pretty Table Set, Yo-yo Bunny

Vicki Blizzard
Dressed-Up Doggies

Jo Ann Burrington
Fluffy Slippers

Debra Caldwell
Brimming With Roses Hat, Needle Me On Pincushion

Jessica Caldwell
Booties for Baby, Key Chain Combo

Maggie Petsch Chasalow
Butterfly's Fancy Table Set, Chain of Daisies Chest, Loves Me, Loves Me Not, Tresses Trio

Sue Childress
Bunny Delight, Cutie Pie Clothespin Dolls, Flower Garden Bolero, Snipper Keeper

Sue Collins-Ottinger
Bag Lady, Fluttering Butterflies Motifs

Dot Drake
Happy Times

Linda Driscoll
Miniature Rose Crib Set, Petite Christmas Coaster

Maureen Egan Emlet
Windowpane Tunic

Katherine Eng
Christmas Treasures, Granny's Scrap Basket, Miniature Coverlet

Darla Fanton
Mended Hearts

Nazanin S. Fard
Forget-Me-Not Trinket Box, Rosebud Hair Accent, Rosebuds 'n' Beads T-Shirt

Connie L. Folse
Angelfish Pillow, Hot Pepper Hot Pad

Laura Gebhardt
Jolly Holiday Cushion, Pastel Garden Centerpiece, Wild Rose Sachet

Janet Giese
Jute Jar Lid Covers

Shirley Guess
Double-Tiered Star Scrunchies

Alice Heim
Accents in Blue Blouse Edging

Tammy Hildebrand
Best-Dressed Bottle, Butterfly Magnets, Granny's Scrap Bag Apron

Frances Hughes
Scrap Happy Pinwheels

Karen Isak
Flower Friends

Dawn A. Kemp
Fashion Doll Fun

Lucille LaFlamme,
Dainty Dishcloths, Diagonal Stripes Rug, Painted Daisies Runner

Melissa Leapman
String of Clusters Pullover, Zesty Zigzag Cardigan

Melody MacDuffee
Autumn Glory

Roberta Maier
Parfait Baby Afghan

Jo Ann Maxwell
Cornflower & Cream Doily

Daria McGuire
Windowsill Tissue Box Cover

Beverly Mewhorter
Decorative Candy Dish

Shirley Patterson
Circles Chatelaine, Confetti Place Mat

Carolyn Pfeifer
Farm Animal Magnets

Rose Pirrone
Pastel Stripes

Barbara Roy
Ho-Ho-Ho Wall Hanging

Hélène Rush
Floral Window Shade Trim, Mini-Entrelacs for Kids

Jennifer Sauter
Citrus Pot Holder, Waffle Pot Holder

Colleen Sullivan
Gold Glitter Stockings

Aline Suplinskas
Dreamy Stripes

Loa Ann Thaxton
Reversible Rag Rug

Michele Maks Thompson
Random Acts of Kindness

Vicky Tignanelli
Christmas Cuties

Judy Treague Treece
Dainty Peach Doily

Sharon Volkman
Country Christmas Booties

Michele Wilcox
Piggyback

Isabelle Wolters
Happy Hair Doll, Starburst Hot Pad, Strawberry Motifs, Tiny Tannenbaum